THE

FUTURE

OF

PUBLIC

EDUCATION

Myron Lieberman

THE

FUTURE

OF

PUBLIC

EDUCATION

 THE UNIVERSITY OF CHICAGO PRESS

Library of Congress Catalog Number: 59-15108
The University of Chicago Press, Chicago 37
Cambridge University Press, London, N.W., 1 England
The University of Toronto Press, Toronto 5, Canada
© 1960 by The University of Chicago. Published 1960
Printed in the U.S.A.

To

LEO MOLINARO

with deepest admiration
respect and affection

PREFACE

Some of the material in this book appeared first in *The Nation* and in *School and Society*. I would like to thank the editors of these magazines and the publishers of the many other works quoted throughout the book, for permission to quote from their publications.

In the writing of this book, I have had the benefit of suggestions and criticisms from many sources. In particular, I would like to express my deep appreciation to the following persons, who read all or a part of the manuscript in draft or periodical form and made comments which helped in some way to improve it: Mr. Charles Cogen, president of the New York Teachers Guild, AFL-CIO, Professor Robert Anderson of Harvard University, Professor B. Othanel Smith of the University of Illinois, Dr. Paul Woodring and Dr. Lester Nelson of the Fund for the Advancement of Education, Dr. Robert M. Hutchins of the Fund for the Republic, Dr. James B. Conant, and Mr. Myrl Herman of Washington University. In virtually all of these cases, one outcome was a friendly agreement to disagree on some issues, a fact which should be emphasized because the views of some of these persons are criticized in the book itself. Likewise, there should be no thought that any of these persons necessarily endorses or approves what I have written concerning any organizations with which they are affiliated; quite often the reverse is the case.

The manuscript was also influenced by conversations over the past few years with many persons in school systems, educational organizations, foundations, and institutions of higher education. Since there were so many persons who helped me in this way, I can only hope that a general but sincere expression of appreciation will indicate the depth of my obligation to them. For the final product I alone must and do take complete responsibility. However, my debt to one other person must be recorded; there would be no book at all, let alone a poor one, without the unfailing encouragement and assistance of my wife, Dr. Mary Arthur Lieberman.

CONTENTS

Chapter I

THE POINT OF VIEW

This book is an attempt to explain and defend a point of view about public education in the United States. The point of view is not crystallized in a label or summed up by a slogan. I am not an advocate of basic education, progressive education, liberal education, the three R's, social adjustment, or stricter discipline in the public schools. I am not going to urge anyone to join a society of the educationally anointed or to subscribe to a magazine which prints only Educational Truth. I shall make no appeal to parents to march on school boards or for Public Spirited Citizens to rise up and clean out the Augean stables of American education. Nevertheless, I believe that public education in the United States is much less effective than it can and ought to be. This book is devoted to explaining why I think so and what I think should be done about it.

Before setting forth my position, I should like to comment briefly upon the contemporary educational situation. Following this, I shall outline the position to be developed in the following chapters, indicating in a general way the points of contrast between this and other analyses of public education. After providing a very general fix on my position, I shall turn directly to the task of relating it to the focal points of current controversy.

To me, the crucial aspect of our educational situation is this: We are at the threshold of a revolution in education, a revolution which will alter drastically every important aspect of education as a social institution and as a profession. In many respects, the directions that this revolution will take are still unclear. Unless the American people, and especially the teaching profession, achieve a better understanding of the problems of public education than they have had in the past, they are not likely to guide this revolution into constructive channels.

I do not predict an educational revolution as a disinterested observer. On the contrary, I will be disappointed if it does not take place. Its absence will reflect upon my capacity as an educational theoretician, but that is not important. What *is* important is the need for such a revolution and the consequences to our society if we do not sense the need for one and carry it out. I have more confidence that an educational revolution is needed than I have that one will actually take place. Nevertheless, what follows is a prediction as well as a hope—and is offered without apologies for either the hope or the prediction.

The future revolution in education may be regarded as having two dimensions. One dimension relates to the fundamental nature of the changes that will take place. There is, of course, no calculus by which we determine whether a change is "revolutionary" or not. Indeed, people often disagree upon whether a particular change in the social order is or is not "revolutionary." At one extreme, changes are so fundamental that no one doubts the propriety of labeling them "revolutionary." At the other extreme, changes are so unimportant that no one doubts their less consequential nature. In between, there are changes that are regarded as "revolutionary" by some people but not by others.

I believe that within the next few decades education in the United States will undergo changes of tremendous scope and magnitude. That is, the changes will affect not only what is taught and how but also such aspects of education as teachers' organizations, professional ethics, teacher education, the theory and practice of teacher compensation, and the many interrelationships between teachers and pupils, parents, communities, and governmental agencies. These changes will be so basic that we will be fully justified in using the term "revolutionary" to describe them.

There is also a temporal dimension to the forthcoming revolution in education. If the federal government were to finance completely the operating costs of private schools, and if it were to do this through a single piece of legislation, such action would undoubtedly be regarded as a revolutionary change in our educational system. On the other hand, local, state, and federal governments frequently adopt legislation which affects the status of private schools. The laws providing for bus transportation at public expense for students in parochial schools are a case in point. It is conceivable that bits and pieces of legislation over a long period of time, perhaps a century or more, would provide for complete governmental support for private schools. Looking back over a century, one might be unable to characterize any particular item as revolutionary, although the impact of all the legislation might be an educational system radically different from that of a century ago.

To generalize from this discussion, at any given time one can, if one peers far enough into the past, justifiably contend that the current state of affairs represents a revolutionary change from a state of affairs in the past. By the same token, one can always correctly predict, by not putting any time limit on the prediction, that there will be a revolution in education. However, merely to assert that our educational system will differ from what it is today, without any indication of the nature or imminence of the changes, is to achieve predictive certainty at the expense of practical value. In this book, the prediction that there will be a revolution in education means more than that, in some remote future, education will be radically different from what it is today. I am asserting that within the foreseeable future—certainly within the lifetime of most readers—there will be fundamental changes in our educational system. Furthermore, in the chapters to follow, I have specifically indicated what I believe will be their nature.

These changes will not take place merely because they are desirable. They will take place as the logical and practical outcome of events and movements which are upon us now. In this respect, to predict their occurrence is analogous to predicting certain developments in the arms race. When the United States produced atomic weapons, its scientists did not know when Russia would also have such weapons. However, that the Russians would develop them within a certain time span was always clear from trends which were obvious to informed persons. Similarly, there are trends which lead to the conclusion that it is no longer a question of whether certain changes in our educational system will occur, but only of when they will occur.

To label a change "revolutionary" is neither to praise nor to condemn it. I believe that the changes predicted in this book will be beneficial to our society. However, they will not be beneficial merely because they are revolutionary. Their beneficent character, if they have any, rests upon other grounds.

The broad framework of our school system was created in and for an era that is fast disappearing. The period in which make-shift compromises can be used to stave off a fundamental overhauling is fast running out. Nevertheless, the fact that a new framework is needed does not by itself settle the question of what is to be its nature and guiding principles. To some extent, these things will be shaped by the impersonal forces that are undermining the current framework. However, once it becomes clear that a new framework for public education must be developed, not one but many alternatives may be suggested. The specific changes I have set forth constitute what I believe to be the best solutions to basic problems that cannot be evaded. The point is, however, that whatever solutions are accepted will constitute an educational framework different from anything we have known in the past.

This assessment, which may be widely disputed, leads directly to the educational position espoused in subsequent chapters. The bare bones of this position are as follows:

1. Public education in the United States is much less effective than the American people, especially the teaching profession, assume it to be. More important, it is much less effective than it can and ought to be.

2. The most important causes of the ineffectiveness of public education are rooted in its anachronistic and dysfunctional power structure.

3. Because most current controversy is concerned with the rightness or wrongness of certain educational policies and not with the power structure within which these policies are made, it is largely irrelevant to the basic problems of education.

4. The basic educational reforms needed in the United States will have to be initiated and carried out by the teachers themselves. It follows from this that the study of teachers' organizations—their programs, leadership, political sophistication, strategy, and tactics—must be accorded high priority by those who wish to bring about fundamental improvements.

5. Appeals to "the public" to solve the problems of education are usually well intentioned, but under present circumstances they ordinarily result in more harm than good to the cause of public education. They will continue to have this effect until the futility of appealing to a diffuse public becomes manifest to educational leadership and until there is established a sensible delineation of the role of the public in the educational enterprise.

To state these convictions is one thing; to defend them is another. The rest of this book is devoted chiefly to the latter task, but I would be the first to insist that this defense is far from complete.

To avoid serious misunderstanding, the reader must always bear in mind the distinction between a claim that proposition X is valid and a claim that the validity of proposition X has been established by a certain set of statements. To be specific, my purpose is to suggest a series of changes which I regard as imperative for the welfare of public education. The arguments for and against each of these changes might well require a book or more. In this one, I have presented only a prima facie case for the proposed changes. My offer to the reader is this: I grant that the arguments in this book are not conclusive. Furthermore, I do not expect the reader to accept conclusions based upon evidence which lies concealed within my nervous system. However, the reader must recognize that the absence *in this book* of conclusive evidence in support of the changes proposed does not justify the inference that such evidence does not exist.

Some kinds of evidence lie in careful scholarship, and only there. Often this evidence is not easily available to the average person, intelligent and public spirited as he may be. There are other cases in which the evidence is all around us, but we do not have the proper "mind set" to recognize it. If you do not consciously entertain a hypothesis, you are not likely to notice the evidence which confirms or disproves it.

Generally speaking, both kinds of evidence are cited in support of the positions taken in this book. At the same time, I have been forced to omit a great deal of the scholarly data upon which my arguments are based. For this reason, I have suggested additional sources for those who may wish to pursue any of these arguments further. My purpose is not to make converts to my point of view but to establish the possibility that this point of view merits further reflection and investigation.

For this reason, it seems to me especially desirable to have the reader test my arguments against the background of his own studies and educational experiences. There are dangers in this procedure. Personal experience can be a very misleading guide unless it is interpreted within a sound theoretical framework. Also, an appeal to personal experience often results in over-simplification, the great curse of educational theorizing. Whether it does so in this case is partly the responsibility of the reader, and perhaps this note of caution will help him to fulfil his responsibility as well as my own.

OTHER EDUCATIONAL VIEWS: SOME
PRELIMINARY COMMENTS

Let me try to locate my position on the spectrum of educational controversy. I hold no copyright on the notion that the situation in public education is not a healthy one. Indeed, if one were to select the most shopworn question in American life today, "What's wrong with our schools?" would undoubtedly be a strong contender for top honors. It would be difficult to suggest more familiar topics than the fifty-seven varieties of progressive education, the fads and frills versus the three R's, why Johnny can't read as well as his grandparents, the underpaid but dedicated teachers, or the need to protect the liberal arts from vocationalism, professors of education, financial impoverishment, and sundry other disasters. The trouble is that these threadbare topics evoke attitudes and arguments which are familiar to everyone. They arouse only the old war horses of educational controversy; everyone else has other fish to fry.

The fact that certain educational problems receive predominant attention in the mass media year after year can be interpreted in different ways. There is a romantic school of thought which holds that certain problems are perennial because of their great importance. Another interpretation is that certain issues are always with us because nobody has come up with a satisfactory solution to them so far. Still another is that any answers to certain educational problems involve an adjustment of conflicting interests; the pressure groups concerned are continually seeking a readjustment to further their own interests. For example, it might be argued that teachers' salaries will always be a problem because of the conflict of interest inherent in any employer-employee relationship.

These and other interpretations may be valid as applied to specific educational problems. Nevertheless, I do not think they provide a satisfactory answer to the question of why we are confronted with so many of the same problems and the same inadequate solutions year in and year out. It seems to me that when a question has been around for a long time and no satisfactory answer to it is in sight, we should begin to question the question instead of the specific answers to it.

This thought prompts me to suggest that the attention given to such old reliables as "progressive education" or "the fads and frills versus the three R's" bears very little relationship to any issues of intrinsic importance. A thoroughgoing skepticism concerning the field of journalism reinforces the suggestion. "Journalists" are not specialists in education, just as they are not specialists in economics, science, government, or any other substantive field of knowledge. Journalists are trained in journalism

—that is, in the methods and techniques of writing news and feature stories. That they should be alarmed about such traditional bogeys as an alleged overemphasis upon methodology when their own training provides a most glaring example of this weakness is ironical but understandable. To assess what is important in a field, one must understand that field. Editors who pontificate about teachers having to be trained in a field in order to teach it adequately seem unconcerned about whether a reporter has to be trained in a field in order to report and interpret it accurately.

It is not that journalists must have a course in methods of teaching in order to report and interpret educational news intelligently. However, they do need a systematic study of the way in which education is financed and controlled, the dynamics of who gets what kind of education, the interrelationships between the local, state, regional, and national organizations which shape educational policies, and the level, direction, and quality of educational research. These are only a few of the subjects which should be studied by persons who exercise the responsibility of informing the public on educational matters. No doubt a reporter can learn some of these things on the job, but the cost in public understanding is too high a price to pay for this way of educating the press. To make matters worse, the level of educational reporting and editorializing in the mass media is not far below the level of these things in the professional literature which most teachers read. In fact, part of the public confusion about education is a direct result of the inability of educators to define clearly just what are the important educational issues.

An issue may be clear, but people may be confused about what to do because the reasons for and against any particular course of action are so evenly balanced. This kind of confusion is often unavoidable. It is really not confusion at all but practical uncertainty. Such a situation differs in kind from one in which the issues are not clear. In the latter, people do not even know what evidence or arguments are relevant to a solution. Education is characterized by many controversies of this kind. Basically, these unclear issues are pseudo-issues, not real ones, because

8

people are not talking about the same thing and therefore cannot be said to be taking issue with each other.

Since World War II and especially since Sputnik, public education has been the subject of considerable discussion. Educators frequently assert that current public interest in education exceeds that of any previous period in history. From reading the mass media and the professional journals, one gets the impression that there is a "great debate" going on. This "great debate" is supposed to be concerned chiefly with the purposes of education; the main issue is commonly thought to be whether the purpose of education shall be intellectual training or social adjustment.

Personally, I am convinced that the so-called "great debate" on education has been mostly irrelevant and that its actual impact on education has been negligible. Without too much oversimplification, we can place the contributions to the debate on a continuum. At one end would be the "critics" of public education. These assert that the public schools have been diverted from their "true" purpose, that they are failing badly, and that drastic changes are necessary to reverse an alleged trend toward educational mediocrity.[1] It is unfortunate but indicative of our educational situation that the phrase "critics of public education" should be widely used to denote a rather specific group. This group consists largely of certain persons who have contended in books, articles, and speeches over the past ten years that the public schools are emphasizing social adjustment to the neglect of their historic and rightful task of intellectual training.[2] The point is that every person who plays a professional

[1] For examples see Arthur E. Bestor, *The Restoration of Learning* (New York: Alfred A. Knopf, 1955); Robert M. Hutchins, *The Conflict in Education* (New York: Harper & Bros., 1953); John Keats, *Schools without Scholars* (Boston: Houghton Mifflin Co., 1957); Albert Lynd, *Quackery in the Public Schools* (Boston: Little, Brown & Co., 1953); H. G. Rickover, *Education and Freedom* (New York: E. P. Dutton, 1959); Mortimer B. Smith, *The Diminished Mind* (Chicago: Henry Regnery Co., 1954).

[2] The organizational focus of the "critics" is the Council for Basic Education, a kind of Progressive Education Association for educational conservatives. The Council is a conglomeration of viewers with alarm who preferred to establish another splinter organization instead of fighting for their point of view within the educational organizations which have the

9

role in public education should be a critic of it. To label specific individuals or groups as "critics of public education" is implicitly to condemn others, who presumably have lost or neglected their critical faculties.

Ironically, some of the "critics" assert that there is hardly any criticism of public education emanating from the educators themselves. When the latter label a small group as "critics," they inevitably reinforce the very point which the "critics" are making; they are saying in effect that the function of criticism is confined to the "critics." This honors the "critics" more than they deserve and constitutes a gratuitous insult to others who are critical of specific aspects of public education. The tendency to identify the function of criticism with a rather specific group has also been unfair to the latter group. It has given rise to the erroneous notion that the "critics" are opposed to public education per se. On the contrary, the "critics" regard themselves as ardent champions of public education, no less devoted to it than those who (according to the "critics") are unaware of the shortcomings of the public schools.

Every social institution needs criticism. We would hardly regard a person as opposed to legislatures merely because he was critical of the overrepresentation of rural areas in our legislative bodies. Such a person might be an extremely valuable supporter of our legislative institutions, in the sense that he might suggest the corrective measures needed to safeguard their continued existence. Analogously, people who support outmoded and inefficient aspects of public education are not its friends in fact, even though they may be in name and spirit. My point is not that the specific individuals labeled "critics" are the saviors of public education; it is that this way of labeling people can be very misleading. We should be concerned with the specific educational proposals which people make, not with the label they may have picked up along the way.

---

membership and resources to influence the direction of public education. Like the Progressive Education Association, the Council will orbit aimlessly in educational space for a few decades and then wither away, claiming the widespread acceptance of its platform as the reason for its dissolution.

The "critics" are at one end of a continuum; at the other end are those who assert that the public schools are doing a good job on the whole. The person who asserts that everything educational is perfect probably does not exist, any more than the person who asserts that everything about the public schools is bad. However, many people see no need for any sweeping changes in the goals, content, methodology, or control of public education. These people are its "supporters" or "defenders."

The difference between the "critics" and the "supporters" does not lie in their acceptance or rejection of public education per se but in their rejection of certain aspects of the educational status quo. While none of the "supporters" denies the possibility and the need for improvement, the group as a whole is quietistic, except on the need for more money for public education.[3]

Then, as might be expected, there are the middle-of-the-roaders to tell us that things are not as bad as the most severe "critics" tell us nor as good as the "supporters" would have it.[4] The middle-of-the-roaders tend to make this error; they often regard *agreement* that a certain policy is sound as *proof* that it is. People can and do agree upon unsound educational programs; this is a possibility which is not envisaged by some educational conciliators and peacemakers.

This is not a "middle-of-the-road" book for several reasons. First, insofar as there are identifiable schools of educational thought concerning the public school crisis, I am more impressed by the fundamental fallacies they share in common than by the valid points they espouse separately. Second, it is naïve to believe that educational theorizing is not affected by the self-interest of the theorizers, at least as they perceive it. I do not mean that everyone deliberately contends that what is good for

[3] Most of the literature of this group is in periodical rather than book form. Despite his many excellent suggestions for improvement, I would place Dr. Conant in this category inasmuch as he himself rejects the notion that there is need for basic changes in our educational structure. See James B. Conant, *The American High School Today* (New York: McGraw-Hill Book Co., 1959), p. 40.

[4] The best known educator in this category is Paul Woodring. See his *One Fourth of a Nation* (New York: McGraw-Hill Book Co., 1957), and *Let's Talk Sense about the Public Schools* (New York: McGraw-Hill Book Co., 1952).

him is good for the country, but few people keep considerations of self-interest from affecting their consideration of national interest. This is certainly true in the colleges, where professors often visualize a one-to-one relationship between the welfare of their department and the welfare of American society.

One thesis of this book is that in order to achieve substantial improvements in public education, we must first make radical changes in its power structure. It is foolish to suppose that everybody's self-interest will be affected in the same way by sweeping educational changes; to the extent that this is so, it is unlikely that a middle-of-the-road position will make either political or educational sense. The groups whose powers should be diminished are not likely to accept such a development as a sound compromise. In some cases, perhaps they will; in others, they will regard any weakening of their powers as synonymous with the decline of American civilization and resist it accordingly.

Some educational moderates are fond of saying that educational controversy "really" consists of "semantic" differences which would disappear if there were agreement upon definitions. Others see conflict as the result of ignorance and blithely assume that controversy will disappear in the sunlight of more knowledge and understanding. The possibility that more knowledge or a better understanding of other positions may increase instead of decrease controversy is ignored. Nevertheless, increased knowledge may be a cause of, as well as a means of resolving, controversy. A better understanding of the other person's point of view may bring out sharp and irreconcilable differences which were obscured by a less penetrating view.

Agreement upon definitions, more knowledge, and better understanding will invalidate some of the claims which currently fill the air and hence they will also weaken drastically the power of those individuals and groups who rely upon these claims to maintain their position. Because this is so, an approach to educational controversy starting with the assumption that any solutions reached must be acceptable to all sides operates under a handicap likely to prove fatal.

The middle-of-the-roaders want to stress open-mindedness, but this characteristic should refer to one's capacity and willing-ness to examine all sides to a controversy. It has nothing to do with any a priori judgment about the distribution of truth and error in the controversy. It is as narrow-minded to assume beforehand that truth lies "between" conflicting positions as it is to assume that it lies with one or none of them. Whether a position is extreme in the sense of not being shared by others is not so important as whether it is supported by valid evidence and sound reasoning.

In one sense, I place myself with the "critics" of public educa-tion. I am convinced that our schools are not as effective as they should be. I mean by this more than the simple idea that im-provement is possible. Improvements are possible in every social institution—our courts, our legislatures, our hospitals, and so on. When I cast my lot with the "critics," I mean to say that the return on our educational investment is too low to be brushed aside by sincere but routine admissions that improvement is pos-sible and desirable. I am asserting that the gap between the achievable and the actual results of public education should be a matter for deep national concern and that this concern must not abate until the gap has been drastically reduced.

"Our schools are not as effective as they should be"—this is a hazy statement. "Effective" according to what criteria? Are all schools or only most schools "not as effective as they should be"? Does the statement refer to all teachers in most schools or most teachers in all schools? Obviously, two people might agree to this statement but upon analysis find that they really did not share the same conclusions about the ineffectiveness of public schools.

My concept of ineffectiveness is this: the public schools do not develop critical thinking, good citizenship, social competence, or creative skills. This statement cannot be applied with equal justice to all school systems, schools, or teachers. If applied to certain ones, it would be a rank injustice. On the other hand, in this book I am not going to try to separate the sheep from the goats in the 50,000 school systems or among the 1,300,000 school teachers in the country. Nor can I give a thorough evaluation of the impact of public education upon every one of the millions of students who attend or have attended public schools.

Clearly, my evaluation of public education is not a model of clarity and mathematical rigor. There is a difference, however, between a generalization which admittedly does not apply to every possible instance and one which is vague and impressionistic. Furthermore, my purpose in stating this generalization is not to lay down a hypothesis to be proved, at least at this particular point. It is to indicate in a crude way the nature of my agreement with some recent critics of public education. When it comes to a diagnosis of *why* public education is ineffective and what should be done to improve it, my views have little in common with those who contend that the liberal arts colleges are a kind of institutional Messiah, come to save the world from anti-intellectualism and the evils of social adjustment. The situation is like one in which two doctors agree that X is critically ill, but one doctor prescribes a bloodletting and the other a blood transfusion. Needless to add, both doctors will have little in common with others who assert that X has only a bad cold or that X is as robust and healthy as the children who eat their Wheaties every day.

Although the point of view set forth in this book is not original with me, it has never been presented systematically to the public or to the teaching profession. What I have to say may give comfort or pain to various groups, but I have no feeling, and certainly no conscious intent, of acting as a spokesman or advocate for anyone else. I hope that I am not making a fetish out of being different. It is simply that no group or organization is advocating the program which I regard as essential for the future of public education. For what it may be worth, this program and its rationale are set forth in the following pages.

Chapter II

WHAT THE PROBLEM IS NOT

The most important educational issue of our time is what should be the purposes of public education. This problem is "philosophical" in nature, in the sense that our answer to it will eventually depend on our vision of the good life and our conceptions of the nature of man, society, truth, ultimate reality, and other philosophical concepts. The determination of the purposes of education is essentially a matter for public rather than professional action.

I wish to dissent from all three of these propositions. The purpose of this chapter is to explain why they are fallacious and how belief in them has been harmful to public education in the United States.

Regardless of whether the determination of the broad purposes of education is *the* major problem of public education, there can be little doubt that most educational theorists think that it is. One of the "critics" writes:

The point I am making is that despite a sometimes fundamental philosophical cleavage, the traditionalists and the modernists believed in content, in a body of subject matter to be taught, but parted company on matters of method. This is no longer the main debate in American education; the controversy today is between those who continue to believe that the cultivation of intelligence, moral as well as intellectual, is inextricably bound up with the cultural heritage and accumulated knowledge of mankind, and those who feel that education's primary task is to adjust the individual to the group, to see that he responds "satisfactorily" to the stresses and strains of the social order.[1]

A recent textbook by four well-known professors of education asks and answers itself:

Why should the teacher know anything about the social role of the school?

First, most of the educational disputes now taking place in many communities center about the essential purpose of the school.[2]

Paul Woodring, a widely known educational theorist who is not identified with any particular school of educational thought, comments:

Today we are engaged in a great national debate over the aims and purpose of education, a debate that has included vigorous criticism of existing schools and of the philosophy of education which lies behind them.

And later, after proposing that "the proper aim of education is to prepare the individual to make wise decisions," he says:

If we can agree on this as our aim, our educational planning will be greatly simplified and the great American debate over education can move on to a profitable discussion of the best means for reaching our goals.[3]

The point of view expressed in these quotations is too common to require further documentation.[4] Nevertheless, despite its wide acceptance in the educational world, I believe that it represents a basic fallacy in our approach to educational problems.

It is true that no *statement* of the broad purposes of education has been accepted by the American people as a whole, but this

[1] Mortimer Smith, *The Diminished Mind* (Chicago: Henry Regnery Co., 1954), pp. 19–20.

[2] William O. Stanley, B. Othanel Smith, Kenneth D. Benne, and Archibald W. Anderson, *Social Foundations of Education* (New York: Dryden Press, 1956), p. 454.

[3] Paul Woodring, *One Fourth of a Nation* (New York: McGraw-Hill Book Co., 1957), pp. 6, 115.

[4] If any more is needed, I suppose that my own advocacy of this position not so long ago should be included. See Myron Lieberman, *Education as a Profession* (Englewood Cliffs, N.J.: Prentice-Hall, 1956), pp. 19–48.

does not mean that there is widespread disagreement about these purposes. There is a difference between agreement with a particular statement of purpose and agreement upon the purposes themselves. It is possible to have either of these things without the other. To the best of my knowledge, the American people as a whole have never agreed formally to a statement of the functions of *any* profession. Nevertheless, the professions are not unduly handicapped by a lack of agreement as to their general purposes. This fact suggests that the absence of any widespread formal agreement on the broad purposes of education must be interpreted very cautiously.

Certainly, there are disagreements concerning the broad purposes of education, just as there are some disagreements concerning the objectives of the medical profession, the legal profession, the engineering profession, the civil service, and many other occupational groups. Sometimes these disagreements present extremely difficult problems for the individual in a given field. Many scientists working on the atomic bomb had grave doubts concerning the purpose of their work. Lawyers are often confronted with situations which force them to decide whether their function is to advance the interests of their client or to see that justice is done. Other examples could be cited. Furthermore, I would agree that in specific instances conflict over the broad purposes of education does constitute a serious problem. My point is that these instances are too infrequent to be regarded as our major educational problem.

Since education is a state and local responsibility in the United States, some people contend that there is no reason why the American people as a whole should agree on its general objectives. Some even go so far as to assert that it would be dangerous to have widespread agreement on the purposes of education. Nevertheless, I believe that the American people are in substantial agreement that the purposes of education are the development of critical thinking, effective communication, creative skills, and social, civic, and occupational competence.

If there is widespread agreement on the broad purposes of education, why do so many people believe that disagreement in this area is so pervasive? The most important reason is the confusion over what are purposes and what are the means of achieving them. In this connection, bear in mind that school subjects are means of achieving certain purposes; they are not the purposes themselves. When we disagree about the inclusion of a subject in the curriculum, the disagreement may or may not arise out of disagreement over educational objectives.

The point of the preceding paragraph is an extremely important one; I shall elaborate upon it on several occasions in later chapters. Here let me suggest a simple example to illustrate the point and to bring out its importance. I believe that one of the objectives of public education is to develop critical thinking. To achieve this purpose, I believe that the study of logic and scientific method should be introduced into the public school curriculum. I also happen to believe that the world history courses so often given at the tenth-grade level are largely a waste of time.

I am not concerned now with defending either of these recommendations. For the sake of argument on the main issue, concede that I am completely mistaken in thinking that the study of logic and scientific method would be more conducive to critical intelligence than tenth-grade world history. I do not see, however, how anyone can question my categorical assertion that I accept and advocate the broad purpose of developing critical thinking. The important issue is whether the study of logic and scientific method would facilitate the development of critical thinking more than the study of world history.

This example suggests that a great deal of argument popularly labeled "controversy over the broad purposes of education" really concerns the means of achieving agreed-upon objectives. This confusion results from the fact that educational theory has not provided a clear-cut demarcation between purposes and the means of achieving them. At this point the reader may ask: "What difference does it make if the disagreement is labeled one of purpose or one of means? Isn't the important fact the one of disagreement, not what it is labeled?" My answer is that in

18

this context, the way we label the disagreement is more important than the fact of disagreement.

Ultimately, the determination of the broad purposes of education is one for our entire society to make. The choice of means is one for the teaching profession to decide. If there is no clear-cut understanding of what are objectives and what are means, people think they are arguing about one when they are really arguing about the other. Naturally, as a result of this confusion, people tend to exaggerate the extent of disagreement over purposes. What is more important, this confusion encourages the public to make decisions concerning means which in its own best interests should be made by teachers. *To generalize: it makes a tremendous difference whether we classify a disagreement as one of purpose or as one of means, because the mode of classification has a crucial bearing on who should settle the disagreement.*

Consider again, for a moment, a few sentences from the education textbook already cited:

In school after school, the teachers and principal are attacked by vociferous groups of citizens who think that the three R's are not given enough time, or that the conventional subjects are neglected, or that the school is not emphasizing moral and spiritual values, or that false and dangerous economic and political doctrines are being taught. . . . Each of these attacks reflects a public concern with what the school is attempting to do. *Each one presupposes that the school should serve one function rather than another—that the role of the school is to teach the fundamental skills and the conventional subjects,* or to develop moral and spiritual character, or to maintain the *status quo* or even the *status quo ante* in economics and politics, and so on.[5]

This quotation illustrates exactly the kind of confusion I am talking about. A controversy over whether "the three R's are not given enough time" is not necessarily a conflict over the function of public education. Such controversy does *not* "presuppose that the school should serve one function rather than another." Assuming that it does so only confuses teachers and laymen alike into exaggerating the extent of disagreement over the objectives

[5] Stanley *et al., loc. cit.* Italics added.

of education and encourages massive interference with academic freedom. If educators themselves tell citizens to debate and settle the amount of time given to the three R's on the grounds that this problem is one of broad purpose, they have in effect abandoned their professional claim to autonomy in this matter. And, in general, academic freedom is muddled away by educators more than it is trampled upon by laymen.

Exaggeration of the extent of disagreement over purposes is compounded by a tendency to assume that people who advocate different subjects in the curriculum necessarily advocate different objectives for education. People often agree on what is purpose and what are means, but then erroneously regard a difference in means as reflecting a difference in purpose. Sometimes it is, but often it is not. Disagreement over the inclusion of a subject may simply reflect differing estimates of its usefulness in achieving an agreed-upon purpose.

Although disagreement over educational purposes is neither the pervasive nor the all-important problem that it is often thought to be, there are some extremely important analytical and practical problems directly related to this problem. In order to effectuate any objective, teachers must develop a set of intermediate objectives which will provide direction for their efforts in the classroom. It is at this point—the point of professional translation of broad purposes into a coherent educational program—that we have some of our major unsolved problems. The failure of the teaching profession to implement certain broad purposes of education has understandably but mistakenly led to the belief that teachers have abandoned these purposes. A failure in performance has come to be regarded as one of intent instead of capability.

For example, one of the objectives of education may be to develop the ability to communicate effectively. However, the first-grade teacher can contribute to this purpose only by setting certain specific goals, such as a vocabulary of so many words or an ability to write the letters of the alphabet, for her students. The English teacher in the high school also contributes to the same broad objective but only by setting intermediate objectives which are different from those set by elementary-school teachers: he works toward such intermediate objectives as an understanding of grammar, an ability to locate sources of information, an appreciation of literary classics, and so on.

Some of the intermediate objectives of the high-school teacher will appear to be the same as those of the elementary-school teacher. For instance, both will accept increasing the pupil's vocabulary as an intermediate objective. In practice, however, the words and concepts taught by one will be different from those taught by the other. Indeed, all teachers should have as one of their broad objectives the development of effective communication. All may contribute toward this objective by increasing the vocabulary of their students. However, each teacher will have a different vocabulary to teach. The history teacher will introduce such new concepts as feudalism or the Industrial Revolution, the physics teacher will introduce such new ones as velocity and ergs, and so on.

The problem here is that the teachers have failed to establish sets of intermediate objectives which would clarify how they propose to fulfil the general objectives of education. The discussion of objectives is usually concerned with the general ones, but this is not where the problem lies. It lies in establishing consistent, defensible, and attainable intermediate objectives which can serve as the basis for evaluating the progress made by the profession.

Let me illustrate this point by examples from other occupations. One of the broad aims of the medical profession is to prolong life. In carrying out this objective, the medical profession has eliminated most communicable causes of death. Of communicable diseases, only tuberculosis and pneumonia are still major causes of death, and the advances made in checking these are impressive. Thus, in 1900 the death rate per 100,000 persons from tuberculosis was 194.4; in 1952 it was only 16.1. In 1900 the death rate per 100,000 persons from pneumonia was 175.4; in 1952 it was 30.5. Again, bear in mind that other communicable diseases have been eliminated entirely or reduced to a negligible factor.

Thus, in carrying out its general purpose of prolonging life, the medical profession has concentrated upon the major causes of death at any given time. Obviously, as some are eliminated, other causes become major. Today, degenerative diseases have largely replaced communicable diseases as the major causes of death, and the medical profession is now beginning to eliminate or substantially reduce the death rate from these. As it succeeds, still other diseases will become major causes of death, and they in turn will be subjected to intensive research with a view to their elimination or substantial reduction.

By thus going from one specific intermediate objective to another, the medical profession has achieved outstanding success in fulfilling one of its broad purposes, the prolongation of life. In the United States, life expectancy at birth was approximately 40 years in 1800, 49 years in 1900, close to 60 years by 1925, and close to 70 years by 1950. Indeed, the success of the medical profession in eliminating one after another of the leading causes of death has led the profession to question whether there are any insuperable biological limits to human life. At any rate, there is every reason to expect greater and greater success in prolonging human life, but always through concrete intermediate goals which lead to the broad goal itself.

Perhaps one other example will be useful. Physicists have as their general purpose the achievement of an understanding of the laws of matter and motion. Their field is usually regarded as encompassing mechanics, heat, electricity, light, and sound. Now, although the general purpose of physicists has remained unchanged for centuries, in recent years they have achieved dazzling success in its fulfilment. For example, when Einstein discovered that $e = mc^2$, he made an enormous contribution to the understanding of the laws of matter and motion. Other physicists have solved one after another of the basic theoretical problems of physics. But the point is that these gains have been achieved because physicists, collectively and individually, have continually set and achieved strategic intermediate objectives which would implement the broad purpose of their profession.

Getting back to education, we see that it too has broad purposes, such as the development of an ability to communicate effectively. Such a purpose is analogous to the general purpose of prolonging life or of increasing our understanding of matter and motion. But whereas doctors and physicists have progressive and feasible intermediate objectives, teachers do not. Therein is a problem of purpose, albeit not the problem which agitates so many of our post-Sputnik philosophers of education.

Let me illustrate what might be done. A student who is capable of earning an engineering degree is ordinarily capable of learning calculus by the time he finishes high school. In practice, such students are not even exposed to calculus until their second or third year in college. Teachers might well accept, as one of their intermediate objectives, the objective of having all students of a certain ability level and career pattern master calculus by the time they have finished high school.

Many interrelated problems would have to be solved to accomplish this intermediate objective. For instance, there are thousands of small high schools which have only one or a very few students capable of learning calculus. Some of these schools have no trained mathematics teachers, and there is little chance that a school system is going to employ a highly paid teacher for a handful of students. Thus, to achieve the proposed objective, it might be necessary to reduce drastically the number of high schools so that the remaining ones could offer appropriate courses with a reasonable teacher-pupil ratio. Obviously, changes in teacher education, in teachers' salaries, in the high-school curriculum, and in many other aspects of education would also be necessary to achieve the suggested intermediate objective. None of these changes is impossible or even impractical, given able leadership.

There are many kinds of intermediate objectives which teachers might set for themselves. Some of them would not involve any improvement in the performance of students. Instead, they would involve only an improvement in the productivity of teachers. Everyone is aware of the fact that maturational factors limit what can be taught to young children. The same student who is capable of learning calculus in the twelfth grade is not capable of learning it in the elementary grades. Of course, when we say that young children cannot learn better or faster, we never know for certain whether we are dealing with a stubborn and eradicable fact of life or with our ignorance of the learning process. In any case, when it is unreasonable to set higher goals for the students, teachers should concentrate upon ways and means of utilizing a smaller number of teachers to accomplish a given educational result. Just as in other fields, productivity may be increased either by a constant labor force which expands its output or by a constant output achieved through a decreasing labor force. In most occupations there are exciting frontiers in both directions. Teachers, however, seem unable to make much progress in either.

It is important to recognize that intermediate objectives should be set by the professions, not by the public. The medical profession is best qualified to decide what specific hypotheses should be subjected to research in order to advance the broad purpose of prolonging life. Surely, physicists are the persons best qualified to decide which particular investigations will deepen our understanding of matter and motion. And in education teachers are, or should be, the persons best qualified to decide what proximate objectives of education should be pursued to fulfil its broad purposes. Unfortunately, while the doctors are making rapid advances in reducing pain and prolonging life, while scientists are exploring the vast reaches of the universe and the nature of the tiniest particles, while our industrialists and our labor force are achieving exciting advances in productivity, in short, while one occupational group after another is soaring to new heights, the teachers seem unable to get off the ground.

Why are the frontiers of public education so static? Why is education lost in a Sargasso Sea, so that from one generation to the next the schools are involved in the same dreary problems with the same dreary kinds of persons advocating the same dreary positions? Partly, I think, because of the misplaced, often pseudo-profound, concern with the broad purposes of education. This concern is the other side of a coin which reveals a shocking unwillingness and inability on the part of teachers at all levels and of all subjects to evaluate their own work.

Are schools today more effective (by any criterion) than they were x number of years ago? This question is important. We cannot evaluate public education without confronting it. Nevertheless, despite the fact that the question is often asked, there is a remarkable lack of systematic reliable data to answer it. The truth is that there is little rigorous evaluation of public education.

We have little evidence to show that the schools today are much more effective than those of an earlier day. Neither do we have much evidence to confirm the belief that there has been a sweeping deterioration in public education. But the important point is that the absence of systematic evaluative data is more remarkable than any conclusion to be drawn from whatever data we have.

An antipathy to evaluation pervades every dimension of the educational enterprise, from the kindergarten to the graduate school. It is reflected in the decline of examinations for a teaching certificate, the fear of any kind of merit-rating for teachers, and the opposition to standardized examinations to test student progress. It is also a cause of the overemphasis upon personality and the downgrading of intellectual competence as a basis for selecting prospective teachers. Personality traits, such as an interest in children, are much more difficult to evaluate than intellectual competence. Reliance upon "personality" as a criterion for evaluating prospective teachers degenerates into reliance upon no criteria at all.

The lack of evaluation in the public schools is the natural and logical consequence of its absence from higher education. Many professors who have been critical of the public schools apparently expect them to apply evaluative criteria which the professors would never dream of applying to their own departments and institutions. For example, in a recent book on the shortcomings of public education, a professor of history points out that (1) the public schools today enrol a much higher proportion of the school age population than they did in previous generations;

and (2) after taking into account the effects of inflation and the fact that the increased enrolments have been most pronounced at the secondary level, educational expenditures per pupil in attendance are much greater today than they have been in the past. The author cites figures to show that educational expenditures per pupil in attendance in 1950 were seven times as great as they were in 1870 and three times as great as they were in 1910. He then makes the following suggestions concerning evaluation:

> It is ludicrous in the extreme to measure the effectiveness of our public schools today by comparing them with the achievements of the wretchedly inadequate schools of previous generations. . . . The present effectiveness of the schools measured against the best that can possibly be achieved, is the *only* valid measure of our educational accomplishment. . . . We must, moreover, measure the achievement of our schools against an even more rigorous standard. Are they giving to the people and to the nation the values that were the promised result of universal education? If the schools are doing their job, we should expect educators to point to a significant and indisputable achievement in raising the intellectual level of the nation—measured perhaps by larger per capita circulation of books and serious magazines, by definitely improved taste in movies and radio programs, by higher standards of political debate, by increased respect for freedom of speech and of thought, by a marked decline of such evidences of mental retardation as the incessant reading of comic books by adults. . . . We should expect school administrators to produce testimonials from employers, professional men, college professors, and officers of the armed services to the effect that young men and women are coming out of high school with sounder intellectual background and greater skill and competence than ever before.
>
> No such claims are being advanced and no such comparisons are being made by the men and women to whom we have entrusted the control of our public schools.[6]

Note that most of the criteria suggested by Bestor are especially appropriate for evaluating the effectiveness of our liberal arts colleges. These colleges enrol a much larger proportion of the population from 18 to 22 years of age than they have in the past. Their level of expenditures per pupil is much higher than

[6] Arthur Bestor, *The Restoration of Learning* (New York: Alfred A. Knopf, 1955), pp. 14, 18–21.

it has ever been. Surely, if they are successfully providing a liberal education, they too should be able to point to "a larger per capita circulation of books and serious magazines, higher standards of political debate," and an increasing number of "testimonials from employers, professional men, college professors, and officers of the armed services to the effect that young men and women are coming out of" (and here let us substitute "liberal arts colleges" for "high school") with sounder intellectual background and greater skill and competence than ever before." [7]

Personally, I doubt whether *all* of the criteria suggested by Bestor are valid for either the public schools or the liberal arts colleges. However, if they are appropriate for one, they are also appropriate for evaluating the other. But there is hardly a hint of this possibility in the prescriptions for educational reform which pour out of the liberal arts colleges. Too many of the professors in these institutions live by a double standard. They are all for evaluation and reform, provided that these things can be confined to the public schools. I do not say this in a "So's your old man" spirit. Despite all the furor over "too many methods courses," let us not forget that most teachers take most of their college training in the liberal arts and sciences. The absence of evaluation in these areas must be regarded as an important cause of the absence of evaluation by teachers in the public schools. Teachers taught by professors who don't practice rigorous evaluation are not likely to practice it themselves.

THE "PHILOSOPHICAL" PROBLEM

We are often told that conflict over the purposes of education is "philosophical" in nature, and that until there is agreement at the philosophical level, there is little hope for agreement at the practical level. Frequently, this idea is expressed in terms of our need for a philosophy of education to provide us with a clear-cut idea of the purposes of education. Having held this point of view myself until a short time ago, I am not in-

[7] For a strong testimonial to the effect that even the best graduates from the best colleges are deficient in the fundamentals of a liberal education, see H. G. Rickover, *Education and Freedom* (New York: E. P. Dutton, 1959), p. 23.

clined to describe its proponents as nitwits. I am inclined, however, to think that they are mistaken and that they tend to confuse rather than to clarify important educational issues.

That educational theorists generally regard the determination of the broad purposes of education as a "philosophical" problem is hardly debatable. A deluge of educational literature, representative of virtually every educational position, can be cited to confirm this point. One author, in criticizing a school board for providing a high-school course designed to train girls to operate beauty shops, says: "Adoption of the course by the county school board was a choice in educational philosophy, and it was presented to the voters as a *fait accompli* but such choices belong to the public that maintains the public school—and to no one else." [8] A former university president writes that "education without a philosophy of education, that is, a coherent statement of the aims and possibilities of education, is impossible." [9]

From the scores of textbooks that echo this point of view, I shall cite only one:

> Part of the function of philosophy of education is to find fault with what we have and to set goals to be achieved. . . . The important role which philosophy has played in the development of education should not be minimized. A statement of purposes provides something to work toward . . . a statement of purpose, a philosophy of education, is needed to guide the invention and to test the tryout of new teaching ideas as they develop. [10]

Sometimes, the same people who believe that the public should determine the broad purposes of education and who regard this problem as "philosophical" will also express the view that it is important for each teacher to have *a* philosophy of education. The difficulty with this point of view is that society, not the individual teachers, should determine the broad purposes of education. To contend that every teacher ought to have "a

[8] John Keats, *Schools without Scholars* (Boston: Houghton Mifflin Co., 1958), p. 8.
[9] Robert M. Hutchins, *The University of Utopia* (Chicago: University of Chicago Press, 1953), p. 52.
[10] Paul R. Mort and William S. Vincent, *Introduction to American Education* (New York: McGraw-Hill Book Co., 1954), pp. 47–48.

philosophy of education," as if every teacher should decide for himself what should be the broad purposes of education which he personally will accept in his classroom, is to be mixed up. It is one thing to have teachers understand the purposes for which schools were established and a totally different thing to have each teacher go off on a tangent pursuant to his private "philosophy of education." Of course, every teacher has the right to advocate that education be devoted to certain purposes not presently accepted in our schools. However, this right is a different thing from the right to substitute one's own purposes for those of the larger community.

A variation on this theme is the practice of having the teachers in a given school or school system formulate their "philosophy of education." Two authorities in the field of educational administration write: "While it is perhaps inevitable that individuals among educational personnel will have a personal philosophy, it is equally true that only one that is representatively and cooperatively arrived at shall be utilized as the foundation for the administrative framework of a school system's or a school's program." [11] But what holds for the individual teacher also holds for all the teachers in a particular school or school system; they do not have the right to substitute their broad purposes for those accepted by our society as a whole.

Like many other terms, the word "philosophy" has more than one legitimate meaning. Nevertheless, the notion that conflict over the purposes of education is "philosophical" would seem strange to most professional philosophers. In professional philosophy today, "philosophical" disputes are distinguished from "scientific" ones. Roughly speaking, philosophical problems are problems of meaning; scientific problems are problems of empirical fact. The question of whether dogs can run faster than horses is of the latter type; there is no way to answer it except by looking to see how fast dogs and horses run. On the other hand, suppose the question is whether there can be a dog who is not an animal. The answer is clearly "No," because part of the

---

[11] Herold C. Hunt and Paul R. Pierce, *The Practice of School Administration* (Boston: Houghton Mifflin Co., 1958), p. 21.

very meaning of "dog" is "an animal with certain characteristics." There would be absolutely no point in looking for a dog who was not an animal; one cannot even imagine such a dog.

I have used simple examples to illustrate the difference between philosophical and scientific questions. Professional philosophers do not argue over whether dogs can be non-animal, any more than scientists argue over whether dogs run faster than horses. As we all know, scientific questions can become technical and complex. Philosophical questions can also; we should bear in mind that mathematics is fundamentally a branch of philosophy. But Plato to the contrary, philosophers are not experts on the purposes of life, and philosophers of education are not experts on the purposes of education.

It is often contended that conflict over the broad purposes of education is "really" rooted in conflict over such complex philosophical issues as the nature of man, the nature of reality, and the nature of truth. For example, Paul Woodring tells us that "A philosophy of education must rest upon a tenable view of the world and of man. It must be consistent with a clear conception of the nature of knowledge, the sources of truth, and a valid ethical theory, and these must be consistent with each other." [12]

The fact of the matter is that the major practical problems of education are not rooted in differences over the nature of man or of society or of reality. Furthermore, we should all be thankful for this fact. These topics have been the subject of irresolvable conflict for thousands of years. Educators would be paralyzed if we had to reach agreement on such ultimate questions in order to operate our schools effectively. Actually, people who have the

[12] Woodring, *op. cit.*, p. 31. "I hope to show that the philosophy of education, by which I mean a reasoned and coherent statement of its aims and possibilities, is a secondary subject, dependent on our conception of man and society, that is, upon our philosophy in general" (Robert M. Hutchins, *The Conflict in Education* [New York: Harper & Bros., 1953], p. 1).

For an example of this approach in a philosophy of education textbook, see Harry S. Broudy, *Building a Philosophy of Education* (New York: Prentice-Hall, 1954). According to Broudy, philosophy of education is "the systematic discussion of educational problems on a philosophical level, i.e., the probing into an educational question until it is reduced to an issue in metaphysics, epistemology, ethics, logic, or aesthetics, or to a combination of these" (*ibid.*, pp. 19–20).

most diverse ideas (or none at all!) about such things as the nature of man and the nature of ultimate reality can agree on practical educational questions. And I might also point out that often people who have identical views on these ultimate philosophical questions disagree on practical educational issues.

There are important philosophical problems in education. For example, it is important to clarify the meaning of such educational concepts as "academic freedom," "equality of educational opportunity," and "indoctrination," to cite just a few. Such clarification is a responsibility of philosophers of education, just as the clarification of such concepts as "sovereignty," "representation," and "totalitarianism" is a responsibility of political philosophers. But it is not the particular responsibility of philosophers of education to tell us what should be the purposes of education. They have no special competence to do so. It is time for citizens and educators alike to abandon this approach and to concentrate upon the organizational, technological, professional, legal, and managerial changes which are desperately needed to make public education effective.

These comments cannot logically be taken to mean that the broad purposes of education are unimportant. Water is important to fishes, but it is not a *problem* for them if they are comfortably ensconced in the middle of the ocean. Shelter for my family is important but it may not be one of my problems if I have just paid off the mortgage. To repeat, I am not denying the importance of the broad purposes of education; I am only contending that their problematic character has been greatly exaggerated.

THE PURPOSES OF EDUCATION AS A
STRATEGIC PROBLEM

Thus far in this chapter, I have tried to explain why I do not regard conflict over broad purposes as the most crucial problem in American education. I have also tried to explain why the determination of the broad purposes of education is not a philosophical problem. At this point, I should like to discuss these broad purposes from what might be called a strategic point of view. I mean by this that I wish to analyze them from the standpoint of the way in which they are formulated, approved, and modified. Previously, I expressed the view that the public should be the final source of authority for the general objectives of education. But this view says nothing about the way in which these objectives come to be proposed, accepted, or rejected.

To illustrate what I mean by a strategic point of view, consider a situation in which a sick man refuses to consult a doctor. Meanwhile his friends and relatives are arguing over whether he has blood poisoning or an allergy. Suppose we ask, what is this man's problem? Obviously, the nature of his illness in one sense constitutes the most important problem for him. But strategically, the problem is not whether he has blood poisoning or an allergy but how to get him to consult a doctor. Given a solution to this strategic problem, we might expect a rapid solution to the substantive medical one.

Much educational controversy has ignored the strategic problems which must be resolved before we can expect to achieve any worthwhile solution of substantive educational problems. As a case in point, consider the reactions of teachers to the recent wave of criticisms of public education. The teachers often regard themselves as the scapegoats. The public is supposed to set the purposes of education, they say, but it is confused, indifferent, and inconsistent in its thinking. As a result, the teachers are caught between conflicting purposes and pressures. They are supposed to train the mind, to prepare students for college, to eradicate juvenile delinquency, to teach patriotism, the brotherhood of man, how to drive, respect for other points of view, to inculcate good manners and morals, to develop social competence, and so on and so forth. And the public not only expects an underpaid, overworked staff to accomplish all these things but shows little respect or recognition for the achievements of our schools under adverse economic and social conditions.

This is the lament of the teachers. Suppose we concede that there is much truth in it. Despite anything I have said thus far, suppose we agree that the public *is* confused, indifferent, and inconsistent and *does* expect too much for too little. But this fact, if it be a fact, often serves to conceal another aspect of the situation which is not so kind to the teachers. Teachers act as if they are supposed to sit around idly while the "great debate" over the purposes of education goes on. Then when the public has decided what it wants of its schools, it presumably will push a button and the teachers will carry out its mandate.

Even if it be granted that the public is confused as to the purposes of education, still this is not where the *strategic* problem lies. The strategic problem lies with the teachers, their bumbling organizations and their ineffectual leadership. It is their responsibility to provide the ideas and the leadership that would enable the public to think and act its way out of the present crisis. The teachers are in the best position to develop, to formulate, and to gain the necessary public support for the broad educational policies that should guide our people as a whole. Of course, in this process, the teachers must themselves be open-minded and capable of change. But if they continue to play a passive role instead of providing aggressive leadership, they might as well resign themselves to a continuation, even a worsening, of the present state of education.

It may be that I have underestimated the extent to which there is disagreement over the broad purposes of education. It may also be that I do not understand the nature of a philosophical problem and that the determination of these broad purposes is such a problem. Even so, I would insist that this determination is a matter for professional action, from a strategic point of view. In this context, public acceptance is not the prior condition of professional action; it is the outcome of it.

Chapter III

LOCAL CONTROL OF EDUCATION

One of the most important educational trends in the next few decades is likely to be the decline of local control of education. Such a development is long overdue. Local control of education has clearly outlived its usefulness on the American scene. Practically, it must give way to a system of educational controls in which local communities play ceremonial rather than policy-making roles. *Intellectually*, it is already a corpse. At least, I propose to treat it as such in this book. The proper way to treat a corpse is to conduct an autopsy upon it and then bury it promptly. Having done this, we can better understand the rationale for the school system which will emerge from the present chaos in education.

An autopsy of local control reveals several reasons for its demise. In the first place, mobility and interdependence have completely undermined the notion that local communities ought to have a free hand in educating their children. Second, national survival now requires educational policies and programs which are not subject to local veto. Third, it is becoming increasingly clear that local control cannot in practice be reconciled with the ideals of a democratic society. Finally, local control is a major cause of the dull parochialism and attenuated totalitarianism that characterizes public education in operation.

Let us analyze these reasons briefly. In order to do so, consider carefully the following question: *Who* should decide whether the children in a given community should be required to learn to read and write?

Some persons would undoubtedly argue that parents should have the right to raise their children as illiterates if they wish to do so. Most people would probably feel that the public ought to have the right of final decision in this matter. Still, there are many publics: local, state, regional, national, international, and even publics which are not defined geographically. Which of these publics should be authorized to have the last word in the matter?

Until a short time ago, every state had a compulsory education law. These laws took the power to decide our hypothetical question out of the hands of parents and local communities. Recently, however, some states have passed standby legislation which would enable them to abolish compulsory education in order to avoid racial integration in their public schools. States cannot be prevented by the federal government from abolishing public education. There is no way that the federal government can force a state legislature or local community to appropriate money to operate public schools. But what about our basic question— should the decision as to whether children shall learn to read and write be properly regarded as one for local communities or even state governments to make?

The reasons why the power to make this decision was taken away from parents and later from local communities will help us to answer this question. One reason was based upon the concept of fair play for the individual child. There was growing acceptance of the belief that a child's chances in life should not depend upon whether his parents or his local community were willing and able to educate him.

Should a child's chances depend upon whether he lives in a state which is willing to educate him? Certainly not as long as we adhere to the concept of an open society, one in which the individual's chances are not determined by fortuitous factors. As far as the individual child is concerned, the extent to which his state government is willing to provide him with an education is as much a fortuitous matter as the socioeconomic status of his parents or the educational values of his local community.

35

Consider the problem from a social standpoint instead of an individual one. We are an extremely mobile people. Most of us eventually move away from the community in which we received our education. In the year ending in April, 1958, 30,800,000 Americans changed their residence. Over 11,000,000 moved from one county to another; about half this number moved to a different state. Thus, on the average, every American moves to a different state two times during his life. Under these circumstances, does it make sense to insist that the citizens of one state have no right to insist upon literacy for the children of other states? Today, we plead for federal aid to education in order to equalize opportunities between states. Tomorrow, we could hardly contend that the federal government must stand by idly while a state legislature compounded the inequity by depriving children of an education altogether.[1]

As an abstract proposition, it has always been clear that it is undemocratic to permit educational opportunity to be determined by circumstances of race, geographical location, or economic status. It has also been clear that our national welfare was dependent upon the extent to which individual talents were able to flourish, regardless of their social, economic, racial, or geographical origins. Neither the ideal of equality of opportunity nor the fact of our interdependence is new. What is new is the urgency of these things. Proposals for federal aid to education in order to equalize educational opportunities between states have been ignored by Congress for generations. The same proposals, advanced as a counterpoise to Russian scientific progress, are now regarded as insufficient by panic-stricken congressmen who never supported them on equalitarian grounds.

Some idea of the bankruptcy of local control of education may be seen in the statistics concerning selective service registrants disqualified for failure to pass mental tests. In 1956 the lowest

[1] My argument treats control of education by the states as local control of education. Fundamentally, this identification is sound although people do not now think of control at the state level as local control. It is only a matter of time before they do so, and then the control of education at the state level will go the way of control at the parental and community levels. In point of time, the decline of community control over broad educational policy will precede the decline of state control over it, but the same forces that undermine the one will eventually undermine the other.

rate of rejection for failure was in Montana, where 2.5 per cent of the registrants failed these tests. The highest rate was in Mississippi, where 44.9 per cent of the registrants failed the tests. In ten states, fewer than one out of every twenty registrants failed to pass; in eleven other states, one or more out of every four registrants failed to pass.[2]

The vast differences among the states in the rate of disqualification are not due solely to the differences in the quality of their school systems. A registrant educated in Montana might take his selective service tests in Mississippi or vice versa. The statistics on rejection include the failures to pass because of inherited mental deficiency, and there are other causes for such failure over which the schools have no control. Nevertheless, the differences between the states cannot be explained solely by noneducational causes. Because some states and communities provide a decent minimum education for only a small minority of their children, we must, in all states, draft persons who, for family or occupational reasons, ought not to be in the armed services at all. This is only a small part of the exorbitant price we are paying for local control of education. The intellectual smog that has obscured our grasp of this fact is being cleared away once and for all by such dramatic events as the riots in Little Rock and the Russian conquests of space.

LOCAL CONTROL AND TOTALITARIAN CONTROL

The prevailing point of view is that anything but local control of education, with perhaps a few concessions made to control at the state level, would be a step toward totalitarianism. This view is profoundly mistaken. Our present system of local control is far more conducive to totalitarianism than a national system of schools would be. I know that this statement is not acceptable to the overwhelming majority of the American people, including the teachers, but I am willing to stand on it.

The assertion that our educational system tends toward totali-

[2] NEA Research Division, *Research Bulletin*, XXXVI, No. 1 (February, 1958), 29.

tarianism seems absurd on its face. A totalitarian system is one which develops a massive uniformity of outlook. It is based upon a policy of intellectual protection for a point of view that cannot stand the test of free discussion. We have a multitude of schools of all denominations or no denomination at all. Among the teachers and students in our public schools, there are adherents to every major political, economic, and religious point of view. What could be further from totalitarianism than this?

In most states the purposes and the content of education are left to local school boards to determine. Undoubtedly, there are some constitutional limits to the purposes for which communities may operate public schools. However, these limits have never been spelled out, and there is great latitude in what a community might require of its schools. Since the purposes of education are set forth locally, the predominant groups in the community tend to establish purposes which accord with their particular religious, political, economic, or social points of view. As a practical matter, therefore, local control results in the same kind of intellectual protectionism that characterizes schools in totalitarian countries.

The basic problem is not that communities define the purpose of education to be the acceptance of the Protestant faith or un-swerving devotion to the single tax or the inculcation of the tenets of the Democratic party. Some communities have not blinked at adopting purposes as sectarian as these, but this is not where the problem lies. Even where a community accepts the most liberal educational purposes for its public schools, its interpretation of what intermediate objectives and what educational programs fulfil these purposes may have the same stultifying effect as out-right adherence to a sectarian purpose. Every pressure group is for the general welfare, but each has its own version of what measures do in fact promote the general welfare. Similarly, every pressure group is for a liberal or a democratic education, but has a special version of what intermediate objectives and what educational programs lead to this result.

What is crucial is that, at the local level, it is relatively easy for a preponderant group to enforce a policy of intellectual protectionism for its sacred cows. Thus the white majorities in

Southern communities exclude instruction that is critical of racial segregation. Communities in which fundamentalist sects predominate exclude instruction critical of evolution. Some communities have prohibited the study of the United Nations or of UNESCO. Ours is a heterogeneous country, but in most communities the predominant racial, religious, economic, or political groups are able to veto whatever in the school program displeases them.

Looking at our system as a whole and seeing the existence of public schools teaching diverse doctrines, one might infer that our schools are free. We do not readily recognize the totalitarianism implicit in our situation because not all schools protect the same dogmas. Nonetheless, a diversity of schools based upon intellectual protectionism for different dogmas does not constitute a "democratic school system." At least, it does not do so if "democratic" refers to the education actually provided in these schools instead of to the legal structure which encourages a variety of one-sided programs.

The diversity of our undemocratic schools is not the only factor which maintains the fiction that we have a democratic school system. No matter how successful a group may be in excluding certain facts and ideas from the public schools, television, radio, and other mass media are almost certain to expose students to these facts and ideas. The power structure of American society is such that no single group is able to enforce or to indoctrinate its dogmas on the population as a whole. People look at this situation and say "Our schools have kept us free." They should say "Our freedoms have survived our schools."

THE MYTHOLOGY OF LOCAL CONTROL

Many persons believe that public education was not made a federal responsibility in the Constitution because the founding fathers feared the potentialities for dictatorship in a federal school system. Actually, education was not included as a federal function in the Constitution because the idea of free public education had not even occurred to the founding fathers. At the time of the American Revolution, the concept of universal public education was receiving attention for the first time and then only from a few frontier thinkers. Our decentralized school system was not an inspired stroke of genius but a historical accident, resulting from the fact that the ideal of free public education for all became widely accepted only long after the American Revolution.

Our schools have never been an important foundation of our free society. Our freedom is partly due to a separation of powers which enables us to transact public business reasonably well while avoiding excessive subjection to government officials. Perhaps for this reason we tend to regard the diffusion of power over our schools as an essential element of our free society. But adherence to the general principle that we must avoid excessive concentration of power does not automatically justify every separation or diffusion of it. Everything depends upon the circumstances— what powers are involved, who is to wield them, and so on. It is preposterous to think that merely because their political genius was expressed through a constitution embodying a remarkably successful separation of powers, the founding fathers would align themselves today with the supporters of local control of education.

People are seldom aware of the non-public character of public education. They tend to regard it as a legal concept and to neglect it as an educational concept. However, the ideal of public education means more than having some governmental unit—local, state, or federal—provide the funds to operate schools. Public education has a referent in the quality of education as well as in its financial basis. The qualitative referent is an education in which the search for truth is carried on regardless of what empires topple, interests collapse, or heads roll. Without this, public education is a delusion, as dangerous as the notion that mere government ownership of the means of production will automatically result in their operation for the public welfare instead of for private interests. The socialization of a service at any level of government is no automatic guarantee that the service will be performed in the public interest. The "new class" should have ended all of our illusions on this score.

Public schools, then, are not necessarily infused with a public spirit. Likewise, the fact that a school is privately controlled does not mean that its program is necessarily sectarian in character. The program of some privately controlled institutions such as Harvard is more free of parochial limitations than the programs in most publicly controlled institutions. In short, we cannot assume anything about the educational program of a school merely from a knowledge of whether the school is publicly or privately controlled.[3] Nor can we infer that the educational program of a school is undemocratic merely because the school is locally controlled or that it is democratic merely because the schools are part of a national system. The relationship between the legal status of a school and the quality of its educational program is never one of strict logical implication.

The system of legal controls under which schools operate is only one factor which serves to shape their educational programs. However, it is an extremely important factor. Because a national system of controls is more likely to broaden the purposes of education and to preserve the professional autonomy of teachers, it is much more likely to provide a truly liberal education than a multitude of totalitarian systems under local control. It is a striking fact that in England, which has a national system of education, the teachers are on record as being opposed to local control of education precisely because they fear that it would undermine their professional autonomy.[4] Meanwhile, teachers in the United States, who lack any substantial measure of professional autonomy, continue to act as if local control must be maintained inviolate lest academic freedom (which they do not possess) be imperiled.

The decentralization of our schools is often justified by an

[3] The notion that private education per se is superior to public education is assiduously cultivated by private school interests at all levels. It is a myth insofar as it pretends to be a generalization or even a statement of probable tendency. This myth results in outright tragedy at the elementary and secondary levels if parents assume that exorbitant fees automatically purchase educational advantages not available in the public schools.

[4] Educational leaders in England are very outspoken in their view that any trend toward giving local boards of education increased control over the financing of education would be a threat to the freedom of the teaching profession. See Sir Ronald Gould, "The Teaching Profession," *The Concept of Professional Status* (London: College of Preceptors, 1957), p. 42.

appeal to the experimental nature of this situation. We supposedly have fifty state school systems, each of which is free to try something different from the others. Each state has delegated considerable power to local school boards, which supposedly multiplies the experimental possibilities. This is thought to make for progress, since each state and each system is not only free to try something new but is free to benefit from the experience of other systems.

There is no doubt that some change for the better occurs in this way. Nevertheless, such enormous decentralization cannot be justified on the grounds that the different school systems constitute a vast pool of educational experimentation. The different schools do not constitute experiments except in the loosest sense of the word. They do not operate under conditions carefully controlled for purposes of analysis and comparison. They just operate.

Much of the experience of different systems is valuable only on the premise that education should be a state or local responsibility. A school board may indeed be interested in how another community put over a school bond campaign. But if funds came from the federal government, the experience of this or that school system in raising money would be academic.

The truth is that local control of education has obstructed rather than facilitated educational research. By and large, only large urban systems allocate funds to research. Even in these cases, the research is generally limited to problems that are of local concern. Very few school systems support any research that is even theoretically of more than local interest.

Educational research is supposed to be a function of our universities, but they also have a tendency to concentrate on local problems. Thus a university will make a study of population trends in a nearby community which desires to know where to build its new schools. Few universities devote any substantial effort to research on teaching and learning which would be of universal interest.

Educators have not learned from the development of industrial research. In industry, most research is conducted by corporations with a monopoly or near monopoly of the market for a particular product. These firms can support research intended to have a national impact because they stand to benefit from it. On the other hand, little research is conducted from private funds on products whose ownership is diffused. For example, individual farmers are generally unwilling to support research from their private funds because they would be adding substantially to their own cost of operation, while the results of the research would be immediately available to all farmers whether they had contributed to it or not.

We have much the same problem in education. Why should a particular school system support research which is for everyone's benefit? If we do not expect an individual farmer to support basic agricultural research from his own funds, neither should we expect him to support an educational research program in his local schools from local funds. The federal government supports basic research in agriculture because of the clearly evident futility of waiting for the small operator to do so. The same policy can and should be followed in education.

The U.S. Office of Education, a branch of the Department of Health, Education, and Welfare, has conducted research on certain administrative problems for many years. However, it was not granted funds for research in the art and science of teaching until 1956. In that year, $3,000,000 was made available by Congress for grants in various fields of education. The National Defense Education Act passed by Congress in August, 1958, included an appropriation of $18,000,000 over a four-year period for research on the educational use of radio, television, and audiovisual aids. It is likely that larger amounts for educational research will be appropriated by Congress in the future. But as long as education is primarily a state and local responsibility, educational research will never receive the support it ought to have. Local communities and state governments will never adequately subsidize research which is clearly universal in application.

How much money ought to be spent on educational research? Public education is a $15,000,000,000 enterprise. Enlightened practice in large-scale industry and government is to spend 3 to 6 per cent of the total budget for research. In education, this would call for an expenditure of from $450,000,000 to $900,-000,000 annually. In fact, it is unlikely that the country is spending more than $25,000,000 a year from all sources for educational research.

The suggestion that it is realistic to think in terms of a twenty-fold increase in expenditures for educational research will be considered a pipe dream by most educators. Nevertheless, such an increase would still leave expenditures for educational research at a conservative level even if we are now spending only $25,000,000 annually for this purpose. Those who blanch at my proposal should remember that we are currently spending well over $300,000,000 annually for medical research. A report submitted to the Secretary of Health, Education, and Welfare in the summer of 1958 by a distinguished advisory committee of medical educators and research executives calls for increasing our expenditures for medical research to the point where the nation will be spending a billion dollars a year for such research by 1970. Foundations which are currently supporting educational research might well support studies and action programs designed to develop more adequate sources of funds on a national basis. It does not take such studies, however, to realize that educational research has been neglected under our system of local control of education.

In this connection, it is interesting to note that one of the most persistent and most pathetic arguments against a national school system is that such a system would not permit experimentation in the schools. The assumption seems to be that centralized administration is necessarily non-experimental or that it necessarily insists upon uniformity down to every detail. Actually, several federal departments which have centralized administration also subsidize programs of research which dwarf anything we have ever seen in education. The departments of Defense and Agriculture illustrate the possibilities.

If the present structure of American education is not conducive to the support of research, it is well designed to obstruct the utilization of it. On this subject, we need only to compare the lag between the discovery and the application of knowledge in education and the lag in other professions.

In the legal profession, important developments such as Supreme Court decisions are taken into account by all lawyers within a very short period of time. When the Bureau of Internal Revenue makes a ruling which affects a substantial number of tax returns, the accountants generally absorb it within a matter of months. Everyone is familiar with the short period of time between the discovery of an effective polio vaccine and its use by doctors everywhere. In education, however, the lags between discovery and practice are scandalous. These lags are reflected in what is taught as well as in how teachers teach their subjects.[5]

The average person is little aware how long it takes for important new knowledge to be reflected in the public school curriculum. The diffusion of teacher education and of the curriculum is so great that it often takes decades before teachers realize the need to add or delete a subject or to make radical changes in the content of an accepted subject. Even after this hurdle has been passed, tens of thousands of school boards must be persuaded that these changes are desirable. "Go ye therefore and persuade all those who are affected by the decision"—thus reads the Word in textbooks on school administration. The Curriculum Committee of the PTA, the school board, the parents, the students—all must have a voice in a decision which affects them. An infinite number of banana peels lie between the professional decision to modify the curriculum and actual practice in the school.

THE BREAKDOWN OF LOCAL SUPPORT
FOR PUBLIC EDUCATION

The case against local control of education becomes more compelling when we consider the practical problems involved in introducing basic changes that require heavy expendi-

---

[5] The need for drastic revision in the mathematics and physics curriculum of the public schools is discussed in Howard F. Fehr, "The Mathematics Curriculum for the High School of the Future," *Teachers College Record,* LIX (February, 1958), 258–67, and the articles on the Physical Science Study Committee in *Science Teacher,* XXIV (November, 1957), 316–29; and *Harvard Educational Review,* XXIX (Winter, 1959), 1–36.

tures. In recent years, our high schools have **been** severely criticized for their real or alleged neglect of science. For the sake of argument, suppose that we required every high-school student who has the ability to do college work to take three years of physics during his high-school career. At this point, consider only the practical problems involved in implementing this recommendation. How would we get from the status quo to a situation in which all these high-school students take three years of physics? Regardless of whether this particular change is desirable, consider its implementation solely from the standpoint of the difficulties of making any basic curriculum reforms under the present system.

There are over 21,000 high schools across the country. In 1956, only 12,000 of these schools offered one full year's work in physics. As late as 1954, 50 per cent of all schools having tenth-grade pupils did not offer physics at all. These were usually the smaller schools, but it is interesting to note that only one-fourth of all high-school students in 1954 took as much as one full year of physics before graduation. We are thus confronted by thousands of school boards which have seen fit to offer one year's work or none at all in physics.[6] Each board must now be persuaded, one by one, to make drastic changes in its curriculum. Since it is unlikely that the additional work in physics will simply be added to the present curriculum, each board must make its own decision about what subjects shall be reduced or eliminated. Each board must decide what to do with the teachers in subjects to be eliminated.

Even assuming that most school boards could be convinced that more work in physics is desirable, can they be persuaded to implement such a change? If a school is to offer three years of physics instead of one or none, extensive remodeling would almost invariably be required. There would have to be substantial expenditures for new laboratory equipment and supplies. Just how substantial these would have to be is evident from a survey

[6] I do not mean to suggest that there is one school board for each high school. Actually, the number of school districts is over twice as large as the number of high schools, even though many districts include more than one high school.

made in March, 1957, by the NEA's Research Division, which covered the needs for instructional equipment in high-school science and mathematics classes. More than half the schools responding to the inquiry from the Research Division reported that they did not even have direct electric current in their physics laboratory. Less than 15 per cent of the schools reporting had a calculator available for mathematics courses. Only one school in five had a graph board in every mathematics classroom; about two out of every five did not have a graph board in any mathematics classroom. The report indicated that 57 cents was the average per pupil expenditure for supplies and consumable equipment in science classrooms.[7]

Before most high schools could offer three years of physics, local school boards would have to adopt salary schedules much more attractive than the prevailing ones. Even though physics is now offered for only one year in the majority of schools which offer it at all, there is already a large and growing shortage of physics teachers.[8] It would be pleasant to think that school boards which have heretofore balked at making minimal expenditures for physics instruction will suddenly be inspired to vote the necessary taxes for an adequate program. Unfortunately, the odds are overwhelmingly against such a development.

Under our present system of financing education, the states and local communities supply over 95 per cent of the funds for public education. Our nation spent a total of $14,827,550,000 for public education in 1957–58. Of this total, about 3 per cent came from federal sources, 40.8 per cent from the state governments, and 56.2 per cent from local sources. On a state-by-state basis, there are wide variations in the relative amounts supplied by local, state, and federal sources. In Alaska, 14.7 per cent of

[7] NEA Legislative Commission, *The Hidden Need: Basic Instructional Equipment for Schools* (Washington, D.C.: National Education Association, nd.). See also n. 8 below.

[8] The National Defense Education Act passed by Congress on August 23, 1958, provided an appropriation of $300,000,000 over a four-year period for science equipment. It will be interesting to see how long it takes for Congress to recognize the futility of waiting for local school boards to institute salary schedules high enough to attract reasonably competent science and mathematics teachers.

the total expenditures for public education came from the federal government, whereas only 0.5 per cent of the total spent in New Jersey were from this source. Also in 1957–58, Delaware raised 88.2 per cent of its school revenues at the state level and 10.3 per cent at the local level. At the other extreme, Nebraska raised 6.9 per cent of its school revenues from state sources and 89.5 per cent from local sources.[9]

In general, the trend has been for local sources to provide a decreasing percentage of the total expenditures for public education. Expenditures by the state governments tend to constitute a much larger percentage of the total, while the percentage from federal sources has been increasing but at a much slower rate than that coming from the state governments. There are several reasons why this structure is not working and can never be made to work.

In the first place, some states have four to five times as much taxable wealth, on the average, as other states. The differences between school districts are even greater; some school districts have several hundred times as much taxable wealth as others. Ability to support education has also been studied in terms of what educators call "personal income payments per pupil enrolled," that is, the total income received by the residents of a state divided by the number of pupils enrolled in its public schools. In 1956–57, "personal income payments per pupil enrolled" amounted to $17,432 in Delaware and $3,754 in Mississippi. Needless to say, there were even greater differences between the richest and the poorest school districts.

For many years, authorities on school finance have pointed out that the poorest states and school districts usually devote a higher proportion of their resources to education than do the wealthier ones. Theoretically, one might argue that this is not very significant because all states and school districts should be making a greater effort to support education. However, this argument overlooks many important considerations relating to our tax structure.

One such consideration is the competitive aspect of state and

[9] Data from Research Division, *Estimates of School Statistics* (Washington, D.C.: National Education Association, 1959).

local taxation. In New York City, there is a concentration of high incomes unequaled anywhere in the country. Nearly 20 per cent of all internal revenue is collected in New York State. Thus it would appear that New York City, which is permitted to levy an income tax but does not, and New York State, which does levy an income tax, could easily have the very best schools in the nation. The difficulty is, however, that many high-income persons and corporations would move if tax rates were raised substantially. This is why it is often fallacious to criticize states and communities for not raising taxes; if they did so, they would lose people and businesses to areas less concerned about education. The need for, and justice of, federal taxation for education would thus remain even if there were substantial equality in wealth and revenues among all states and school districts. The fact that a federal tax cannot be evaded at the expense of children in a particular school district is one of the most compelling reasons why we must move toward an educational system financed by the federal government.

Still another factor makes it very unlikely that an adequate educational system could be financed without massive federal support. School districts have been forced to raise most of their funds (54 per cent in 1953–54) by means of the property tax. Unlike most other taxes, property taxes must usually be submitted to popular vote. As is usual in this type of situation, the people who are badly hurt by a substantial tax increase are more effective politically than the diffuse majority which benefits from the increase. The result is that an increasing number of bond issues for school funds are being defeated in communities sympathetic to public education. Here is some indication of the rising (and often justified) tide of resentment against such discriminatory taxation.

The need for federal support of public education, if not for a federal system, is also related to the way in which the federal government supports non-educational activities. In the new highway program, for example, the federal government will spend $9.00 for every dollar appropriated by the state governments. Obviously, this will result in a bigger share of the state dollar being spent on highways. And, in general, states are tending to appropriate funds for projects which will receive substantial support from the federal government. Thus the only way that education can compete for funds, even at the state level, is for the federal government to assume a much larger share of the educational budget.

THE CENTRALIZATION OF PUBLIC EDUCATION: PRELIMINARY CONSIDERATIONS

The preceding discussion has by no means covered all the practical difficulties inherent in our present system of educational controls. To continue with our hypothetical change for a few more paragraphs, bear in mind that more and better physics teachers in high schools require more and better physics teachers in institutions of higher education. However, our colleges and universities are already confronted by serious shortages of qualified physics teachers. In the United States, there are about 1,200 institutions of higher education which train teachers. Who will see to it that a sufficient number of these 1,200 institutions will have enough money to retain good physics professors and adequate supporting facilities?

If the high schools drop certain subjects to make room for additional physics courses, the colleges which prepare teachers must do likewise. What are the colleges going to do with their faculties and their facilities for training teachers in the subjects no longer taught in the high schools? There is no assurance that the colleges will produce teachers prepared to teach three years of high-school physics just because the high schools would like to have such teachers. In fact, the colleges are not even producing enough physics teachers to offer one year of high-school physics. Many colleges are able to keep going only because they enrol large numbers of prospective teachers for inexpensive subjects. They would be devastated if required to increase their offerings in physics and decrease them in such inexpensive subjects as history and speech.

Perhaps these complex problems can be solved within the

framework of local control of education. Somehow, we might just muddle through the last half of the twentieth century with an eighteenth-century educational system. The chances are, however, that the practical sense of the American people will be forced to assert itself and that they will develop a centralized school system while simultaneously reaffirming their faith that any such system is un-American.

It is difficult to predict the form which centralization will take. It is possible that centralization may take place while much of our present educational structure is formally left intact. To understand this, bear in mind that a national system of education is not necessarily the same thing as a federal system of education. A federal system would be one in which the schools were operated by the federal government. However, education might continue to be the legal responsibility of states and local communities, while it also became substantially similar over the country as a result of non-governmental pressures.

The point can be illustrated by the situation in medicine. Legally, medical education and licensure are controlled by the various state medical boards. In actuality, these state boards are so dominated by the American Medical Association that we have a national system of medical education. There are some variations from state to state, but nothing compared to the chaos in teacher education and licensure. There are other occupations wherein the legal control of professional training and entry is a state function but wherein the activities of national professional organizations and accrediting agencies have brought about a national system of professional training and licensure.

The same possibility exists for elementary and secondary education. That is, even though education at these levels may continue to be the legal responsibility of state and local governments, various organizations and social pressures may force the different states and communities to adopt the same basic educational program. Under these circumstances, it would make sense to speak of an educational system that was national but not federal.

It is unlikely that in the next few decades we shall have a

federal school system covering the entire country. Such a development would occur only if the failures of states and communities to carry out their educational responsibilities were to be brought home dramatically to the American people by some such event as the abolition of public education in the South. I am convinced, however, that we are about to move rapidly toward a national system of education. What is certain is not the form but the fact that we shall have a much more centralized system of education in the future than we have had in the past. The idea that the present chaos in education is the price one has to pay for living in a democracy, or the even more nonsensical notion that the prevailing educational chaos is one of the foundations of democracy, will linger on but without any real force in our society.

Unquestionably, the most important barrier to a centralized system of public education is the notion that any such system would be "totalitarian" or "undemocratic." We are warned that a centralized system would provide an opportunity for one particular group, say a political party, to seize control of the schools, and by indoctrinating its point of view, maintain itself in power. Since this line of reasoning is undoubtedly the basis of our fear of a centralized school system, I wish to consider it at some length in this and the following chapter.

Those who think along these lines usually point to Soviet Russia to illustrate the dangers of a centralized system of education. But it should be obvious that one cannot assume that a centralized system per se is more likely to be totalitarian than our own. England, France, and the Scandinavian countries all have national systems. In all of these, there is less political interference with teachers than there is in the United States. Put positively, there is more freedom to teach and to learn in all of these national school systems than there is in the overwhelming majority of schools in the United States.

In the United States, how would any particular group, be it political, religious, or economic, achieve such complete control of all schools that it could produce a generation of unthinking disciples? To develop such a generation would require complete control of our mass media. This in turn would presuppose fairly complete control of the government. Any pressure group which could achieve such controls would have no need to control the schools. Indeed, it could safely permit schools to operate as they do now, preparing generations of civic illiterates who firmly believe they have fulfilled the highest obligations of citizenship when they have flipped a lever in a voting booth.

We already have many schools supported by the federal government. What evidence is available indicates that the teachers in these federal schools have more, not less, freedom than teachers elsewhere. For example, there is as much or more academic freedom at Howard University, which is supported by federal funds, than there is at the overwhelming majority of institutions of higher education.

People are opposed to a centralized system of schools for many reasons, not all of them noble ones. Some of the opposition comes from private school interests which would not share in the federal funds which will undergird such a system. We need private schools, but the arguments which some private school spokesmen make against federal aid or a federal school system are unrealistic. Private educational institutions whose *raison d'être* is to keep the faithful from being exposed to heretical points of view oppose federal aid to education on the grounds that such aid would mean mass conformity and indoctrination. The free and independent mind which these institutions claim to nurture is what some of them fear above everything else.

Nonetheless, it must be conceded that many people have a gnawing fear of a centralized school system which is quite unrelated to any thought that their particular points of view might not survive in such a system. These people do not fear for their points of view in an atmosphere of intellectual freedom. They would not exclude a fair presentation of other points of view in the schools even if they had the power to do so. Their fear is for the integrity of the system, not for the fate of their particular views on political, economic, religious, racial, or other controversial issues.

Ironically, these fears often are based upon experiences with local control. Every inadequacy of a local board reinforces rather than weakens the fear of a federal system. Under the present system, the worst blunders are confined to a limited area. What would happen, people ask, if a national school board or federal school administrator were to engage in the educational follies which characterize some local school boards?

The answer is that it would be a calamity, but the more we centralize our school system (up to a point, of course), the less likely it is that such a calamity will occur. The crucial point is that at the national level, no one group has the kind of power to interfere with the educational program that one sees every day under a system of local control. The rabble rousers who can successfully frighten a large city school system like that of Los Angeles into dropping an essay contest on the United Nations would not have a chance in a federal school system. Nor would the more powerful pressure groups be able to shape the educational program to their own ends. None has sufficient power by itself to do this. Each would be watched and checked if necessary by all the others if it attempted any massive interference with the educational program or with educational personnel. Since no non-professional group would have the power to dictate the educational program or personnel policies, and since teachers would not be subject to local censorship, the teachers would be free to discuss points of view which are now proscribed by local boards of education.

The fact, if it be a fact, that no pressure group would be able to dominate a centralized system might not sound very appealing. Would the integrity of such a system rest upon a balance of power among large national pressure groups, all of whom would subvert the school program to their own ends if they could? If so, what assurance is there that tomorrow, or the day after, the balance of power will not change so as to provide one of these groups, or a combination of them, with the opportunity they seek?

If by "assurance" is meant an ironclad guarantee, of course there is none. We are choosing between practical alternatives, not between mathematical solutions, one of which is the perfect answer. It is local control of education which provides a greater opportunity for national pressure groups to dominate the educational programs of the public schools, on a *national* basis. The reason is that local school boards are unable to withstand the pressures which can be generated by powerful national organizations which know what they want from our schools. However, there is another factor which seems to me to clinch the case for a centralized school system, at least insofar as the criterion of academic freedom is concerned. This factor is the impact which centralization is likely to have upon teachers' organizations and the role which they would play in protecting the integrity of a centralized public school system.

Chapter IV

PUBLIC AND PROFESSIONAL
DECISIONS

Within the foreseeable future, local communities will no longer determine what subjects are to be taught or what textbooks and teaching materials are to be used in the public schools. Because this power will be taken away from local communities, it will also be taken from parents, PTA's, citizens' committees, veterans' organizations, and other individuals and groups which currently exercise their power over the curriculum through local school boards. The purpose of this chapter is to explain why authority over the curriculum will be taken from local school boards, with whom this authority will be lodged, and how these developments relate to the alleged dangers of a centralized school system.

At the present time, the power to decide what subjects should be offered rests primarily with local boards of education. In some states, certain subjects are required by state law. In other states, local school boards have unlimited freedom to determine the curriculum. In still other states, a state government may make its financial support to local school districts contingent upon compliance with state regulations concerning the curriculum. Legally, local boards are free to go their own way in this type of situation. Practically, they seldom do so.

Of course, in approving curriculums, local boards must give some thought to a variety of pressures. The curriculum policies of accrediting agencies must be respected. Otherwise, students will not be given credit for their work when they transfer to other schools or apply for admission to college. The colleges exert heavy pressure on the public school curriculum through college admission requirements. The effect of such requirements varies from community to community. A community in which a high proportion of graduates goes on to college will be more responsive to college admission requirements than a community from which no one goes on to college. However, granting the existence of these and other pressures, it is the local school board which ordinarily has the final word on what subjects are to be taught in its schools.

The history of spelling as a school subject illustrates why this is a harmful procedure. For a long time, spelling was offered as a separate subject. Just before 1900, a number of studies indicated that the time devoted to spelling soon reached a point of diminishing returns. That is, beyond a certain period of time, students did not learn to spell appreciably better by devoting more time to the subject—two hours a day devoted to spelling did not seem to produce appreciably better spellers than fifteen minutes devoted to it.

As a result of such studies, proposals were made to reduce the amount of time devoted to spelling as a separate subject. The reaction to these proposals was often uninformed and foolish. Many people thought a new breed of teachers, opposed to spelling, had taken over. Actually, the proposals were made by educators who fully accepted the objective of developing good spellers but who also were critical of the traditional way of achieving this purpose. Nevertheless, proposals to change the amount of time devoted to spelling had to run the gauntlet of every school board whether or not they knew or cared particularly about the evidence on the subject.

We have similar problems today. English as a school subject usually includes two subject matters, grammar and the study of English literature. With respect to grammar, evidence indicates that its formal study is not as important as the extent to which a person is accustomed to hearing and reading good grammar in his daily life. Furthermore, although time should be set aside for the study of grammar, there is some question as to the best distribution of time. The typical way of teaching grammar is to have students write essays which are corrected by English teachers. Instead of regarding grammar as a separate subject called "English," it may be better to put more emphasis upon grammar as it is used in all subjects. The history or geography or science teacher ought to insist upon good grammar as much as the English teacher.

If there were more emphasis upon good grammar in *all* subjects, teachers might reasonably decide to devote less time to English as a *separate* subject. Their purpose would not be to undermine high standards of grammar and composition but to achieve high standards in a more efficient way. Nevertheless, no matter how clear and convincing the evidence, can anyone doubt the public reception that would be accorded proposals to reduce the amount of time devoted to English as a school subject? Undoubtedly some school boards would approve the change. But many others would not, or would not until the teachers had spent more time in persuasion than they do in research. The businessmen, reading only the conclusion and not the evidence or the rationale for it, would be up in arms. The schools are already turning out illiterates, and here is a proposal to reduce the time devoted to English! Some proponents of private education, never too squeamish about the basis of their criticisms of public education, would point to the proposal as proof positive of what they had been saying all along about the public schools. Nor can much help be expected from our newspapers, few of which publish any research reports relevant to the educational proposals that receive wide publicity.

Actually, there is no need to use hypothetical examples to illustrate the folly of according non-professional boards of education the power to set the curriculum. Thousands of school systems do not offer any foreign language. This is not as foolish as the thousands of others which offer a foreign language for only one or two years. There is no real point to the study of a foreign language unless the students acquire the power to use it. Such power cannot ordinarily be acquired in less than three or four years of study. Nevertheless, only a very small number of school systems offering foreign languages provide more than one or two year's work in the languages they offer.

Strictly from the standpoint of efficiency, it does not make sense to force the professional employee to justify his every means to reach an end which everyone accepts. If there were a serious question whether teachers should develop students who can read and write clearly, that would be one thing. But if there is agreement on the purpose, then it is the task of the professional to evaluate the means employed. He is not paid just to be in the classroom; part of his job is to keep abreast of current research in his field. It also does not make sense to expect school boards, which are non-professional bodies, to keep up with all the research in all subjects. Common sense calls for placing the decision-making power over the curriculum with the persons who are being paid to know more about it than the layman does.

The notion that most school boards are satisfied to accept professional advice concerning the curriculum is not warranted by their performance to date. What advice educational personnel give school boards is heavily influenced by their need to cater to the prejudices of these boards. In many communities, the teachers dare not recommend curriculum changes which are professionally sound because the changes are not politically expedient.

A common technique employed by superintendents is to organize a committee of the school board or a citizens' committee on the curriculum. Such committees are used to study and recommend changes in the curriculum, and they usually include some teachers or have teachers assigned to work with them. Eventually, the committees often make the same recommendations which the teachers would have made immediately. But the whole procedure is unfair and inefficient. If the citizens differ from the teachers, the latter naturally feel that their professional expertness has been disregarded or called into question. If the citizens always accept the views of the teachers, the citizens inevitably come to feel they are being used for window dressing.

Sometimes the rationale for including lay citizens on curriculum committees is that this is the way to prevent "excessive professionalism." The non-professionals are supposed to act as watchdogs on the teachers, who might otherwise abuse their professional autonomy. However, the practice of including lay citizens on agencies designed to answer professional questions rarely works well, either in education or in other professions. The public interest is almost invariably better served by leaving professional questions to the professionals. I say this in the full knowledge that some public school personnel have made indefensible curriculum proposals. The curriculum that must be justified to a larger professional community will often be much different from the one which must be justified to a board of non-professional persons.

Many prominent critics of public education believe that public school personnel are responsible for introducing trivial subjects past the unsuspecting guard of school boards. The school boards have allegedly been taken in by the professional pretensions of their superintendents and curriculum experts. No diagnosis could be more fallacious. The "modern" school administrator believes that public opinion determines what is professionally defensible. Nothing could be further from the minds of most school administrators than a firm determination to provide a curriculum that is professionally defensible, regardless of public opinion. School administrators ought to try to shape public opinion concerning the curriculum, but, in fact, school administration in the United States is degenerating precisely because school administrators *ask* instead of *tell* the public what should be taught in the schools. It is their catering to public opinion, not their attempt to ignore it, that should be criticized.

Virtually all of the "what's wrong with public education" books end with a clarion call for citizens to attend PTA and school board meetings to achieve this, that, or the other reform. Such appeals have a certain plausibility; in the mind's eye, we can see an aroused citizenry resolutely marching on the school board to safeguard the education of children. In reality, the citizen-watchdogs often turn out to be PTA mothers, professional Legionnaires, people who want the school bus to stop closer to (or farther from) their homes, young men on the make politically, and other groups and individuals with assorted axes to grind. Most have a sincere interest in the welfare of public education, but this interest gets so intermixed with their private interests and their hobby horses that the net result of their participation is not especially beneficial.

The quality of the recent books on public education varies a great deal. Good or bad, none of the books has made a dent in the status quo.[1] The significant thing about them is not their impact, which has been virtually nil. It is that regardless of their educational position, the authors uncritically accept the thesis that educational reform is, in the first instance, a matter for public instead of professional leadership. The appeal to a diffuse citizenry to save our schools is futile, not because the schools do not need saving but because most worthwhile educational reforms will have to be initiated and carried out by the teachers. Books that urge citizens to exercise a closer rein on curriculum and methodology merely reinforce the absence of professional autonomy in public education; in doing so, their impact, if they have any, is to make it more difficult to carry out needed educational reforms.

[1] I am referring to such books as Irving Adler, *What We Want of Our Schools* (New York: John Day Co., 1958); Arthur Bestor, *The Restoration of Learning* (New York: Alfred A. Knopf, 1955); James B. Conant, *The American High School Today* (New York: McGraw-Hill Book Co., 1959); Alfred Lynd, *Quackery in the Public Schools* (Boston: Little, Brown & Co., 1953); Robert M. Hutchins, *The University of Utopia* (Chicago: University of Chicago Press, 1953); John Keats, *Schools without Scholars* (Boston: Houghton Mifflin Co., 1958); H. G. Rickover, *Education and Freedom* (New York: E. P. Dutton, 1959); Mortimer Smith, *The Diminished Mind* (Chicago: Henry Regnery Co., 1954); and Paul Woodring, *One Fourth of a Nation* (New York: McGraw-Hill Book Co., 1957). The one possible exception might be Dr. Conant's book. However, this book was published only after Dr. Conant had worked with school boards all over the country on his findings and recommendations for action. It is as accurate to think that Dr. Conant's prestige and organizational spadework made his proposals effective as it is to think that the logic of his position is responsible for their impact.

PROFESSIONAL AUTONOMY IS NOT
UNDEMOCRATIC

Quite frequently, the supporters of professional autonomy in education are thought to be persons who have an
authoritarian bent. Be this as it may, there is nothing undemocratic in the proposal that teachers and not school boards should
decide the subjects to be taught. However, the reasons why
people think the proposal is undemocratic are not difficult to
understand. The relevant cliché here is that the public should
determine what should be taught, and the teachers should determine how to teach whatever it is that the public wants taught.
Like most educational clichés, this one has just enough plausibility to stay alive despite the abuses to which it leads.

The crux of the matter lies in the words "what" and "how."
The public determines *what* to teach in the sense that it sets the
broad purposes of education. The fallacy lies in regarding the
what as a list of subjects instead of a set of purposes. "Teachers
should teach students to communicate effectively" is one thing.
"Teachers should teach penmanship one hour per day in the
sixth grade" is something else again. The first statement is one
of purpose, which should be made by the public; the second
is a statement of the means to be employed and should never
be legislated by a non-professional agency.

At any time, research may justify changes in the time devoted
to a subject or the grade levels at which it is taught. This is why
it is foolish for a state legislature to prescribe the curriculum.
It is like legislating that drug X must always be employed to
cure a certain illness. Imagine the predicament that doctors
would be in if they had to have a new law passed every time they
wished to employ a new and better drug for this illness.

The other side of this coin is the confusion over *how* in "how
to teach." If people were clear that the public should determine
the broad purposes of education, then it would be understood
that "how to teach" refers to subjects as well as teaching methods.
When we say that a doctor knows how to cure, we do not mean
to limit the *how* to a bedside manner. We mean it to include the

substantive knowledge which the doctor applies to achieve a desired end.

The public expects the medical profession to prolong life and to reduce physical pain. No one in his right mind assumes that the public should decide what drugs should be used and that doctors should decide only how to apply them. Absurd as this would be, it is exactly analogous to the notion that the public should determine the subjects to be taught and teachers should decide how to teach them. "How to teach" should be interpreted to mean "how to achieve the goals set for the profession by the public." It would then be clear that non-professional determination of the curriculum is a threat, not a safeguard, to our democratic institutions.

How does one know what purposes the public has set for education? At the local level, the school board can state what they are. The state legislatures can do this at the state level. There is no inherent reason why Congress cannot and should not do this at the national level. In fact, we are likely to get a much better statement of purpose from Congress than we are from a local board.

Theoretically, it is possible for the American people to accord the schools a very narrow purpose. Instead of saying that one of the purposes of education is to develop an understanding and appreciation of our democratic heritage, they might say that the purpose of education is to insure that every student can recite the Bill of Rights from memory. We would regard such a statement of purpose as a mistake. Our thought would be that what the people specified as an end (memorizing the Bill of Rights) should have been regarded only as a means to a larger end. Whether memorizing the Bill of Rights is the best means to this end should be left up to the teachers to decide.

Still, it is logically possible that the American people could define the purposes of education in such a way that the curriculum would not be a matter for professional decision. I hope this will not happen, but it remains a possibility. No matter how often it is pointed out that memorizing the Bill of Rights should be regarded as only a means, and not a very effective one at that, people might insist that this is what they want their schools to accomplish above all else.

It should be clear, however, that the danger of having such narrow purposes decreases as we have a larger and larger community set the purpose. In particular localities, people might insist the purpose of education to be the rejection of the theory of evolution, or an understanding of the history of Oklahoma, or an appreciation of the importance of dairy products, to cite only a few things that have been prescribed by state laws. But, at the national level, such narrow purposes would be manifestly unfeasible.

In the abstract, practically everyone agrees that our schools should teach students to think critically in important areas of concern—politics, economics, international affairs, and so on. What subject matters and what teaching methods will develop such critical thinking? You cannot develop critical thinking if the students and teachers cannot criticize anything. Teachers who are serious about developing critical thinking must have the freedom to be critical of points of view learned at home, in the community, at church, and so on.

A teacher who wishes to develop critical thinking in the area of international relations must stimulate students to analyze the concept of sovereignty. I do not say the teacher should persuade students that national sovereignty is outmoded or even that what was good enough for McKinley's day is not good enough for ours. These are conclusions which a student might or might not reach after he has studied the matter. The point is that if the teacher does his job properly, some students may get the idea that national sovereignty is not the unmixed blessing that the local American Legion post makes it out to be.

The development of critical thinking, of an understanding and appreciation of our democratic heritage, of dedication to the truth wherever it may lead—these purposes take precedence over any particular political, economic, racial, religious, or social point of view. This means that in principle no point of view should be above analysis and criticism in the public schools. However, as things stand, teachers do not have the power to act on this principle.

In the long run, we must see to it that non-professional determination of the curriculum is as unthinkable as non-professional determination of the techniques of brain surgery. In the short run, the solution is to resist non-professional interference in every way possible while working toward a system in which such interference would be impossible. However, there is no thought that individual teachers should seek martyrdom. The problem is essentially one of institutionalizing professional autonomy rather than leaving it to heroic individual defenders to protect. And it should go without saying that there is a difference between non-professional interference with the curriculum and non-professional advice concerning it. My contention is that teachers should have the power to decide what subjects are to be taught. This does not mean that teachers would be justified in ignoring every suggestion from non-professional sources or in adopting a "To hell with the public" point of view.

If teachers should decide what subjects should be taught, then clearly they should decide what instructional materials should be used in teaching these subjects. The power to determine the choice of instructional materials is in fact the power to determine the subjects. Nevertheless, some people persist in the view that the school board should decide on teaching materials.

The absurdity of having school boards, parents, or citizens' committees evaluate and pass on the fitness of instructional tools is most clearly reflected in controversies over "subversive" materials. It is or ought to be obvious that instructional materials are neither subversive or non-subversive in isolation. The Constitution can be utilized for subversive purposes, just as the *Daily Worker* can be used to expose the nature of the Communist party.

Suppose a high-school history teacher decides to have his class study whether the Communist party in the United States is or is not a tool of Russian foreign policy. What materials should he use in the classroom? He should have the official statements of Russian foreign policy and those of the Communist party in this country. For the latter purpose, he would need copies of the *Daily Worker*. By reading them, students could see for themselves how the Communist party in the United States did in fact follow every turn and twist of Russian foreign policy.

All this seems reasonable enough—or does it? I doubt whether a single public school teacher, superintendent, or school board in the country would dare to order such materials, even though they provide the most devastating information on the Communist party obtainable anywhere. The teachers are not going to take any chances with a school board which, if it is typical, divides instructional materials into such ridiculous categories as "subversive" or "patriotic." And the board is not likely to "take any chances" on a teacher who requests such materials. SCHOOL BOARD APPROVES *Daily Worker* IN THE SCHOOLS—a millennium of explanations would not undo the damage of one such headline.

In a country where the professional autonomy of teachers cannot be violated with impunity, it is respected. Where it is respected, newspapers do not print such headlines. Both the public at large and the teachers would be amused by them. In fact, a situation giving rise to such a headline would never arise where teachers had professional autonomy. What would be news would be the foolishness of some non-professional agency in classifying instructional materials as "subversive" or "non-subversive."

Fundamentally, the confusion between public and professional decisions in education is one aspect of our failure to clarify the role of the expert in a democratic society. As a result of this failure, we count noses to answer questions which should be settled by reference to experts, and we rely upon experts to answer questions which should be settled by counting noses. In education, the first type of mistake is the most prevalent. Public education developed in the United States in the absence of a teaching profession. Teachers simply accepted without question the idea that the community had the right to decide subjects, instructional materials, and methods as well as the broad purposes of education. Teachers often questioned whether the community was exercising its rights wisely, but they never questioned the legitimacy of these rights.

66

The precarious employment position of public school personnel, especially school administrators, is another important factor contributing to the absence of professional autonomy in education. Superintendents are often hired on a year-to-year basis. Few have contracts running for more than two or three years, and practically none has tenure. This being the case, few superintendents are going to insist upon their professional autonomy when they know that such a stand may cost them their jobs.

What is worse, the exposed position of superintendents inevitably weakens their support for the professional autonomy of teachers. Suppose a teacher uses a textbook which the school board regards as subversive. Since the superintendent has to please the board, not the teachers, to hold his own job, he is not likely to take the attitude that instructional materials are strictly a matter of professional autonomy. He is much more likely to tell the teacher to drop the textbook. This will, of course, be done in the name of democracy. The elected representatives of the people have the right to say what goes on in their schools; if they have said that *Robin Hood* tends to justify stealing from the rich to give to the poor, we must drop *Robin Hood*—or else.

The real tragedy in this situation is that superintendents and teachers accept it as the way things ought to be. Those who submit curriculum proposals to their school boards are not fuming inwardly at their lack of professional autonomy. In their own eyes, they are following the democratic process when they permit, even encourage, school boards to tell them what subjects to teach and what instructional materials to use. Thus a power structure and an ideology which antedates any serious thought of teaching as a profession is precisely what stands in the way of its becoming one today.

Schools of education, and especially their departments of educational administration, have propagated the notion that public school personnel should not make an important change in the curriculum without first securing community support. This counsel is typically labeled a "democratic theory" or a "democratic philosophy" of education. Advocated as it usually is without any conception of professional autonomy, its effect has been to make any insistence upon autonomy appear undemocratic to the teachers themselves. In all seriousness, the damage has been even worse. The concept of professional autonomy has been eliminated from the consciousness of teachers. In effect, the schools of education tell teachers they are "professionals" while simultaneously undermining the independence which is an essential ingredient of professional status.

Much of the opposition to determination of the curriculum by teachers is due to certain misconceptions about the rationale for professional autonomy. First, it should be emphasized that the justification for taking authority over the curriculum away from local boards and giving it to the teachers is not that the teachers are always right or that the school boards are always wrong, even on admittedly professional matters. Professional autonomy does not result in the absence of error but in the reduction of it.

Opponents of professional autonomy often point to particular instances wherein teachers have made indefensible curriculum decisions. Such instances are cited to justify the denial of teacher control over the curriculum. Such reasoning demolishes only the nonexistent position that perfection is the rationale for professional autonomy. It is like saying that laymen should prescribe drugs because doctors make mistakes.

This brings me to a related point. Professional autonomy does not mean the absence of any control over the professional workers. On the contrary, it means that controls requiring technical competence are exercised by persons who possess such competence. To be specific, if the issue is whether a teacher is choosing appropriate instructional materials, the issue should be settled by persons competent to judge this, not by irate parents or American Legion posts or even intelligent and responsible school boards. Professional autonomy, then, does not imply the absence of all controls. On the contrary, it logically calls for the development of a wide range of professional controls. These are often much more rigorous than those exercised by lay boards.

People tend to think that giving professional autonomy to public school teachers is tantamount to turning over public business to private interests. Actually, it amounts to turning over public business to the kind of public employees most likely to conduct it properly. It can safely be stated that more unwarranted inferences have been drawn from the fact that teachers are publicly employed than from any other single fact about public education. Teachers should not control entry to teaching, should not determine the subjects taught or the instructional materials to be used, should not be permitted to bargain collectively, should not have the right to strike, do not need to formulate and enforce a code of professional ethics—the list of *non sequiturs* that invariably follows the "point" that teachers are public employees constitutes a fairly complete catalogue of what's wrong with American education.

When the average citizen thinks of himself as an employer, he tends to think of public servants as a group that should be servile. The public (which is "I") puts up the money, so "I" have the right to tell teachers what to teach. But it is not an unqualified good for employers, public or private, to be able to coerce their employees. Surely, we can learn this much from what is going on in other parts of the world. When the private patient says to his physician: "Restore me to health, but I shall tell you what drugs to use and the dosage," the physician is ethically obligated to withdraw. The reason is that the physician cannot take responsibility for the health of his patient under such circumstances. The same reasoning would apply in the case of a publicly employed physician—he would be obligated to withdraw from employment wherein he had to submit to lay interference in professional matters.

This is the way teachers should regard the matter. If school boards prescribe subjects and teaching materials, the teachers should withdraw as employees on the grounds that it is not in the interest of their client, the public, to permit it to make professional decisions. Teachers cannot accept responsibility for educational outcomes under such circumstances, any more than physicians can accept responsibility for medical outcomes when laymen tell them how to diagnose and what to prescribe for the sick. It is not in the public's interest as an employer to insist upon lay control of professional matters. The teachers have no moral obligation to acquiesce in the actions of any employer, public or private, who violates their professional autonomy; on the contrary, their obligation to the public interest is to resist such action with all their might.

THE SIGNIFICANCE OF PROFESSIONAL AUTONOMY IN A CENTRALIZED SCHOOL SYSTEM

There are many other misconceptions concerning professional autonomy in public education. However, instead of going into all of them at this point, I should like to relate the analysis to the decline of local control of education and to the possible dangers of a centralized system of schools.

Considerations of national security and fair play require an unprecedented educational effort in this country. Many states and communities will not make this effort—some because of last ditch opposition to integration, some because they are too poor, some because they do not put a sufficiently high priority on educational needs, and some for other reasons. Meanwhile, the national stake in good education will become much more urgent in the near future. The problem then becomes how to reconcile the national stake in an adequate educational system with state and local options to have an inadequate system. Such options, heretofore taken for granted as in the national interest, will inevitably be recognized as contrary to it in the near future.

Every argument made for federal aid to education will gain added force as the disparity between imperative educational needs, on the one hand, and state and local efforts, on the other, grows wider and wider. Consider these arguments: federal aid is needed to equalize educational opportunity, to insure that we have an adequate supply of trained manpower, to equalize financial responsibility as well as educational opportunity, to eliminate the tensions and conflicts resulting from large numbers of uneducated citizens in a mobile society, and so on. If states refuse to strengthen their schools, if they weaken them, if they abolish them altogether to stave off integration, do all these reasons for federal support for education become invalid?

The answer is that they do not. If there is no state or local school system, or if such as exists does an inadequate job even with federal aid, every argument for federal aid becomes an argument for a national system of education.

In the near future, the American people will realize that they have been misled by both proponents and opponents of federal aid to education. The proponents have argued for federal aid on the grounds that some states and communities simply do not have the resources to support good schools. The opponents have opposed federal aid on the grounds that states and local communities do have the financial ability to support good schools. However, the idea that federal aid to education should be dependent upon the ability of states or communities to support education will soon be recognized for the hoax that it is. Some children in wealthy communities are being denied a decent education because their communities refuse to support their schools adequately. Is the national loss any less than if these children had been denied an adequate education because their communities were too poor to provide it? Is it any less unfair to the individual child to let him be deprived of an education because his community refuses to tax itself than to let him be deprived of it because the community has no resources to be taxed? The answers to these questions must be to place the national welfare and the equities of individuals above the financial condition or educational caprice of states and local communities.

As the pressures for a national school system continue to grow, many thoughtful people will take a new look at the problem of federal controls. As they do so, they will become aware of certain basic changes in our society which bear upon the problem at hand. When our nation was founded, the American people were a much more homogeneous group, in terms of their occupations, than they are today. In 1789, over 90 per cent of the people made their living directly or indirectly from farming. At that time, therefore, the problem of avoiding an excessive concentration of federal power required a geographical, rather than an occupational, distribution of power.

Today, however, the problem of avoiding an excessive concentration of federal power must be solved in occupational rather than geographical terms. A cotton farmer in Mississippi has more interests in common with cotton farmers in neighboring states than he does with engineers or teachers or grocers in Mississippi. Thus he attempts to advance many of his major interests through his occupational group rather than through state or local communities. I do not wish to oversimplify this process, but the distribution of power among occupational groups has tended more and more to overshadow its distribution among geographical groups. When the people of a state take important action, usually they are strongly influenced by the attitudes of occupational organizations.

As occupational specialization increases, so does our interdependence. As our interdependence increases, the regulation of occupational affairs becomes more and more a federal instead of a state function. And as this happens, it becomes apparent that avoiding an excessive concentration of federal power requires the development of powerful occupational organizations. Thus a larger and larger portion of industry and commerce has become interstate rather than intrastate. There is more and more regulation of industry and commerce at the federal level. But the factor that stands in the way of arbitrary federal action is the emergence of occupational autonomy and strong national organizations of employers and employees.

These considerations are appropriate to education, and especially so because it is or should be a profession. A profession is an occupation which possesses some kind of expertness. It is in the public interest to accord the professional worker the autonomy to make the decisions which require this expertness. This is why it is undesirable to have non-professional control over the curriculum in any school system. We already have a tremendous amount of non-professional control over the curriculum, a fact which should not be ignored in assessing our present way of doing things. If a centralized system of education places the power to decide curriculum content with appropriate professional persons, it will be a great improvement over the present system.

In asserting the need for professional controls in a centralized system, I do not mean to contend that *all* professional decisions, such as those relating to the content of the curriculum, should be made at the national level. Some professional decisions should be made at state or local levels. Others should be regarded as the prerogative of the individual teacher. The same point should be made with respect to non-professional educational decisions. Some of these decisions should be made at the national level, others at state or local levels, and still others should be made by parents or students.

Regardless of whether a decision is professional or non-professional, the extent of state, local, or individual option to make the decision must be decided in the first instance at a more inclusive level. This is only common sense. The American people as a whole have made national defense a federal concern. It would be senseless to permit individual citizens to decide for themselves whether the country was at war or whether they should bear arms in its defense. Nevertheless, within the limits of national policy, we permit individuals to choose their branch of military service or to enlist in the regular army. In education, there is an urgent need for a clear-cut, comprehensive national policy outlining the educational decisions to be made at the national level and those to be made at state, local, or individual levels.

Our chief concern should be the way in which professional opinion is recognized and articulated in a centralized educational system. For example, the fact that some educational decisions may be made by federal officials is not important per se. What is important is who are these officials, how are they appointed, what specific decisions do they have the power to make, to what extent is their tenure dependent upon satisfying professional opinion, and so on. We must not attempt to settle concrete questions of power and authority in education by generalized appeals to the virtues of a particular level of control.

At present, there is confusion in every direction. The line between professional and non-professional educational decisions has all but disappeared. The main result of this has been a tremendous amount of professional decision-making by non-professional agencies. In addition, the emphasis upon local control has given local school boards the power to make all sorts of non-professional decisions which should be made by non-professional agencies at state or national levels.

It must be clearly understood that both professionalization and centralization can be overdone. There is no pat formula by which we can classify decisions. Each must be evaluated on its own merits to determine whether it is professional in nature and also whether it should be made at the national, state, local, or individual level. We will never make educational sense until we stop using phrases like "local control of education" or "federal control of education" or "academic freedom" as substitutes for clear thinking about the decision-making structure of education.[2]

For example, there has always been *some* federal control over public education, which, like any activity of state or local government, must be carried on within the limitations set by the Constitution. All the furor over racial integration in the schools should not blind us to the fact that the Supreme Court has been deciding such issues as whether or not children in public schools must salute the flag in school, must be released for religious instruction, or must sing Christological Christmas carols. And although some may have questioned the wisdom of its decisions, no one has seriously questioned the Court's constitutional right, its duty even, to make *a* decision on these matters.

Under our present system, people are accustomed to having pressure groups of every kind and description shape the school program to their own ends. They presuppose that the same policy would prevail under a centralized system. Obviously, if the educational program in a centralized system were to be placed under congressional control, or under the control of a politically dominated national school board, the ensuing political

[2] For a more thorough analysis of this point see Myron Lieberman, *Education as a Profession* (New York: Prentice-Hall, 1956), chap. IV.

melee could be disastrous. But the way out is to realize that the problem is not which public—local, state, or national—should establish the educational program, but how to make certain that it is in the hands of the teachers, where it belongs. Once the American people understand the occupational dimension to the distribution of power in our educational system, they will have overcome a major psychological barrier to a centralized educational system.

It is not just a question of whether a more centralized system would be better *if* it were characterized by professional autonomy. The crux of the matter is that centralization itself will hasten the establishment of professional autonomy in education. In the long run, the integrity of public education in a centralized system can and must be protected by the rise of a teaching profession. Nevertheless, it is not altogether germane to fear centralization because the professional organizations of teachers are abysmally weak at the present time. Centralization will dramatize the weaknesses of teachers' organizations and put in motion the forces that will eliminate these weaknesses. Centralization and professionalization are inevitable, not in spite of what people think but because enough people will eventually think long enough and hard enough about public education to realize that no other policy makes sense.

Chapter V

THE MYTH OF THE TEACHING PROFESSION

Education has been bypassed by the professional revolution which has done so much to transform our society. However, such a revolution cannot be delayed much longer in education. Even if the teachers are content to work with a nineteenth-century personnel structure, the facts of modern life will compel them to abandon it.

According to the present personnel structure in public education, all public school teachers are members of the same profession. Since teachers really constitute a number of highly diverse occupational groups, the policy of treating every teacher as a member of the same profession leads to a superficial and self-defeating unity among them. It is as if we were to lump together the directors of General Motors and laborers on the assembly line and call them both "automobile manufacturers." For most purposes, the use of a common occupational label would tend to cover up important differences rather than to reveal basic similarities between the two groups. This is precisely what has happened in education as a result of the policy of treating all teachers as members of the same profession.

The tendency to regard all teachers as members of the same profession has resulted in more than semantic confusion. It has lowered the quality of education and all but nullified the development of a strong teaching profession. For this reason, we must develop educational policies that frankly recognize the basic differences between various kinds of teachers. To be specific, instead of regarding teachers of all grade levels and all subjects as specialists within a single profession, we must regard them as a cluster of related but different professions. This cluster must work together in the schools just as doctors, nurses, psychologists, pharmacists, dietitians, and therapists work together in hospitals. But the present situation in education is as absurd as the situation would be in medicine if all the medical occupations just mentioned were labeled "doctors" and treated as specializations within the same profession.

In order to understand the harmful consequences of regarding all teachers as specialists within the same profession, we must first analyze professional specialization in a general way. What determines whether two occupations should be regarded as specializations within the same profession or as two separate professions? If we are clear on this point, we shall be in a better position to appreciate the need for drastic changes in the teaching profession.

To clarify the problem, compare two persons who are in different occupations with two persons who work in specializations within the same profession. The first situation can be illustrated by A and B, who are both salesmen. A sells refreshments at baseball games. B sells electronic computing machines, the cheapest one selling for $250,000. The second situation can be illustrated by X and Y, who are both lawyers. X is a specialist in corporation law. Y is a specialist in the law of wills and trusts. Why do we think of A and B as members of different occupations although both are "salesmen" and of X and Y as members of the same profession despite their specialized interests?

In the case of A and B, the category "salesman" reveals superficial similarities but covers up basic differences. It takes no formal training to sell refreshments at baseball games, but to sell enormously complex electronic computers does require a considerable amount of specialized training. B must have a background in mathematics and engineering. As a person dealing with the top executives of large corporations and government agencies, he must have a thorough grasp of data-processing systems. In short, B is a mathematician or an engineer who sells. There is nothing in common between A and B in such matters as their training, the organizations to which they belong, the occupational literature they read, the conditions under which they work, the social and economic status of their jobs, and so on. To regard them as members of the same occupational group because they both sell would be patently absurd.

The situation with respect to X and Y is much different. They have a substantial amount of common training. If their professional training was at all divergent, the divergencies represented only a small portion of their total education. Although X and Y may belong to a few different occupational organizations, they also share membership in city, state, and national bar associations. To some extent, they read the same professional literature. They are governed by the same governmental and professional agencies and work under the same code of ethics. There is no inherent difference in their social and economic status, as there is in the case of A and B. In short, although there are differences between X and Y, we are referring to basic occupational similarities in referring to both as "lawyers."

In the case of our two salesmen, nobody is fooled by the common label. The very fact that "salesmen" covers so many diverse groups who sell inhibits us from making any judgments about an individual because he is a "salesman." For this very reason, salesmen who must have a technical background and who operate at the upper echelons of industry try to appropriate some other label (e.g., sales engineer) to distinguish themselves from the huge undifferentiated mass of "salesmen." Persons at the bottom of the sales group are only too glad to use the broad label "salesman" to cover up their specific place in the hierarchy of salesmen.

Now the situation in education is that basically diverse groups do use the same label, to wit, "teacher." However, unlike the situation with respect to salesmen, people are misled by the common label "teacher" into according the same treatment to these diverse occupational groups. These groups have two characteristics in common; they teach and they work in the same building. But these common characteristics are extremely superficial. They can be compared to the similarities between a man who sells at a cigarette counter and one who sells electronic computing machines in the same building.

To illustrate what happens when we regard all teachers as members of the same profession, I wish to analyze briefly some aspects of the increased attention being given to driver education in secondary schools. I have selected driver education for this purpose because it is probably the fastest growing subject in American high schools. A study conducted by the NEA in 1954 indicated that 47 per cent of our high schools had some kind of offering in this area; about 80 per cent of these schools offered driver education as a separate course or devoted an equivalent amount of time to it.[1] To simplify the analysis, I shall consider the impact of this growth only upon high-school teachers of physics.

Physics teachers and driver-education teachers are supposed to be specialists within the teaching profession. In the overwhelming majority of school systems, both kinds of teachers are paid exactly the same salary so long as they have the equivalent amount of training and years of teaching experience. They belong to the same local, state, and national educational associations. (They may, of course, also belong to organizations limited to teachers in their field of specialization. However, such organizations for specialized groups coexist with the comprehensive organizations for all the practitioners in all the professions.) At the state level, the requirements for licenses for both groups are regulated by the state education department. On the surface of things, it appears that these two groups of teachers represent specializations within the same profession. What is wrong with this situation?

It does not take professional training to teach people how to

[1] NEA Research Division, "The Status of Driver Education in Public High Schools," *Research Bulletin*, XXXII (April, 1954), 55–56.

drive a car safely. Most of us learned how to drive from relatives or friends who were not licensed teachers of driver education. Our "teachers" simply passed on a skill which required very little formal education to learn or to teach. This is borne out by the fact that it has never been deemed necessary to insist upon a college degree for people who operate private driving schools. Such schools are ordinarily permitted to operate without any governmental regulation whatsoever, in the same way that private language, music, or dancing schools are conducted.

Perhaps the most conclusive evidence in this matter is in the amount of specialized training actually taken by teachers of driver education. The 1954 NEA study of driver education included a summary of the specialized training of driver-education teachers.[2] Of the driver-education teachers, only 32.4 per cent had had a one-week intensive course, and 14.5 per cent had no special preparation in driver education at all. Only 12.6 per cent had one full semester course (that is, not a summer-school course) in driver education.

When it comes to physics teachers, the situation is altogether different. The person who has had only a one-semester course in physics cannot teach physics to high-school students—and everyone knows that he cannot. The physics teacher needs a considerable amount of specialized training; the driver-education teacher needs so little specialized training that it is unrealistic to accord him the same professional recognition.[3]

Bear in mind, however, that in the overwhelming majority of school systems, physics teachers and driver-education teachers are accorded the same financial and professional recognition. They are paid the same, and they participate equally as faculty members and in the professional organizations of teachers at local, state, and national levels. Obviously, one possible result of these policies is to upgrade the status of driver-education teachers. Such upgrading has happened to some extent. And if

[2] *Ibid.*, p. 67.
[3] It is true that the specialized training of teachers includes more than their training in the subjects they teach. However, it is difficult to believe that teachers of driver education need to study much of anything besides driver education to do their job properly.

the only effect of the inclusion of driver education teachers within the teaching profession were to upgrade their status, perhaps no particular harm would be done. However, let us analyze what happens in practice when driver education is included in the teaching profession.

First, what are the academic and intellectual standards for the occupation of teaching going to be, now that we have added driver education to it? It takes less intellectual ability and training to teach driver education than to teach physics. Ostensibly, this need not matter. Standards for becoming a driver-education teacher could be maintained at such a high level that such teachers would be on a par with the physics teachers. In practice, however, the inclusion of driver-education teachers in the teaching profession is certain to depress the standards for the teaching group as a whole.

As a general rule, the larger an occupational group becomes, the more difficulty it has maintaining high standards for entry. In the instant case, if the intellectual standards for a teaching certificate are maintained at the level required for good physics teachers, it becomes impossible to recruit enough teachers of driver education. The result is that standards are lowered to the point where it becomes possible to recruit an adequate supply of both kinds of teachers. This weakens the quality of physics teaching and the professional status of physics teachers.

The deterioration of the teaching profession as a result of the inclusion of subprofessional teaching groups can be a rather subtle process. We want teachers who can do a good job of teaching their subject. However, our notions of what constitutes good teaching can and do vary, and they depend in part on the available supply. Thus in teaching fields characterized by extreme shortages, there is a tendency to revise downward our idea of what constitutes good teaching. Conversely, in areas where there is an oversupply of teachers, we raise our standards. The supply of teachers for a given subject thus affects our notion of the appropriate minimum level of competence a teacher should have. In this way, deterioration of the quality of teachers is often hidden by lower standards.

If we lower the standards for teaching a particular subject, then teachers who were unsatisfactory according to the old standards may be satisfactory according to the new ones. Thus whether it takes as much ability to teach driver education as it does to teach physics depends upon what standards we accept for a good job of teaching each subject. By insisting upon extremely high standards for driver-education courses and very low ones for physics courses, we might produce a situation in which there was no significant difference in the ability required to teach one subject or the other.

Despite the difficulties of comparing the intellectual abilities required to teach different subjects, it should be obvious that more intellectual ability and training are required to teach high-school physics than to teach driver education. Bear in mind that the intellectual abilities and training required to teach a subject bear a functional relationship to the performance expected of the students. We could insist upon very rigorous requirements for teachers of driver education. We might require them to have a Ph.D. degree and ten years of safe driving experience and to be able to disassemble and assemble automobiles blindfolded. But we would quickly agree, I think, that these requirements would be absurd. The reason is that they would not be reflected in the results which driver-education teachers achieve in their teaching. True, the requirements might make some difference, but the difference would not be enough to justify the requirements. It would be like requiring a janitor to have a master's degree in sanitary engineering.

Sooner or later, we come to a point where the benefits to be expected from additional formal training are not worth the costs to the individual and to society. There is no simple way to determine where this point lies. It varies from one occupation to another. Sometimes it is very difficult to decide the cutoff point. But, conceding all this, it must be clear that we are overtraining the driver-education teacher by requiring him to take four to seven years of higher education, whereas we are not overtraining the physics teacher by these requirements.

These comments most definitely do not mean that every high-school physics teacher is intellectually superior to every driver-education teacher. My supposition is that as a group the physics teachers are intellectually superior to driver-education teachers but that there is some overlap between the two groups. The crux of the matter is, however, that this overlap has been achieved by overselecting and overtraining driver-education teachers and underselecting and undertraining physics teachers.

THE INTEREST-IN-CHILDREN MYTH

Most people believe that the common characteristic of good teachers is their desire to work with children. The majority of teachers, school administrators, and schools of education share this view. In most education textbooks, the teacher's attitude toward children is commonly stated to be the most important characteristic of good teachers.

The truth is that a person's attitudes toward working with children are a relatively useless criterion of his success as a teacher. What is most important, and here I am speaking primarily but not exclusively of high-school teachers, is the teacher's knowledge of and interest in the subject he teaches. This is an unpleasant truth in many places. It is a truth which has been misunderstood in the liberal arts colleges and ignored in the colleges of education. It is a truth that may be misinterpreted. But it is a truth that must and will be clearly recognized in the near future.

Several tests have been devised to use in counseling students about their choice of careers. These tests have been constructed from studies of the interest patterns of people who have been successful in a particular occupation. These studies indicated that there are rather common patterns for persons in particular occupations. For example, forest rangers will tend to be more interested than the average person in some things and less interested in others. If a person shares the same interests as successful forest rangers, there is some basis for thinking that he might well consider becoming a forest ranger. Similarly, if a person's interests appeal to few forest rangers, then there is considerable doubt whether the choice of a job as a forest ranger would be appropriate for that person.

The research of Strong, who was a pioneer in the field of vocational interests, is of particular relevance. In the early years of his work, Strong assumed that the interests of high-school teachers, principals, and professors of education would be similar. Later, he came to the view that:

> The theory upheld by most departments of education that all teachers should be interested in teaching young people first and only secondarily interested in their subject matter may possibly be a worthy ideal. But the facts of the case are that these two types of men [high school social science and mathematics-physics teachers] have quite different interests. . . . The same situation holds true with respect to women high school teachers . . . Evidently teaching per se, like managing per se, is less significant than the specific kind of teaching or managing.[4]

It can be stated categorically that the point of view expressed by Strong is now the accepted point of view in vocational counseling, though not in the schools of education themselves. In assessing a person's potentialities for becoming a good teacher, vocational counselors today give more weight to a person's interest in a subject area than they give to his interest in working with young people.

These comments should not be interpreted to mean that a person's attitudes toward children are completely irrelevant to his success or failure as a teacher. The point is that insofar as teaching is concerned, the key consideration usually is whether the person has a strong interest in his subject field. Granted, some people who have a strong interest in a particular subject would make poor teachers because of their negative attitude toward children. However, as a rule, persons with the necessary subject-matter interest and ability regard the school as one of many environments in which they can fulfil this interest. "Working with children" is generally not the decisive factor, one way or the other.

Let me explain the point in a different way. Suppose that from all the persons who have the necessary interest in physics to be good physics teachers, we choose one hundred at random. If this

---

[4] Edward K. Strong, Jr., *Vocational Interests of Men and Women* (Stanford, Calif.: Stanford University Press, 1943), p. 161.

is done, only a small number, perhaps twenty-five at most, will be unfit for high-school physics teaching because of their disinterest in or negative attitude toward children. On the other hand, suppose that from all the persons who have a strong interest in working with children, we again select one hundred at random. Suppose also that from this number, we wish to exclude those who would not be good physics teachers because of their insufficient interest in physics. This time, we would have to exclude a very substantial portion of the group, perhaps seventy-five or more.

In other words, a person might be unfit for teaching either because of a lack of interest in working with children or a lack of interest in the subject. At the high-school level, however, it is the subject factor which most often rules the person out. The emphasis upon interest in children is misplaced—not because the prospective teacher does not need it, but because its absence is seldom the reason why people are poor teachers. It is the same mistake that characterizes concern with loyalty of teachers. Of course, teachers should be loyal to their country, but it is not reasonable to say that loyalty is what you are looking for in teachers, when only one teacher out of a million is disloyal. Loyalty is important, but it is not selective in this context. Similarly, an interest in working with children is important, but it is not much of a selective factor in assessing whether or not people will make good teachers.

I do not wish to contend that the interest tests currently in use are infallible or even that they are of very great value. They are, however, widely used in vocational counseling and they seem to serve a useful purpose, so long as they are used with good sense. In most universities, the training of guidance and vocational counselors is a function of the department of education. It hardly behooves these departments to question the value of the tests at this late date merely because they implicitly contradict the dogma that a strong interest in working with children is the chief criterion of a good teacher. The surprising thing is that the departments of education should be the last instead of the first to abandon this dogma.

Consider the problem from the standpoint of recruitment. If teaching required the same ability level, regardless of subject, and if a strong interest in children were the common denominator of teachers, it would be surprising to find extreme shortages in some fields and a surplus in others. This is what we do find, and the reasons should be obvious. The college student who has the ability and interest to be a physics teacher is the same person who has the ability and interest to be a physicist in private industry. There is no particular reason why he should enter teaching if his salary as a teacher is going to be substantially lower than it is in industry.

THE ECONOMICS OF A UNITARY
PROFESSION

The worst consequence of regarding every person who teaches in public schools as a member of the same profession is that this policy weakens the quality and quantity of instruction in areas where good teachers are most urgently needed. The present crisis in high-school physics is an illustration of this fact.

If we accept the view that teaching should compete with other fields, we should be in a position to offer physics teachers starting salaries of $6,500 to $7,500 with good prospects of making $10,000 within five years and opportunities for outstanding persons to make $25,000 to $50,000 a year before retirement. Actually, the highest salary schedules for teachers in the entire country do not even begin to compete with this salary range. In New York City, which has a moderately high schedule, the top salary for a classroom teacher with a Ph.D. degree and thirty years of teaching experience is $8,700—about $2,500 more than starting salaries for persons with a bachelor's degree in physics. No wonder the potential physics teacher turns his back on a teaching career.

To get more and better physics teachers, we must provide substantial increases in their salaries. However, since the overwhelming majority of school systems pay all teachers the same amount regardless of the subject taught, they find it necessary to raise the salaries of all teachers just to attract those who are most needed. And as might be expected, school systems are re-fusing to pay all teachers the salaries needed to attract good physics teachers. The result is a shortage of physics teachers, a shortage that will become more acute as long as we adhere to the fiction that all teachers are members of the same profession.

Consider what happens when a school budget is presented to a school board. The addition of driver education has increased the total budget, thereby making it more difficult to get approval of higher salaries for physics teachers. The more teachers there are, the more difficult it becomes to increase their compensation. This helps to explain why the uncritical accretion of more teach-ing specializations has had a disastrous effect upon the economic status of those teachers who should be getting paid at a profes-sional level. To raise the salaries of all teachers a few per cent a year makes a substantial difference in any school budget. This is why the inclusion of a new subject is a matter of the greatest importance to the teaching profession.

In addition to increasing the total budget, and thereby making it more difficult to pay any teacher a professional salary, the addition of subjects like driver education has a harmful effect on the public's attitude toward the teaching profession. A school board is not going to pay teachers $10,000 a year to teach adoles-cents how to drive safely. The fact that these salaries must be paid to get good high-school physics teachers is never going to overcome the public aversion to overpaying the driver-education teacher. In short, the teacher who should be paid as a professional is bound to suffer when his salary is geared to salaries for teachers who do not require professional training.

Teachers ought to be the first to scrutinize critically proposals to expand educational offerings, since they are the first victims of unwarranted educational inflation. Nevertheless, teachers are currently the chief advocates of educational inflation in our society. They wish to add innumerable subjects, increase the services offered, extend education for all downward to the nursery level and upward to the graduate school—and they lament their economic and professional problems! The crucial point, however, is that quite apart from the welfare of teachers, or of some teachers, what the country needs is not so much more and better teachers in general but more and better teachers in specific areas of instruction. Of course, it is always good to have better teachers, regardless of grade level or subject. Certainly, all teachers should be striving to improve their teaching. But it is time to confront the possibility if not the fact that certain of our efforts to improve teaching at all levels and subjects have actually weakened it in some of the most important areas of instruction.

Note that the problem must eventually plague the colleges as well. If there are to be high-school teachers of driver education, there must be college professors to teach the prospective high-school teachers what and how to teach in driver education. And so the entire process is repeated at the college level. Professors of physics are bound to suffer when college budgets include professors of driver education, their secretaries, their offices, their supplies and equipment, and so on. The inclusion of professors of driver education (usually labeled professors of safety education) has the same adverse effects upon the social and economic status of physics professors as the inclusion of driver-education teachers has upon high-school physics teachers, and for exactly the same reasons.[5]

It is as if medicine and nursing were combined in one profession. Obviously, to secure enough physicians and nurses, it would be impossible to adhere to present standards for admission to medical school. The desperate need for nurses would force medical schools to lower their standards for entrance and for graduation in order to produce an adequate supply of the two specializations. If admission standards were lowered to accommodate a larger group, then the standards to pass each course would also be lowered because of the lower caliber of the student body. Inevitably, standards for graduation would also be lowered. As this happened, public expectations and attitudes vis-à-vis the medical profession would change and public respect for it would

[5] The devastating effect of proliferating courses in higher education upon the economic status of professors is set forth in Beardsley Ruml and Donald H. Morrison, *Memo to a College Trustee* (New York: McGraw-Hill Book Co., 1959).

decline. People could not pay physicians as well as they do now because they would also have to pay nurses similar fees. For these and other reasons, the inclusion of nurses would destroy the medical profession as we now know it. True, the nurses might be better off, just as the driver-education teachers are better off as a result of the false unity which regards them as the professional equals of physics teachers. But make no mistake about it, society as a whole would suffer along with the "real" physicians from any such movement to treat medicine and nursing as a single profession.

In many cases, it is difficult to say whether a certain kind of work should be regarded as a specialization within a profession, albeit the easiest and the one with the least prestige and economic rewards, or as a subprofessional occupation not to be included at all. Technically, the policy of according physics teachers the same treatment as driver-education teachers might be regarded as an inequity *within* the teaching profession. It might be argued that the shortage of physics teachers is due to the fact that their economic status is tied not to that of a subprofessional group but to that of a different specialization within the same profession. Perhaps my analogy should have been to a hospital which insisted upon hiring surgeons, the highest paid medical specialists, at the same salary as anesthesiologists, the lowest paid specialists. If the hospital wanted to get good surgeons, it would have to overpay the anesthesiologists. If it insisted on paying only the salary needed to get good anesthesiologists, it would go without surgeons or perhaps with less able ones.

Now a single salary schedule does result in inequities between some teaching groups which should rightfully be considered as specializations within the teaching profession. However, this fact has not been overlooked in proposing to exclude driver-education teachers from the teaching profession. Embarrassing as it may be, we must face up to the fact that many teaching fields currently regarded as specializations within the teaching profession should be regarded as outside the profession altogether.

In advocating the exclusion of certain kinds of teachers from the profession, I do not wish to minimize the importance of what these groups teach. The severest critics of driver education as a school subject agree that safe driving is important. However, its importance is not the only factor to be considered in deciding whether or not to include it in the curriculum. Its proponents think that if students who take driver education have a lower accident rate than students who do not, this justifies its inclusion in the curriculum. This is an erroneous, or at least an oversimplified way of judging the matter. Perhaps the time and money that go into driver education could accomplish more for safe driving if devoted to stricter enforcement of the traffic laws or better examinations for drivers' licenses. We must also consider what students could be studying instead of driver education. Perhaps our society would be better off if students accelerated their technical or civic training during the time they devote to driver education.

I can summarize my analysis here by saying that the functions of the school system need not be identical with the functions of the teaching profession. Since the schools bring together all the children, it may make sense to provide certain health and welfare services through the schools, or to use them whenever we must deal with all children. But whenever this is done, we should not deprofessionalize education by enlarging it to include every group that works in the school.

THE EDUCATIONAL PROFESSIONS

The breakup of education as a single profession will involve much more than the exclusion of certain fields from "the teaching profession." I doubt whether it makes sense to think of "the profession" merely as an entity from which subprofessional and semiprofessional groups have been excluded. It makes more sense to think of education as a cluster of professions, which include many that are of equal status. For example, science and mathematics teachers might constitute one profession and social science teachers another. There need be no invidious distinctions between them; it might simply be the case that although the same minimum level of intellectual ability is needed for both, the training for them is so different that it is unwise to lump them together.

Anyone who adheres to the notion that teaching is a unitary profession ought to consider current certification requirements. For example, in the state of New York, the permanent certificate for both elementary and high-school teachers requires a master's degree. Elementary teachers are required to have thirty-six hours of education courses and high-school teachers twenty-four hours. A minimum number of credit hours for each high-school teaching field of specialization is also specified. Both certificates require a certain distribution of courses outside the field of education.

Now insofar as the state requirements are concerned, it is quite possible for elementary and high-school teachers to get a permanent certificate without taking one course in common. This statement is not even restricted to those courses which are part of the professional training of teachers. It is, of course, unlikely that this will occur during the entire five-year period of higher education required for permanent certificates, but the state requirements leave it as a theoretical possibility. As a matter of fact, we could add a school principal and a school superintendent to this example and the statement would still hold—insofar as New York state certification regulations are concerned, it would be possible for all four of these persons to get permanent certificates without having taken one professional course or one course of any kind whatsoever in common. And yet elementary teachers, secondary teachers, principals, and superintendents are supposed to be members of the same profession!

Even this situation does not fully reveal the extent to which present certification policies are inconsistent with the view that all teachers and school administrators are members of the same profession. It is possible for two high-school teachers to receive permanent certificates without having taken so much as one course, professional or otherwise, in common during their five years of study. And in other specialized areas, such as elementary education, the amount of work which must be taken in common by all prospective teachers is negligible.

These comments are in no way intended as a criticism of the certification requirements for teachers in New York State. On the contrary, the more defensible these requirements are, the more they demonstrate the hollowness of a teaching profession that includes teachers of all subjects and grade levels. The New York certification requirements are typical of those prevailing elsewhere. There are few if any states in which teachers of different subjects and grade levels are required to have a significant amount of common training. There are many states in which even teachers of the same subject and grade level need have very little common training or none at all.

We cannot continue to have it both ways. If teachers of different subjects and grade levels are really members of the same profession, then this fact must be reflected in their training. In medicine, law, architecture, and other professions, most of the training program is taken by all practitioners, regardless of specialization. Specialized or elective study constitutes only a small portion of the total program. On the other hand, if current certification policies for teachers are at all correct, education is really a host of professions instead of a single profession with many specializations.

The more one analyzes current certification policies, the clearer it is that they are inconsistent with the notion of a comprehensive teaching profession. In medicine, law, dentistry, pharmacy, architecture, and practically every other profession, the practice is for the appropriate state agency to issue one certificate, regardless of specialization. A lawyer does not get a license to practice criminal law or corporation law; he gets a license to practice *law*. Specialization is chiefly a matter of employer-employee relations; it is not something regulated by a professional license. Thus the professionals identify themselves chiefly as members of the profession as a whole, not with a particular segment of it. In education, the tendency is to have a multitude of certificates which limit the holder to specific areas. This is more consistent with the view that education is a group of separate professions than it is with the view that it is a single profession.

How many different teaching professions should there be? Clearly, there should not be one for each subject. It is just as harmful to create separate professions which should be merely specializations within a profession as it is to ignore basic differences between professions. There is already overspecialization in some areas of education and we must constantly be on guard against the establishment of educational requirements that bear little or no functional relationship to the work involved. Education is not the only field in which unnecessary educational qualifications have been established for certain kinds of work, but it is well on the way toward being one of the worst offenders in this respect. (In this connection, for example, I question the growing trend to require a substantial amount of course work in educational administration for positions in that field.)

In the long run, we should expect the teaching professions to be built around subject areas. There will be border-line cases in which it will be difficult to decide the professional status of teachers of a particular subject. At the secondary level, there will be a few professions of co-ordinate status. There will also be a few of varying status, their number depending upon the functions which are assigned to the schools.

Perhaps the most fundamental change will be the development of elementary education as a separate profession. Historically, elementary education was so regarded until the 1940's. It was not only different but somewhat lower than high-school teaching in social and economic status. Elementary teachers were naturally unhappy about this situation. They emphasized the importance of good teaching during the first years of school. The Freudian emphasis upon the crucial early childhood years was enthusiastically indorsed by the elementary teachers; the cult of the child never carried so far in the high schools as it did in the elementary schools.

However, the most potent factors tending to equalize the training and compensation of elementary and secondary teachers probably had little to do with the functional requirements or importance of the two fields. Elementary teachers far outnumbered secondary teachers in local, state, and national teachers' organizations. As a result, these organizations inevitably came to advocate the elimination of salary differentials between the two groups. This development coincided with the need for more elementary teachers immediately after World War II. For this reason, school boards found it expedient to accept a single salary schedule, since by doing so they were able to meet their immediate needs for more elementary teachers.

As previously pointed out, in most states elementary and secondary teachers are already members of different professions insofar as certification requirements are concerned. All that needs to be done is to recognize this fact in other aspects of education. The United States is now the only major country in which the two groups are placed on an equal footing within the same profession. Partly as a result of this policy, the professional status of high-school teachers in the United States has suffered a drastic decline in the past fifty years. It is questionable whether substantial improvements in secondary education can be achieved if every improvement accorded high-school teachers must be accorded the elementary teachers as well.

Twenty-five years ago, only a handful of states required elementary teachers to have a bachelor's degree. Today, most states require it. However, the higher requirements for elementary teachers have resulted in substantial increases in their non-professional, not in their professional training. And this in turn suggests that the effort to treat elementary and secondary teachers as specializations within a single profession is not based upon actual job requirements in these two fields.

Perhaps it is true that we need to strengthen drastically the education of teachers at all levels. However, the non-school demand for people who can teach well in high school is far greater than the non-school demand for those who can teach well at the elementary level. In the days when a pool of unemployed was taken for granted, there was a plentiful supply of teachers for any level or subject. In an economy geared to full employment, the effort to attract enough good high-school teachers by conditions of employment geared to the elementary group is almost certain to fail.

Before leaving this subject, let me add a few important qualifications to my comments thus far. First, if we took the various kinds of teaching positions currently in existence, I am certain that elementary teaching should not rank lower in its professional standards and requirements than *all* secondary teaching positions. To put the matter in another way, the occupational differences between certain secondary teaching fields are as great or greater than the differences between elementary and secondary teaching. In fact, I would argue that it is fallacious to compare elementary with secondary teaching per se; the particular kind of secondary-school teaching that is involved makes a considerable difference. For that matter, I am not altogether certain that elementary teaching as such should be regarded as a homogeneous field from an occupational standpoint. My other main qualification is that this entire discussion could be invalidated by the development of a personnel hierarchy built around the teaching of a single subject. Let me turn briefly to this last possibility, since it may upset quite a few of our present policies relating to educational personnel.

THE TEAM CONCEPT

Up to the present time, the emergence of different professions has been discussed solely in relation to the various teaching fields of specialization. Thus it was suggested that teachers of science and mathematics might constitute one professional group, teachers of the social sciences another, and so on. At this point, let us consider the possibility of a professional hierarchy *within* a single subject rather than *between* teachers of different subjects.

My analogy here is again to the medical situation, wherein the doctor is the head of a medical team which includes nurses, psychologists, pharmacists, dietitians, and other specialists. The latter groups are not specializations within the same profession; they constitute a hierarchy of professions which operate under the direction of the doctors. I believe it is possible to introduce such a personnel hierarchy into education. Such a development would change the teaching profession in a revolutionary way.

For illustrative purposes, consider an elementary school which requires twenty teachers. Since superintendents usually prefer teachers who have graduate degrees, let us assume that all twenty have a master's degree. It might be possible to provide a better education for the children in this school with three teachers holding a Ph.D. and seventeen holding a bachelor's degree. (This is an arbitrary breakdown which I am using merely to illustrate the possibilities of a hierarchical structure.) Let us suppose that the persons with Ph.D. degrees are the "teachers." They are the educational equivalent of physicians. The persons with bachelor's degrees are the educational equivalent of nurses. Let us call them "assistant teachers" or "auxiliaries." They work under the direction of the "teachers," who have seven years of training. Without making any unreasonable assumptions about the situation, we can visualize a number of ways in which a staff of three "teachers" and seventeen "auxiliaries" might be more effective than one comprised of twenty teachers each with a master's degree.

1. It would provide for a higher level of technical competence in the school itself. For example, one of the Ph.D.'s could be an expert in the teaching of the basic skills. Another might be an expert in child growth and development, and in the diagnosis and treatment of psychological and physical blocks to learning. The third might be a person with considerable training in certain subject-matter fields, whose responsibility it would be to supervise curriculum planning. Or one of these "teachers" might be a person with training in arts and crafts and in teaching them in the elementary school. These "teachers," each with seven years of training, would be available in the school to help with any problem requiring expert diagnosis and treatment.

2. A good deal of the professional training for elementary teachers is often given in schools of education, far removed from any children or classrooms. Some of this training could be shifted to the school systems with great profit to everyone. This will be apparent if we consider present training programs. The average elementary teacher takes about eighteen semester hours of work in elementary education; certainly the average is not much more than this and it is possibly less. This means that each prospective teacher takes the equivalent of six courses carrying a credit of three semester hours per course. Now the typical professor of elementary education teaches three or five courses per semester.

Thus it is not unreasonable to suppose that elementary teachers currently receive their professional training from no more than two to four professors.

Bear in mind that the "teachers" in our hypothetical school will have academic and professional training which is at least equivalent to that possessed by professors of elementary education. This means that each "teacher" is able to teach the equivalent of two to four courses. In other words, the three "teachers" in our example would encompass more technical expertness in the field of elementary education than the typical elementary teacher is currently exposed to during her entire program of professional training. If each "teacher" were to teach the "auxiliaries" the equivalent of two courses, the latter would have the equivalent of eighteen semester hours of college work.

One might raise certain objections: for example, the typical elementary school will not have the library facilities which are available at a college. But facilities for scholarly study are not needed to learn to teach every practical skill. For that matter, many subjects in medical school are taught with reference to a single textbook and practically nothing else. Similarly, one might object that the "teachers" could never find time to teach the "auxiliaries." However, school systems could employ the "teachers" and "auxiliaries" on an eleven or twelve-month basis, rather than for nine or ten months. Part of the work of the "auxiliaries" would be studying under the direction of "teachers," perhaps before and after the school term. Classes could also be held for the "auxiliaries" during the school year. Instead of rushing off for an extension course on elementary methods, taught in a university classroom without a child in the building, the "auxiliaries" could be taught on the job by persons who would also be around to supervise their classroom work. In other words, the "auxiliaries" would receive some of their training as a regular part of their duties.

3. Since there are only three "teachers" who are recognized from the outset as professionals, they could easily be paid $10,000 to $20,000 a year. This would enable the schools to attract top quality personnel who would have completed a program of

professional training as long and as rigorous as that which is required for any other profession.

4. Turnover would be largely confined to the people with four years of training—those at the "auxiliary" level. This is the level at which turnover comes in other professions. The existence of the professional hierarchy would reduce its damaging effects, which would come chiefly in the lower echelons.

5. The high salaries paid the "teachers" would make it possible to attract more men into elementary teaching.

6. The hierarchical plan would cost less despite the higher salaries paid the "teachers." In the first place, there would be no need to pay all twenty persons a "professional" salary. Nurses and technicians do not receive and do not expect to receive salaries equal to those paid doctors; similarly, the "auxiliaries" would not expect to be paid as much as the "teachers." As a matter of fact, it would probably be less expensive to have three persons with seven years of training plus twenty with four years of training than it would be to have twenty each with a master's degree. That is, a hierarchical personnel structure may require more persons but still provide better education at less cost than the present system.

7. Although the hierarchical plan would provide for a higher level of technical competence in the school, it would represent a substantial saving in the over-all cost of professional training. The conventional way of staffing the school calls for twenty teachers, each with five years of college training. This comes to a total of one hundred years of college training. The suggested plan calls for seventeen teachers with a bachelor's degree (68 years of training) plus three teachers with a doctor's degree (21 years of training), or a total of eighty-nine years of college training.

Note that we could add two more "auxiliaries" and still be operating with less *total* training (ninety-seven years) but a higher level of specialized training in the school. If any hierarchical structure could reduce the total amount of time devoted to higher education, the savings to our society would be enormous. Any unnecessary prolongation of higher education represents a double loss—the expense of the unnecessary education and the loss of the productive labor which both professors and students would otherwise render.

This three "teacher" and seventeen "auxiliary" plan is illustrative only; my basic argument for a professional hierarchy would not be invalidated merely because this particular arrangement might prove less effective than our present one. Certainly, the possibilities for developing a new personnel structure are not limited to elementary education. My own conviction is not that the particular hierarchical arrangement I have suggested is the answer, but that we will develop a personnel structure in education radically different from the prevailing one. How many skill levels it will have, and what will be the proportions of professional, semiprofessional, and subprofessional personnel, are matters for research and experimentation.

Whenever I have suggested to teachers that one of our educational frontiers is the development of a hierarchical personnel structure, the character of their objections has tended to confirm my conviction that such a structure is feasible. I have been told that it is undemocratic, that there would be no way for "teachers" to work with the "auxiliaries," that Dr. Smith, who has a Ph.D. in the teaching of reading, knows less about it than Miss Jones, who does not even have a bachelor's degree, and so on.

One of the most common reactions is that it is all right to have teacher aides but they must not be permitted to teach. The assumption is that teaching is always the professional part of the teacher's job. This is questionable. In medicine, there are situations in which the difficult task is diagnostic, and the work after diagnosis may be as simple as giving the patient a pill. On the other hand, there are situations in which the diagnosis is obvious even to a nurse, but the action called for requires the highest levels of professional skill and judgment. As a practical matter, therefore, one cannot say that the medical aides should never do any diagnosing or that they should never do any medicating. The only limitation that makes sense it that whatever role they are given be appropriate to their training and experience.

Similarly, there are educational situations in which diagnosis is extremely difficult but "teaching" quite simple. For example, it might be very hard to diagnose a reading difficulty but relatively easy to supervise the remedial action needed once the diagnosis becomes clear. There are other situations in which diagnosis may be relatively simple (e.g., grading and scoring standardized tests may indicate certain academic weaknesses) but the teaching required after this point may require the highest level of skill and expertness. People who "know," before any systematic experimentation with professional teams designed to teach a single subject, that teacher aides must never be permitted to teach are not showing the open-mindedness expected of good teachers. And, in general, the intellectual level of the objections to a personnel hierarchy in education shows clearly that teachers have never even considered a personnel structure different from the prevailing one.[6] This gives me hope that when they do think about the matter, something much better will emerge from the present situation.

[6] The hostile reactions of teacher organizations to the teacher aide project in Bay City, Michigan, illustrate this point. In brief, this project was designed to find out whether a teacher with an aide could teach a large class as effectively as two teachers assigned separately to classes of regular size. Teacher organizations should be the first to propose and support such projects; instead, their negative attitude toward the very idea of experimentation in this area has been rather poorly disguised as criticism of the research design and alleged results of the Bay City project.

Chapter VI

THE MISEDUCATION OF EDUCATORS

Let me begin my discussion of teacher education with a confession of avoidance. I am not going to argue for or against the proposition that teachers take too many methods courses and too few courses in their subject fields. One reason is that I am bored by the stale and sterile academic wrangling over this red herring. Such genuine issues as are occasionally involved in this controversy will be better understood if we begin with the genuinely important problems of teacher education.

The most important problem in teacher education is this: Who should determine the content and duration of programs of teacher education? I grant that the decision-making authority, whoever it rightfully may be, will be confronted by many difficult questions. Under any structure there will be disagreements, just as there are disagreements about medical and legal and engineering education. Such disagreements are fruitful, however, only when they can be raised and settled within a sound decision-making structure. Teacher education lacks such a structure.

Most of the current controversies over teacher education are carried on apart from any thoughtful consideration of who ought to have the operating power to resolve them. It is the neglect of this issue that is primarily responsible for the perpetual chaos and confusion in teacher education. Once this issue is settled on a sound basis, we will see the orderly resolution of current controversies in this area. But unless and until it is properly settled, we might as well resign ourselves to a continuation of sterile bickering on the subject.

Let us analyze briefly how decisions concerning the education of teachers are made at the present time. This is difficult to do because the decision-making structure in teacher education is so diffuse. Every state has its own procedure, and the variations among and within states are almost beyond description. In a brief discussion, the most that can be achieved is to convey some idea of the chaos that prevails in this field.

The most common procedure is for the state legislature to delegate to a state board of education the power to prescribe the requirements for a teaching certificate. These state boards are usually non-professional bodies, appointed by the governor, and serving without pay. The certification requirements they prescribe vary widely from state to state, but whatever they are, teacher-training institutions must respect them in planning the content and duration of programs of teacher education.

Quite frequently, the legislatures set forth special requirements which the state boards of education cannot abolish or modify on their own authority. Thus some state legislatures have required applicants for a teaching certificate to have a course in the history or the constitution of their particular state. Some have required prospective teachers to take a loyalty oath. In still others, there is a legislative requirement that an applicant for a teaching certificate be a citizen, or that he have applied for his first papers.

There are also states in which the legal responsibility for prescribing the requirements for teaching certificates rests with the chief state school officer, most commonly known as the superintendent of public instruction or the commissioner of education. Frequently, it is the responsibility of this officer to recommend the requirements to the state board of education, which has the power to approve or to reject these recommendations.

There is tremendous variation in the extent to which the requirements are spelled out by the state authorities, whoever they may be. For instance, in Colorado, a prospective teacher of English needs only twelve semester hours in the "area of English" and only five in the specific subject taught (English, speech, drama, etc.) to qualify for a teaching certificate; in Kentucky, a prospective English teacher needs forty-eight semester hours in the area and thirty in the specific subject field. The requirements in other states vary between these limits.[1]

Note, however, that the course requirements laid down by the state authorities seldom go beyond specifying the required total number of hours in the subject taught, in general education, and in education courses. Thus it is usually up to each teacher-training institution to decide what specific courses will be used to meet the state requirements. This gives them a great deal of operational control over programs of teacher education.

For purposes of illustration, we may note that as of 1957 there were fifteen states which required 24 semester hours of English for a permanent secondary certificate to teach English. Now, in each of these states, it is the responsibility of the teacher-training institutions to decide what courses in English will be used to meet the 24-hour requirement. There is considerable variation among institutions on the courses actually utilized for this purpose. Such variations frequently exist even between teacher-training institutions within a particular state. In fact, students at the same institution preparing for the same license often fulfil the state requirements by course patterns which differ from student to student.

The same pattern holds with regard to the requirements in general education or in education courses. That is, despite a state regulation requiring a certain number of hours in these areas, the training institutions usually decide which courses will in fact be used to meet the state requirements. The over-all result has been sheer chaos, and even within a given state, let alone when any two states are compared, there is no assurance that the teachers who have met identical state requirements have actually had very much training in common.

Sometimes the discretion accorded the teacher-training in-

[1] W. Earl Armstrong and T. M. Stinnett, *A Manual on Certification Requirements for School Personnel in the United States* (Washington: National Education Association, 1957), pp. 29–30.

stitutions even goes beyond the freedom to decide what courses will be used to meet the state requirements. In some states, such as Nevada and Washington, the number of semester hours required to teach academic subjects is not spelled out. Instead, the state requires that the teacher shall have a "major" in the subject, and the number of hours required for a major is left to the teacher-training institutions to decide.[2]

The chaos with respect to course requirements for a teaching license is paralleled by chaos with respect to the method of selecting or appointing the state authorities which set the requirements. Even when there are similarities in title between these authorities, there are often wide divergencies in the ways in which they are appointed or elected. A state superintendent of public instruction may have substantially the same power to regulate teacher education in each of three different states. In one state, he may be chosen in state-wide elections, in another, he may be selected by the state board of education, and in still another, he may be appointed by the governor. Similarly, state boards of education may have identical powers to determine the content and duration of teacher education, but from state to state there are the widest divergencies in the constituencies and in the methods of selecting members of the board. In some states, various state officials are ex officio members; in others, there are certain limitations on who can be a member. Some states expressly exclude teachers from the board; others expressly include one or more educators. In some states, appointments are made on a geographical basis, whereas in others there is no geographical restriction or distribution required by state law.

We can summarize the situation in this way: From state to state, the power to regulate the requirements for a teaching certificate is haphazardly divided between legislatures, boards of education, education departments, superintendents of public instruction, and teacher-training institutions. The policies adopted by each of these agencies are often shaped by chance factors which should have no influence at all on teacher-education. In

[2] *Ibid.*

other words, when we take into account not only who makes the decisions affecting teacher education at the state level but also the processes by which these persons acquire their positions, it becomes clear that there is neither rhyme nor reason to the way in which teacher education is controlled in the United States.

But who *should* control it? Let me approach this question first from a professional point of view. In other professions, the practitioners themselves exercise the decisive role in shaping programs for their own training. Entry to the profession is controlled through state board examinations, and the professional schools must offer a curriculum that will enable their graduates to pass these examinations. The scope of the examinations is so broad that the professional schools have little discretion to offer electives or to require subjects not required by the state boards. The crucial point, however, is that the state boards which prescribe and evaluate the examinations are controlled directly or indirectly by the practitioners of the profession concerned.

Professional control over professional training takes different forms from state to state and from profession to profession. Sometimes it is indirect and depends more on the pressure which the profession can bring to bear upon state authorities and schools than it does on any explicit mention of practitioner control in the laws regulating professional training.

On many occasions, teachers have asked me why teachers must control entry if teaching is to be regarded as a profession. The question is really like asking why a bridge player has to take thirteen tricks to make a grand slam. The fact that teachers think they are asking a question of fact instead of a question of meaning is in itself a reflection of their widespread naïveté concerning professionalism. By definition, an occupational group is a profession only when it controls entry to that occupation. To ask whether teachers should control entry to teaching is tantamount to asking whether teaching should be a profession at all; to oppose teacher control of entry while advocating that teaching be a profession is to be confused.

One might argue that if expertness is the criterion, then we should leave professional training to the faculties of the professional schools. We cannot do this because it is necessary to have some check upon the schools themselves. This check is supplied by the state board examinations controlled by the practitioners. The very purpose of these examinations is to make sure that the self-interest of the schools does not thwart the public and professional interest in high standards of professional training. Granted, the practitioners are also affected by the standards of professional training for their profession. However, the self-interest of the practitioners is usually served by high standards, whereas the self-interest of the institutions offering professional training is often served by low standards. The state board examinations controlled by the practitioners provide a very necessary safeguard against commercialism in the professional schools.

What about commercialism on the part of the practitioners? Many observers regard control over entry largely as an attempt by professional groups to enhance their own economic position by limiting the supply of persons eligible to practice the profession. This point of view is not supported by past experience with professional controls (despite some popular prejudices against the American Medical Association in this regard). It is undebatable that there are some needless or questionable requirements for entry to many occupations. What is debatable is (1) the extent of such requirements, (2) the extent to which they would be eliminated by removing occupational control over entry, and (3) whether the harmful consequences of unnecessary restriction due to professional control outweigh the harmful consequences of permitting laymen to regulate entry into a highly complex and essential social service.

Probably the reason why most people, including most teachers, reject teacher regulation of entry is the fact that teachers are publicly employed. It is thought that this would permit public decisions to be made by a private group. The fact that most teachers are publicly employed supposedly indicates that the public has a stronger interest in the requirements for teaching than for medicine. But this fact is irrelevant. It is in the public interest to place the control of professional training in the hands of those who are best equipped to decide what is required for successful practice. This is the basic issue. Surely, it would not make sense to turn control of medical education over to plumbers and salesmen if and when most physicians are publicly employed. The analogy is appropriate; given a reasonable projection of present trends, most physicians will be publicly employed within a few generations.

Parents are every bit as concerned about the competence of doctors for their children as they are about the competence of teachers. Indeed, the final irony here is that while teachers argue for non-professional control of entry and for financing educational services from public funds because teaching is so important to society, doctors insist upon professional control of entry and a non-governmental system of financing medical care for the same reason. Of course, even if people were more concerned about the quality of teachers than about the quality of doctors, it would still make little sense to argue that the proper way for them to express their concern is by having laymen decide what doctors must study in order to be admitted to practice.

Certainly, the dangers of unjustifiable occupational protection are no greater among publicly employed professions than among privately employed ones. Unjustifiable restrictions upon the supply of doctors would be as harmful as unjustifiable restrictions upon the supply of teachers. If anything, not to be able to get a doctor when one is needed is a more serious calamity than not to be able to get a teacher. The point is, however, that there is absolutely no difference in the economics of the two situations. If the supply of doctors is restricted for the benefit of the doctors, citizens pay higher medical fees. If the supply of teachers is restricted for the benefit of the teachers, citizens pay higher taxes.

To summarize, one cannot show a single danger in professional control of admission to a publicly employed profession that is not present in a situation of private employment. By the same token, the benefits that accrue to the public from professional control in fee-taking professions would also be reflected in the publicly employed professions as well. Insofar as entry is concerned, it should not make the slightest difference whether the profession being licensed is publicly or privately employed.

THE MYTHOLOGY OF TEACHER
EDUCATION

As things actually work out, programs of teacher education are a hodgepodge which reflects the irrational controls to which they are subjected. This hodgepodge has been rationalized by the teacher-training institutions as "the freedom to experiment" with different programs. In fact, serious experimentation in teacher education is practically at a standstill. Even more important, the extreme diffusion of controls over teacher education has created a situation wherein it is practically impossible to place the education of teachers on a professional basis. This comes out most clearly when we consider the claims and counterclaims made by various types of colleges which prepare teachers.

Professors in teachers' colleges contend that these institutions are ideal for teacher training because, unlike the universities, they concentrate upon training instead of research. This is a completely antiprofessional point of view. The best professional schools, whether they be in medicine, engineering, dentistry, psychology, or anything else, are located in the universities which are centers of research. The best physicians, the best engineers, the best professionals in any field, are trained in institutions where the professors are advancing the frontiers of knowledge in the basic disciplines of the profession. The medical professors who are carrying on the most advanced research in the cause and cure of illness are going to produce better physicians than those who concentrate on teaching. For that matter, a physician could not become a medical professor, at least in a first-rate medical school, unless he were advancing the science of medicine.

Teachers should be trained only in institutions where the professors are engaged in research in the subjects studied by the teachers. If a student is going to be a chemistry teacher, he should be trained where the professors of chemistry are engaged in the study of problems in their own field. Likewise, he will be better trained if his professors in subjects which he will utilize but not teach, such as educational psychology, are engaged in significant research.

Of course, if teacher education is to be conducted on a professional basis, it must be taken away from the four-year liberal arts colleges as well as from the teachers' colleges. Furthermore, it should be taken away from them for the same reason that it should be taken away from the teachers' colleges. The four-year liberal arts colleges also lack the research orientation which an institution must have to be an adequate center for professional training.

I do not wish to give the impression that nobody in a teachers' college or liberal arts college ever does any research, nor do I mean to suggest that every professor in every university is engaged in research, constructive or otherwise. But the point is that the university is designed for research, or should be, at any rate. The existence of particular individuals who do not implement the university ideal does not alter the basic case for placing the education of teachers in the university setting, where it belongs if it is to be genuinely professional.

The squabbling over what type of institution is best equipped to train teachers is generally carried on with the most naïve assumptions concerning the professional aspects of teacher education. Professors of education have been prone to argue that the professional portion of teacher education is to be found solely in the education courses taken by prospective teachers. This is fallacious on at least two grounds. First, a teacher's professional training includes his specialized training in the subject he is to teach. In the second place, many education courses are not professional courses at all.

For example, the course labeled "Introduction to Education," which is probably the most widely offered course in education, should hardly ever be regarded as a professional course. Practically all colleges require students to take a course in political science. However, nobody regards introductory courses in political science as professional training, to be studied only by political scientists. Similarly, students are often required to take an "Introduction to Economics," in which they are supposed to acquire some insight into our economic system. Again, nobody contends that such courses are professional in nature, to be taken only by prospective economists. By the same token, I do not believe that a course which involves the introductory study of our educational system should be regarded as a professional course in education.

The fact that certain education courses are not professional must be interpreted carefully. One should not infer from this fact that these courses should not be taken by prospective teachers. Prospective teachers should be required to study our educational system. Indeed, I think it makes sense to require *all* students to study it, just as it makes sense to require all of them to study our political and economic systems. But I am equally convinced that that study of education at this level is no more professional than the courses in political science or economics which are required of all students. What puzzles me is to hear so many "academic scholars" talk about the crucial importance of education and then restrict its study as much as they possibly can. To label such academicians "confused" is to take the most charitable interpretation of their actions. At any rate, as long as professors in departments other than education persist in the untenable position that only prospective teachers should take courses in education, and not even then if it can be helped, the mistaken tendency on the part of professors of education to classify all education courses as "professional" will continue.

While many professors of education delude themselves that a teacher's professional training consists of his education courses, professors in other areas exhibit an equally naïve view of the basic principles of education for other professions. It is common to hear complaints outside departments of education (and sometimes within them) that state certification regulations interfere with institutional autonomy. Of course they do—but not as much as they should. To read all the complaints about the fact that there are state requirements for a teaching license, one would never suspect that the curriculum in other kinds of professional schools is not determined by institutions of higher education but by the state boards which control entry to the professions.

All this is not said to justify any particular certification requirements. On the contrary, I think most of them are indefensible. But the point is that many individuals, especially in higher education, do not grasp the full implications of their argument that teacher education ought to be largely the province of each institution which trains teachers. This argument may be sound, but it cannot be reconciled with the notion that teaching is a profession.

It may make sense to accord institutional autonomy to the liberal arts college, which we might justifiably permit to set its own requirements for a degree. But professional schools are supposed to operate on an altogether different basis. Here, the major concern is not with the student so much as it is with the future clients of the professional worker. In the professional school, what the student wants to study, or even what the institution would like for him to study, must give way to what the student must know and be able to do in order to carry out his professional tasks effectively. Experience shows rather conclusively that it is as unsound to permit each institution to set the requirements for professional training as it is to permit individual students to set them through an elective system.

It is true that even in professional schools students have some choices. Most notably, they can choose their area of specialization, if the profession lends itself to specialization. But even in these situations, the state boards or extralegal professional boards will frequently determine what the student must study to be proficient in his specialty. In education, every teacher is a specialist; there is no such thing as general practice. Although a qualified student should be entitled to choose his own special field, neither he nor the institution should have much discretion to determine the content of programs of teacher education. If there are rigorous state board examinations covering the minimum essentials for successful teaching, teacher-training institutions can be given considerable freedom to develop their own programs. However, this is not likely to be a major practical concession, since few institutions will find it feasible to require much more training than is necessary to pass the state board examinations.

Teacher-training institutions will object strenuously to this point of view, but they must be ultimately overruled. Their argument is that we must wait until specific patterns of teacher education prove their worth before we require all teachers to take them. The rejoinder must be that the present diffuse and dysfunctional structure of teacher education makes it all but impossible to develop better patterns or to have any pattern gain acceptance against the vested interests which would be swept away by a system of professional controls. To delay changing the present structure until we get better programs of teacher education is unrealistic. We are unlikely to get the better programs until we change the structure.

INTEGRATING THEORY AND PRACTICE

Common usage often classifies education courses as either "theoretical" or "practical." The basis of the distinction has never been too clear. The most common interpretation seems to be that "theoretical courses" are the ones with little or no classroom application whereas "practical courses" supposedly are useful in the classroom. This interpretation has had unfortunate connotations. It suggests that theory is not practical and that what is practical is devoid of theoretical content.

The "theoretical-practical" distinction should not be used to refer to the results of courses but to the context in which they are taught. Some courses, such as those in mathematics, are theoretical in the sense that their content is a body of theory. They are also practical in the sense that they are useful in application to professional problems. However, they need not be taught in a practical context; students do not have to practice manipulative skills to grasp their content.

There are other courses which are both theoretical and practical, in the sense just described, but which do require a practical context to be taught effectively. To go outside the field of teacher education, a course in surgery, like one in mathematics, has theoretical content and is certainly useful in practice. However, unlike mathematics, it must be taught in a context of application. In order to learn theory as well as skills, the prospective surgeon must be taught where there are cadavers, sick people, instruments, machines, drugs, and other accouterments. However, this fact does not mean that surgery has no theoretical content.

Good programs of teacher education should include both theoretical and practical courses as I have described them. For example, a prospective teacher should take courses in mathematics and education. The mathematics courses are purely theoretical in the sense that they need not be taught in a practical setting. But what about education courses?

Some education courses require a practical context, others do not. There are still others which would be difficult to classify. Some might be improved by having the theoretical content taught in a practical context, but the need to teach them this way may not be clearly decisive. It is in these courses that the instructor may require a few field trips or assign projects which involve some practical experience.

Let me illustrate: Courses in the history of education need not be taught in a practical context. They can properly be classified as theory courses, according to the usage I have proposed. Most courses in methods of teaching should be taught in a practical context. Prospective chemistry teachers should be taught methods of teaching chemistry while they have an opportunity to observe the subject being presented to the kinds of students they will eventually teach. Their opportunities for observation, and perhaps even for trying out what they learn in a methods course, should not be deferred until a later time.

In the actual structure and sequence of education courses, little attention is typically paid to the need to teach certain courses in this way. Prospective teachers take most of their courses at a college of education, far removed from the kinds of classes they are supposed eventually to teach. Occasionally an instructor may require some observation of schools as part of a course, but this is usually sporadic, even in the courses where practically all the teaching should be done in a practical context.

Student teaching is commonly thought to make up for the absence of demonstrations and applications in other parts of the teacher-education program. For this reason, most states require a period of student teaching for a certificate, the amount varying from state to state, grade level to grade level, and subject to subject. Nevertheless, it is doubtful whether student teaching, as it is currently taken by prospective teachers, is really of much help to them. It is usually undertaken after all other education courses have been completed or during the semester when the student teacher is completing his course work. This procedure cannot make up for the sterile way in which the other education courses are taught. Prior to the time they take their student teaching, prospective teachers have taken courses in methods, educational psychology, tests and measurements, and others in which the content requires a practical setting to be grasped effectively.

The failure to teach certain education courses in a practical context has more serious consequences than the student's failure to acquire methods and techniques. Even the theoretical content of many education courses cannot be thoroughly understood as long as they are taught apart from demonstrations and applications. Therefore, when the prospective teachers come to their period of student teaching, they have already forgotten whatever theory they may have learned in previous education courses. The effort to integrate theory and practice during student teaching fails, not because the theory is erroneous (although this is often the case) but because the students never really grasped the theory or the skills and techniques which they were supposed to have learned.

Note also that deferring the student's practical experience until his period of student teaching eliminates most of his opportunities to discuss this experience with his instructors in a systematic and fruitful way. Since he will have finished most of his course work prior to the student teaching period, the prospective teacher brings the questions generated by student teaching to the supervising teacher or the director of student teaching. These people, however, are not usually the specialists to whom his questions should be directed.

My point may also be made by an attempt to visualize how professional training in other fields would be conducted if it followed the pattern of teacher education. If the procedures currently followed by education students were followed in medicine, medical students would study anatomy, surgery, obstetrics, and other medical subjects chiefly as textbook courses. They would see no broken limbs in the surgery course, no women in labor during the obstetrics course, and no mentally ill persons during the psychiatry course. They would be told about medical principles and techniques, but all or practically all firsthand experience with sick persons would be deferred until their internship.

Of course, one shudders at the thought of what this would do to medical education. When a medical professor explains the principles, techniques, and drugs required to keep patients alive during an operation, he does not confine his activities to talking about these things. He makes sure that his students are confronted within the day or week with concrete illustrations of them. However, if medical education were like teacher education, there would be very little integration of theory and practice in the medical courses themselves. The demonstration and applications exemplifying the content of the course would be deferred, not just for days, weeks, or months but for years. In such an event, the medical students would have forgotten most of what they had learned, or were supposed to have learned, by the time they began their internship.

Teacher education should be changed to make it accord with sound principles of professional training. This will require an end to the practice of deferring practical training until the period of student teaching. A much larger measure of practical training must be included in some (but not all) of the courses which precede student teaching or teacher internships. Teacher-training institutions must put aside the notion that they can teach theory in one course, practice in another, and have the prospective teacher splice them together properly during a period of student teaching.[3]

The fact that practical experience is deferred to the period of student teaching might not be so unfortunate if it also were not bungled so badly. The student teacher usually works under the supervision of a regular teacher. The university director of student teaching or one of his assistants usually visits the student a few times during the months of practice. Even under ideal conditions, this is an unsound arrangement. Although an effort is made to get good supervising teachers, this often turns out to be a hit-or-miss proposition. The supervising teachers are generally not paid for their supervision; hence many look upon the task of overseeing student teachers as an unnecessary interruption of their work. The choice of supervising teachers frequently depends on a chain of fortuitous factors—what school systems are available, whether the principals and the teachers are interested in having any student teachers, where the student teacher lives, how far the participating school is from the college of education, what teachers are available at the times which the student teacher can spare from his other subjects, and so on.

Going back to our medical situation again, note that the very same professor who gives the lectures also supervises the practical demonstrations and applications. This fact eliminates the possibility that differences in theoretical orientation between the person giving the course and the person supervising the practical experience will leave the student without any orientation whatsoever. Even with the best of intentions, it may be very difficult for the supervising teacher to know what was taught by the professors of education, just as it is impossible for the professors to get more than a fleeting glimpse of the supervising teacher at work.

The fact that the practical demonstrations and applications and the supervision of the prospective teacher's practical training are

[3] Robert M. Hutchins has long contended that the institutions of higher education should provide the theoretical training and the professions the practical training needed for incoming members of a profession. In my opinion, this point of view overlooks the extent to which a practical context may be desirable, or even essential, to learning the theory which the professional man should know. See Robert M. Hutchins, *The University of Utopia* (Chicago: University of Chicago Press, 1953), p. 40.

not handled by the same persons who provided the theoretical content is a basic weakness of virtually all teacher-education programs. The professors are never sure of what the supervising teachers are going to do. The activities of the supervising teachers may or may not illustrate the points which the professors were trying to make in their college courses. The result is that there is little articulation between the practical experience gained in student teaching and the college courses which supposedly provide the theoretical basis for that experience.

This problem is compounded by the fact that the teachers responsible for day-to-day supervision of student teachers usually do not possess the same amount of training as the professors who give the courses. It is as if medical professors were to teach the courses and then turn over the supervision of interns to medical technicians. It does not make sense to leave the supervision of the trainee's practical experience in the hands of persons who have less training than those who teach the theory.

Many classroom teachers, especially those who supervise student teachers, would take strong exception to these comments. They would contend that the teacher-training institutions frequently send out student teachers who know a lot of unworkable theory and nothing else. They would argue that the lack of articulation between the supervising teachers and the college professors is due not to the fact that the former have an inadequate theoretical orientation but rather to the fact that the professors of education have forgotten, if they ever knew, what it was like to teach in elementary and secondary schools.

I have a great deal of sympathy with this point of view. After all, it is only what might be expected under a system where the professors of education only talk about teaching but no longer have to do any work themselves below the college level, even for demonstration or research purposes. The situation is as if upon becoming a professor of surgery, a medical professor never conducted another operation in his life. Yet the fact is that those professors of education whose responsibilities include instruction in the art and science of teaching in elementary or secondary schools rarely teach again at these levels once they have assumed their professorial positions. It should be no surprise that what they have to say becomes divorced from some of the harsher realities of the classroom. I would suggest as evidence for this the fact that classroom teachers are rarely as permissive as they were urged to be by some professors of education. The teachers simply could not retain control of their classrooms while permitting their students the freedoms which were advocated by the professors.

Student teaching is often regarded and justified as a kind of internship, comparable to that which is undertaken by future doctors before they enter medical practice. In this connection, it is interesting to note that internship programs are being abandoned by the medical schools. In 1956, only one medical school still required an internship for an M.D. degree. The medical schools have found internships inefficient, and for the same reasons that student teaching is ineffective in teacher education. All too often the future doctor would take his internship at a hospital where the supervisors were not acquainted with the training program in the medical school. Often the supervising doctors did not know as much as the interns they supervised. Many hospitals used interns as cheap labor and had no systematic training program for them. Frequently there was little articulation between the internship and the courses taken in the medical school. If the intern was confronted by a situation which led him to question something which he was taught in medical school, it was too late to raise the issue with the professor who was responsible for teaching it.

The solution in medical education has been to introduce more practical experience in the courses in the medical school, where the same persons could present theory and supervise practical demonstrations and applications. I believe we must accept substantially the same solution to the problem of integrating theory and practice in teacher education.

At the present time, teaching internships are a growing practice in teacher education. The internship ideal is viable, and under certain conditions its widespread adoption could be a boon. Unfortunately, too many programs of teacher education labeled "internships" are such in name only. The quality of these programs varies considerably. Many amount to nothing more than taking some education courses simultaneously with paid teaching. They reveal little or no articulation between the courses taken in the university and the school experience that would make them meaningful.

Actually, some internship programs have really gone off the deep end in their uncritical notions of articulating theory and practice. They have operated as if such subjects as "history of education" need to be integrated with practice in the same way as courses in "methods of teaching." However, it is as unwise to try to teach every course in a practical context as it is to teach none of them this way. On the whole, the content of a history of education course lies in a good university library. It should be sought there, without naïve attempts to teach it in a practical context. We must scrutinize each subject matter, whether in an education course or not, to evaluate the extent to which it must be taught in a practical context to be learned effectively.

These comments are relevant to the issue of whether future teachers should take their professional courses as undergraduates or whether these courses should be deferred until the student has acquired a bachelor's degree or completed preprofessional training. In most professions, students devote their full time first to preprofessional studies. When these are completed, regardless of whether they include a bachelor's degree, the students devote their full time to studies in the professional school. Training in law, medicine, and dentistry illustrates this point. Personally, I favor this policy, partly because the professional school needs the full day to do its job properly. It seems difficult to believe that our best professional schools could operate effectively if they had students for only half the day, even if the students were enrolled in these schools for twice as many semesters as they are now. There is also the fact that studies taken during the undergraduate years, especially the freshman and sophomore years, are hardly regarded as professional by the outside world.

Many people in teacher education would accept this analysis. The trouble starts when they add to it the unwarranted notion that all education courses are "professional." The result is that courses like "Introduction to Education," which should be taught to freshmen and sophomores as a part of a general education sequence, are postponed to the fifth year, where they look rather anemic compared to fifth-year work taken by law or medical students. Furthermore, the policy of deferring all education courses to the fifth year results in a situation wherein this year is often pre-empted by education courses, making it difficult for students to take graduate work in their field of specialization.

On the other hand, the situation is not necessarily improved by the inclusion of education courses in the undergraduate program. All too often, the courses so included are the ones which should be deferred to the period of professional training. Thus many schools give courses in methods of teaching early in the undergraduate years. By the time the student goes out to teach, he has forgotten whatever he might have learned in the methods courses. The period between the end of professional studies and the beginning of professional practice should be as brief as possible.

FACILITIES FOR TEACHER EDUCATION

Most current thinking about teacher education is concerned chiefly with changing the course requirements for a teaching certificate. "Reforms" usually consist of juggling the course requirements to accord with the prejudices of whoever happens to be in the saddle at any given time. Other aspects of teacher education, such as its need for more adequate facilities, are not receiving the attention which they deserve.

Teacher education should have available schools which are geared to that purpose without sacrificing any educational rights or privileges of students. Many teachers' colleges and schools of education established laboratory schools partly for this purpose. These laboratory schools were also established to provide research facilities for professors interested in studying children and how they learn. In most laboratory schools, however, the research function has all but disappeared. For this reason, these schools are not the advanced centers of teacher education that they were originally supposed to be.

The basic weaknesses of the typical laboratory school are clear from comparing its operations to those of a teaching hospital. The teaching hospital is deeply interested in the most difficult and unusual cases, for such cases are the most valuable from the standpoint of research and experimentation. On the other hand, the student body in most laboratory schools is bright and well behaved. In many institutions, the laboratory school has an unusually large percentage of faculty children, so that it takes on the character of a private school. I know of more than one school where this fact created special problems because the teachers in the laboratory school were in the same academic department as the parents of the children in their classes.

Some laboratory schools try to enrol a "normal" school population, a procedure which is questionable on at least two grounds. In the first place, a student body representative of the population as a whole is practically never found in any particular school. And, in the second place, unusual children or classes often provide the best illustrations for learning how to teach average ones. At any rate, because of their lack of a research orientation, their fear of tough cases, their tendency to assume utopian conditions of employment for the future teachers, and their use of demonstration teachers with less than the top level of training, the laboratory schools are but another illustration of the way in which teacher education apes the appearance while avoiding the substance of professional training.

The fact that many teacher-training institutions do not have any laboratory schools at all, and that existing laboratory schools are not being used effectively in training teachers, emphasizes the need to reconsider the relationships between public school systems and teacher-training institutions. In recent years, the Fund for the Advancement of Education has been supporting programs of teacher education in which public school systems play a much more active role than they have in the past. In these programs, school systems are being encouraged to provide financial assistance to teaching interns, to make available staff time for teacher education, and to work co-operatively with teacher-training institutions in the selection, training, and evaluation of prospective teachers.

These efforts are a step in the right direction. There is no doubt that public school systems must develop closer relationships with teacher-training institutions for the sake of better teacher education. At the same time, however, I have come to believe that one hard fact severely handicaps most of the efforts to bring about a really effective working relationship between school systems and teacher-training institutions: there is no unified control of public education and teacher education. The result is that the institutions which train teachers do not have enough control over the schools to develop a first-rate program of teacher education. Communities support their schools to educate children, not to train teachers. The public school systems are geared to this purpose, and teacher education must be adjusted to it.

Most school systems are willing to accept student teachers, although not necessarily on the conditions that are best from the standpoint of teacher education. When a school system is asked to do more than this, the school board is likely to raise several objections. "Why," they will ask, "should we provide our money, staff, and resources to train teachers who will not necessarily come into our system anyway?"

For various reasons, some school systems are willing to do more for teacher education than to accept student teachers. They provide paid internships for prospective teachers, release some staff time for working with teaching interns and with personnel from teacher-training institutions, and participate extensively in the selection and evaluation of prospective teachers. They recruit able new teachers, provide recognition for their own outstanding teachers, or have related purposes in authorizing such extensive participation in teacher education.

Nevertheless, teacher education cannot be effectively reorganized without some basic changes in the legal and administrative relationships between school systems and teacher-training institutions. The extent of financial participation by school systems in teacher education is still an open question. The main problem here is to make sure that the school systems get a reasonable return on their investment. Aside from this difficulty, public school personnel are acutely sensitive to community reaction to teachers in training. Parents want their children taught by experienced teachers, not by student teachers or interns. Even if the children are learning as well as they would under their regular teacher, it may be very difficult for public school administrators to convince parents of this or to resist parental requests that the regular teachers take over.

Simply put, the dilemma is that teacher-training institutions must be able to control some schools for training purposes, but such purposes are secondary to those for which the communities support the schools. The solution to this dilemma will have to be similar to the solution reached in medical education, where teaching hospitals are used to train future physicians. The patients in these teaching hospitals generally receive better treatment than they do in ordinary hospitals. The services performed by medical students are closely supervised by outstanding professor-physicians who are always available for emergencies which are too much for the students. The professor-physicians check the medical progress of patients so that no patient actually suffers from being used for educational purposes.

If teacher education were to follow this example, the pupils in the schools used to train teachers would be better off educationally than pupils in other schools. The teacher-training schools would have the best teachers and the most up-to-date facilities, so that the pupils (as well as the student teachers) would be taught at the frontiers of the science and art of teaching. Although the student teachers and interns might do a substantial amount of teaching, the professor-teachers would closely evaluate the progress of pupils to insure that the latter do not suffer because they are being taught as part of a teacher-training program.

The necessary arrangements could be worked out with school systems in several ways. For example, a community might sign a contract permitting a teacher-training institution to operate a particular school, paying the institution what the community would ordinarily pay to operate that school. A community which needs a new school might make an agreement with a teacher-training institution whereby the latter built and operated the school with some reimbursement from the community. The institution would have to provide the additional funds needed to make the school an educational showcase; however, it would be reimbursed for the costs which the school system would otherwise have to pay from its own funds.

This practice has already been established in medical education. Cities often pay medical schools a certain amount to operate a hospital, which is then used by the medical school for teaching purposes. The medical school puts up additional funds to insure that the hospital will provide the very latest in medical care. I know of no important reason why a similar procedure cannot be worked out in teacher education. Such a procedure would give communities a strong practical incentive to support teacher education.

As I have suggested, one of the problems of teacher education is the development of a corps of teachers who have a high degree of theoretical training and who can also do the demonstration teaching in elementary and secondary schools. These teachers must be key members of the university faculty. Teacher-education responsibilities should not be superimposed on teachers whose primary responsibility lies to a school system. We must also give up the practice of having prospective teachers "supervised" by university personnel who spend each day in a different school with a different student teacher and a different regular teacher. There must be supervising professor-teachers devoted to teacher education on a full-time basis. The load for such persons could be one demonstration class and one class of student teachers, with the rest of their time devoted to research and experimentation.

Anyone who thinks that the basic reforms needed in teacher education consist of adding or deleting certain courses is only deluding himself. The basic reforms needed are structural, not curricular. Important curricular reforms are needed, but they will follow, not precede, the structural reforms. We must develop a new system of controls over teacher education, including an examination system interposed between graduation from a teacher-training institution and the receipt of a teaching certificate. Teacher training must be confined to institutions which have the resources to carry it out on a professional basis; this calls for a drastic reduction in the number of institutions which train teachers. The authority to issue teachers' certificates must be vested in educational authorities who are responsive to professional opinion. The requirements for a teaching certificate must not be enacted into state legislation but must have the force of law. The certification structure should be flexible, so that it is not necessary to get an act of the state legislature every time professional opinion supports a change in the certification requirements. As for the current controversy over whether teacher education is putting too much emphasis on "how to teach" at the expense of "what to teach," I can only say again that it is sad and pitiful thing to see this treated as a basic issue in teacher education.

Chapter VII

WHY LIBERAL EDUCATION DOES
NOT LIBERALIZE

Public education, teacher education, and liberal education are so intertwined that a discussion of one quickly involves analysis of the other two. Thus far, however, liberal education has been largely ignored, at least by name, in the preceding chapters. Let us try to analyze what it is and how it relates to public education.

Like progressive education, liberal education suffers from an overdose of definitions. As I view it, the idea of liberal education has a great deal in common with the idea of public education proposed in previous chapters. The common core of these ideas is an education that extends the horizons, that relates to basic ideas and problems, that develops the ability to think, that heightens sensitivity and perception in areas of deep human concern. When I refer to liberal education, I refer to a kind of education which is sabotaged in public schools when students are not allowed to analyze the beliefs which prevail in their homes and local communities.

Historically, the task of inculcating a liberal education has been the responsibility of the "liberal arts college." This college is not necessarily a separate institution of higher education. It can be a separate college in a multipurpose institution, such as a state university, which also includes professional schools, research institutes, and other administrative units.

We must never overlook the distinction between liberal education as an ideal and the liberal arts college as an institution. Criticism of the institution is not necessarily criticism of the ideal. In this discussion, at least, such criticism is intended only to implement that ideal. I raise this point because some critics of liberal education as it now operates have been unjustifiably accused of being hostile toward the ideal of liberal education. This is like saying that a person is opposed to representative government merely because he criticizes the overrepresentation of rural areas in the state legislatures. Still, in the present climate of educational controversy, one cannot be too careful; if you do not say specifically that you believe in motherhood and patriotism, someone is likely to infer that you are against these things.

Whether or not public education and liberal education should be regarded as ideological twins, there is widespread agreement that teachers ought to be liberally educated. Whether they are is something else. The most obvious way to assess the actual extent of their liberal education is to see how much of their total academic program is in the liberal arts. Unfortunately, we can make only guesses on the subject. There are differences in the amount and kind of academic work taken by teachers from state to state, institution to institution, subject to subject, grade level to grade level, and teacher to teacher. Sometimes courses classified as in the liberal arts by one institution are classified as professional by another, or vice versa.

Granting all the difficulties in making an estimate, I would say that about 80 per cent of the academic work of classroom teachers has been in the liberal arts. This estimate is probably a little low for secondary teachers and it may be somewhat high for elementary teachers. In both categories, there will be many individuals who have either a much higher or a much lower percentage of their total program in the liberal arts. Nevertheless, I do not believe that any conclusion reached in the following discussion would be invalidated by the exact figures, whatever they may be.

If about 80 per cent of the academic work of teachers is in the liberal arts, the effectiveness of public education will be closely related to the effectiveness of the liberal arts colleges. Indeed, our concern here should not be limited to the effectiveness of the liberal arts college in preparing future teachers. Its impact upon all who pass through it is a matter of the utmost importance to American education.

One's first thought is apt to be the difficulty of evaluating the influence of liberal arts colleges. There are so many of them, with so many variations in resources, staff, and student body, that one hardly knows where evaluation is to begin. One of the most common procedures has been to test students before and after their attendance at a liberal arts college. Sometimes the students are tested at various intervals during their college careers and after graduation. The idea is to see what changes have taken place in the values and intellectual habits of the students during their college years.

To spell this out a little more, an entering freshman will have certain political, economic, religious, and cultural ideas. He will have certain reading habits relating to the number and quality of books, magazines, and newspapers he reads. He will have a certain stock of information about the world and his place in it. It seems reasonable to assume that if the liberal arts college is doing its job, there will be some basic changes in the values and intellectual habits of students during their four years in a liberal arts college. We should not expect every student to change his point of view on everything, but we certainly should expect that every student will have changed his position on some crucial issues by the time he graduates. Also, we should expect some changes in the intellectual habits of the students after four years of college. For instance, we should expect changes in what they read or in the kinds of radio and television programs which engage their interest.

Before analyzing the results of these "before and after" studies, bear in mind one possible weakness in them. One might find certain changes in students during their years in college, but how is one to know that the changes are due to the influence of the college itself? After all, some people who have never attended college broaden their horizons, acquire new tastes, or change their reading habits.

Unfortunately, it is not possible to compare each college graduate to an identical twin who did not attend a liberal arts college. But rather strenuous efforts have been made to approximate this situation by utilizing a matched-pair technique in which an attempt is made to set up two groups which are as much alike as possible; the only difference between the groups is that one attends a liberal arts college and the other does not. Then the activities of the two groups are compared over a period of years.

To illustrate this procedure, we might take X, who is a high-school graduate about to enter a liberal arts college. He will have a certain grade record, scholastic aptitude, religion, political outlook, socioeconomic status, interest inventory, physical makeup, and so on. The researcher puts X in one group. He then tries to find another person, Y, who is like X in all these respects, but who does not go on to college. Of course, the very fact that Y is not going to college indicates that there may be important differences between him and X, but the researcher tries to keep these differences to a minimum.

Now if the liberal arts college is having an impact upon its student body, there should be differences between the X's and Y's as the years go by. The Y's will not all be growing up in the same environment while the X's are attending college. Some will be in non-academic environments conducive to intellectual growth, some will not. Nevertheless, we should certainly expect substantial group differences between the X's and the Y's—differences in vital information, in ability to think clearly, in awareness of social issues, in reading habits, in participation in civic and cultural activities, and so on.

What, then, do the studies show? They show that the impact

of the liberal arts colleges on the values and intellectual habits of their students is negligible.[1] Regardless of curriculum, location, or reputation, the liberal arts college typically does not produce any profound changes in its student body.

Of course, some students do change their views and values. But to say that they change while attending college is not to say that they change *because* they are attending college. In short, the changes are not more numerous or more fundamental than we would expect if the students had not attended a liberal arts college at all. In the words of the Jacob study:

> This study has not discerned significant changes in student values which can be attributed directly either to the character of the curriculum or to the basic courses in social science which students take as part of their general education.
>
> For the most part, the values and outlook of students do not vary greatly whether they have pursued a conventional liberal arts program, an integrated general education curriculum or one of the strictly professional-vocational options. The more liberally educated student may take a somewhat more active interest in community responsibilities, and keep better informed about public affairs. But the distinction is not striking and by no means does it occur consistently among students at all colleges. It does *not* justify the conclusion that a student acquires a greater maturity of judgment on issues of social policy or a more sensitive regard for the humane values because he had a larger dose of liberal or general education.
>
> Even fundamental revisions of the formal content of the curriculum designed to confront students more forcefully with problems of personal and social conduct and to involve them in a searching examination of value issues rarely appear to have brought about a marked difference in students' beliefs and judgments, let alone their actual patterns of conduct. Nor is there solid evidence of a delayed reaction or "sleeper effect." The alumnus of several years exhibits no unusual trademarks identifying the character of his undergraduate curriculum.[2]

The conclusions of the Jacob study, as well as of practically every other major study which has tried to assess the impact of

---

[1] The most recent summary of the evidence is to be found in Philip E. Jacob, *Changing Values in College* (New York: Harper & Bros., 1957). I have confined my quotations on the impact of the liberal arts college to this book because it takes into account, and is consistent with, previous studies on the subject.

[2] *Ibid.*, pp. 5–6.

the liberal arts college, are not new. They have never been a surprise to persons who believe that the educational claims of liberal arts colleges ought to be evaluated just as rigorously as the educational claims made for the public schools. However, most people find it difficult to believe that an educational institution to which so much obeisance is paid can in fact be so ineffective. Rigorous evaluation of its own effectiveness ought to be an integral part of the operation of every liberal arts college. In practice, however, it is much more convenient to take its effectiveness, and hence its mode of operation, for granted.

This unwillingness to face the facts is most clearly reflected in the claims which are made for the liberal arts college by its professional supporters. Many a college president has cited a host of alumni prominent in business and the professions as proof of the virtues of a liberal education (at his institution, of course). This evaluative technique has even been reduced to an exact science by taking the number of alumni listed in *Who's Who* as the criterion of institutional excellence.

It is no accident that the above technique is embraced most enthusiastically by certain Ivy League colleges. The competition to be admitted to these colleges is based upon prestige considerations which have nothing to do with their alleged educational superiority; it is essentially like the competition to be pledged to a powerful fraternity. The very fact of being pledged is a strong indication that owing to the wealth, power, and prestige of the pledger's family, his chances in life are far above the average. And just as it is not fraternity life that enables him to "succeed" later on, so it is not his attendance at a prestigeful liberal arts college that does it either. His later "success" is due primarily to the factors that enabled him to attend such a college and pledge such a fraternity in the first place. A college which caters to students from rich and powerful and prestigeful families should be able to cite more than rich and powerful and prestigeful alumni as proof of its educational effectiveness.

Interestingly enough, the same kind of fallacious argument is often used to "prove" the value of public education. The fact that the average high-school graduate earns more than the average non-graduate is often cited to demonstrate the value of a high-school education. The possibility that the same factors which enabled certain students to complete high school would, independently of their attendance, enable them to achieve a higher than average level of income is quietly ignored. The higher average income of high-school graduates vis-à-vis non-graduates is undoubtedly due at least in part to several factors other than what they learned in high school, such as their higher average intelligence, the higher average socioeconomic status of their families, and so on. The existence of a high correlation between graduation from high school and later success does not establish a cause-and-effect relationship.

Even if such a relationship were established, we would have to evaluate it carefully. If large corporations employ only college graduates for the positions which lead to the top, the college graduates are bound to show up better than the non-graduates regardless of the ability of the non-college group. If a sizable number of large corporations prefer graduates from certain colleges, such as the Ivy League colleges, then the graduates of the preferred colleges are likely to be economically more successful than graduates of the same ability from non-preferred colleges.

It is true that the firms involved believe that they will get superior personnel in this way. However, even if such a result were established, it would not necessarily prove the *educational* superiority of the preferred colleges. It might prove only that a higher percentage of superior students enrolled in certain colleges for reasons that had nothing to do with the educational program of these colleges. The corporations might well be justified in their recruitment procedures while erroneously attributing the superiority of their personnel to the educational programs of the preferred colleges. Essentially, it is the old story of faith in a fact creating the fact. If employers believe attendance at a particular college is valuable, and therefore require it, then such attendance does become valuable even if the educational program of that particular college is in fact no better, even if it is worse, than the educational program of other institutions.

Obviously, the technique of citing a long list of successful alumni is not equally useful to every liberal arts college. This fact may help to explain why the last-ditch defense of so many liberal arts colleges often lies in an appeal to ethereal considerations. The values of the liberal arts college are said to be not subject to measurement, or to objective analysis of any kind. "We develop moral and spiritual values," the argument runs. "Even though these goals are not subject to measurement, they are the most important part of man's cultural and spiritual heritage."

The trouble with this point of view is that it makes evaluation completely impossible. Whatever the liberal arts college is supposed to accomplish must eventually be observable in somebody's behavior. If there is no observable behavior which can fairly be attributed to the college program, there is no basis for assuming that the college is liberalizing its student body. The same intangibility which is cited to defend the liberal arts college also demolishes its claim to be achieving anything.

Indeed, how could a professor know whether he was successful as a teacher except through what his students write, say, and do? It is absurd to have a student take thirty to forty courses, in each of which he is presumably evaluated according to some observable standard of judgment, and then contend that the objectives of the college program as a whole are so intangible that student behavior affords no clue to the success or failure of the college. And it must be pointed out that the burden of proof here is on the liberal arts college. It accepts the student, encourages him to spend four years of his life under its tutelage —and for what? Certainly not for objectives which are so intangible that nobody can ever know whether or not they have been accomplished.

It is always an interesting experience to challenge liberal arts graduates on the values of the education they have received. I have done this in graduate courses many times and the patterns of response are fairly predictable. Invariably the students assert that the average college graduate makes more than the average non-graduate. Of course, this assertion is true, but as previously pointed out, one cannot infer from it any educational superiority of the liberal arts colleges. But aside from this, it is interesting that graduates should fall back so quickly upon an economic justification for the kind of education they have received.

When pressed for new ideas they have acquired in college, the students rarely respond with a substantive answer. They "know" they have broadened their outlook, met so many different kinds of people, and learned to adjust—but practically never can you get them to set out in clear analytical language an idea they have acquired. Indeed, it can be a shattering experience to listen to these graduates evaluate their college experience. Girls whose only interest in a grade was its role in sorority life tell you in earnest tones that they have learned so much just from the different people they have met in college. These same girls live their entire college careers in sorority houses from which girls of unlike religion, race, socioeconomic status, or social values are rigorously excluded. Listening to their defense of college life, one would never realize that intellectual and social conformity are predominant characteristics of the liberal arts college—that is, if one could ignore their comments on social problems or intellectual issues.

There comes a time when the students finally grasp the question which has been put to them. They realize that they are being asked a very simple thing—what new insights do they have which can reasonably be attributed to their liberal arts program? As a rule, there are none, but the students stubbornly refuse to accept this conclusion, even when they are unable to offer proof to the contrary. "Do you mean to say," they ask, "that we have wasted all the time we were in college?"

Of course, they have not wasted it. They have landed the husband or secured the necessary polish or degree without which they cannot get a good job. But, intellectually speaking, the liberal arts college has failed to do a job. As Jacob puts it in discussing the impact of a college education upon student values:

> Changes are rarely drastic or sudden, and they tend to emerge on the periphery of the student's character, affecting his application of values rather than the core of values themselves.
>
> To call this process a *liberalization* of student values is a misnomer.

The impact of the college experience is rather to *socialize* the individual, to refine, polish, or "shape up" his values so that he can fit comfortably into the ranks of American college alumni.[3]

The situation with respect to the liberal arts college reminds me of student reaction to a well-known philosophy professor in a midwestern university. This professor was an avowed atheist who made it a point to tell his classes that he had an affirmative belief in the non-existence of God. Nevertheless, he was unable to get students to believe that he was really an atheist. The students would merely nudge each other, secure in the belief that the old boy was just spouting atheism to stir up some class discussion. The students "knew" that underneath it all, he believed in God like everybody else. Similarly, if you tell students that there is no strong evidence to indicate that the liberal arts college is liberalizing, their reaction is that you are just saying this to stir up some class discussion. The students may not have any evidence to contradict the assertion, but they retain a sublime faith that such evidence exists.

The ineffectiveness of our liberal arts colleges is too pervasive to be solved by tinkering with their course structures. From college to college or even within the same college, students take a wide variety of courses in virtually every conceivable sequence. The results are consistently unimpressive. In its insistence that even fundamental revisions of the liberal arts curriculum have no discernible impact upon the values and intellectual habits of students, the Jacob study only echoed the results of other major studies devoted to this problem.

THE IMPACT OF LIBERAL ARTS
COLLEGES ON PUBLIC EDUCATION

There is a tendency in some quarters to regard the public schools as a deleterious influence upon the liberal arts colleges. The colleges are supposedly fortresses of high academic standards and intellectual training which are being overwhelmed

---

[3] *Ibid.*, p. 4. It would seem that the large number of professors in liberal arts colleges who are worked up to a fever pitch over an alleged emphasis upon social adjustment in the high schools have plenty of homework to do.

by the illiterate, undisciplined graduates of the public schools. If you think of education at one level primarily as the foundation of education at a higher level, it seems logical to regard any weakness in elementary or secondary education as a cause of the same weakness at the college level. But this way of looking at the matter often overlooks the reverse, the impact of higher education upon elementary and secondary education.

Actually, there is a reciprocal influence between all levels of education. That is, what is done at each level has some influence on what is done at the others. The tendency to regard each level as preparatory for the next is valid in certain contexts and for certain purposes, but we must not overlook the influence of the higher levels of education upon the lower ones. The graduate and professional schools have had a tremendous impact upon the undergraduate colleges; the undergraduate colleges have always been greatly influential in shaping the policies of the high schools; and so on. With the exception of professors in the graduate schools, the teachers at one level of education almost always receive at least some of their training at higher levels of education. Equally important, the examples provided by higher education in terms of such things as academic standards and professional sanctions have had a lasting influence on these things in elementary and secondary education.

It is with these thoughts in mind that I suggest a long and hard look at the impact of higher education, especially of the liberal arts colleges, upon elementary and secondary education. The interrelationships between the various levels of education make it unlikely that major weaknesses in any one of them do not have some roots and causes in others. This is particularly true of public education; my conviction is that every major weakness of public education has its roots in higher education, and especially in the liberal arts colleges. For example, overemphasis upon athletics, social graces, and "adjustment," the favorite whipping boys of our contemporary custodians of culture, are strictly hand-me-downs from the liberal arts colleges.

We may take the development of football as a case in point. Intercollegiate football made its first appearance in November,

1869. The first game was between Princeton and Rutgers. The emphasis accorded football by our leading liberal arts colleges is suggested by the rosters of the first All-American teams: it was not until 1894 that the most authoritative All-American team, the one selected by Walter Camp, included anyone not from Yale, Princeton, or Harvard. In that year, one player from the University of Pennsylvania was chosen by Camp for his annual All-American team. The building of stadiums instead of class-rooms, the recruitment and glorification of athletes instead of scholars, the marching bands and the cheerleaders, the practice of recalling the alumni on a day set aside for athletics instead of for intellectual achievement and stimulation—these things originated and flourished in liberal arts colleges long before they became a part of the high-school scene.

Likewise, the current outcry against education for "life adjustment" comes with poor grace from the liberal arts colleges. While their presidents are extolling the intellectual life upon their campuses, their admissions officers may often be found looking for "good all-around students" instead of "just bookworms." More than one "A" student from Brooklyn has been denied admission to an institution which allegedly emphasizes the intellectual life on the grounds that he "would not adjust satisfactorily" to life at a particular college. Others have been turned down because of the college's alleged need for a "better geographical distribution" for its student body.[4] And we might also note the fact that our undemocratic and anti-intellectual fraternities and sororities were established in liberal arts colleges. They flourished there and eventually became a disruptive and miseducational influence upon our public high schools.

I should not wish to condemn liberal arts colleges today for the mistakes that they made generations ago. Some colleges have

[4] "Professor Henry Steele Commager, of Columbia and Amherst, was discussing the problem of students anxious to get into the *best* colleges. He said that colleges prefer students who would give the school a geographic, social and scholastic balance. One dean of admissions told him: 'If we wanted to, we could have our entire student body composed exclusively of students who all have "A" averages, all from Westchester, and all studying to become doctors' " (from Leonard Lyons' column in the *New York Post*, August 19, 1958).

adopted various measures to eliminate or check the undesirable trends just mentioned. If a professor or an administrator in a liberal arts college criticizes public education, we should evaluate these criticisms according to the logic and evidence which support them, not according to the critic's institutional affiliation. The point is, however, that many of the reforms needed in public education will be delayed, or will not take place at all, unless and until these same reforms are made in liberal arts colleges. It is futile to expect high schools to stress intellectual achievement if the liberal arts colleges do not.[5]

Indeed, much of the pointing with alarm at public education by professors and administrators of liberal arts colleges constitutes sheer effrontery on their part; their own institutions are often directly responsible for the evils which these academicians find in the public schools. For instance, recently I read about a high-school basketball player who was besieged with offers from over a hundred colleges. The pressure upon him had become so great that he finally announced that his choice of college would be made at a press conference in a few weeks. Press conferences called by high-school athletes to announce their choice of college are rare, but intensive recruitment of these athletes by liberal arts colleges is not. And yet who ever heard of these colleges making a similar effort to enrol outstanding high-school scholars? Perhaps the public schools have ceased to stress intellectual achievement, but to whatever extent this criticism is valid, the liberal arts college bears the major responsibility. It has provided most of the education of the teachers. The educational policies governing most of the public school population are set by school board members who graduated from a liberal arts college. And by its own example and influence, the liberal arts college sets the standards and climate for the public schools.

[5] It is illuminating that the more education people have, the more likely they are to regard social adjustment as the most important function of education, and the less likely they are to regard mastery of school subjects as most important. Persons with some college education are five times as likely to regard social adjustment as the most important function of education as are people with only a grammar-school education. See *The Public Looks at Education* (Report No. 21 [Denver: National Opinion Research Center, 1944]), p. 15; and also Myron Lieberman, *Education as a Profession* (Englewood Cliffs, N.J.: Prentice-Hall, 1956), p. 31.

Regardless of the origins of non-academic activities in our educational institutions, it would be futile to try to eliminate all of them in either our colleges or our public schools. Furthermore, I question the wisdom of such a policy even if it could be put into effect. If intercollegiate athletics could be abolished overnight, our institutions of higher education would not thereby become beehives of intellectual activity. What is needed is not so much a de-emphasis upon non-academic activities but a new and effective emphasis upon the intellectual aspects of education.

This is not just a play on words. There is no need to abolish the activities and ceremonies which honor non-academic achievers. The task is to find ways of doing this for intellectual achievers as well. There is also a need for better ways of according prestige to intellectually outstanding teachers. Because athletic coaches in the public schools are in the public eye more than teachers, they are better known and have better chances of getting administrative positions. This is undesirable because it leads to a situation wherein the persons least qualified academically tend to get the key leadership positions. However, this problem will not be solved by the abolition or de-emphasis of interscholastic athletics. It will be solved when other teachers achieve positions of respect in their communities. If teachers were really intellectual leaders, if their opinions were important to the community at large, and if they had their own ways and means of becoming public figures, they would not feel any need to de-emphasize non-academic activities.

At the present time, the academic posture toward many non-academic activities is tinged by frustration and jealousy. Occasionally, a diffuse resentment against the higher financial rewards and greater public recognition accorded football coaches finds expression in a speech or article which receives wide publicity; there is no easier way to achieve a reputation as a crusading intellectual than to lead a "Down with football" movement on the campus.

One professor who achieved immediate if fleeting fame by this tactic explains his crusade in this way: "My only charges against football were that football was becoming symbolic of anti-intellectualism (a fact which nobody questioned during the entire hullabaloo), and that football has practically nothing to contribute to the purposes of a university." [6] Aside from the likelihood that much of what the professors themselves do "has nothing to do with the purposes of a university," the rationale for crusades of this type is dubious. Oxford and Cambridge were competing in rowing matches long before our own universities were participating in football, yet the excellence of these English institutions of higher education is rarely challenged. I have never seen it suggested that they must raise their intellectual level by abolishing rowing, which presumably has as little to do with the purposes of a university as does football.

Instead of baying in the manger, the professors should set high academic standards in their courses, departments, and institutions. They need only insist upon these things and they can blithely ignore what students do outside the classroom. Whether a student plays football, joins the glee club, or attends a beer party nightly should be of no concern to the professors, individually or collectively. On most campuses, non-academic activities do not replace the intellectual life; they flourish because there is no such thing as intellectual life on these campuses in the first place.

PUBLIC AND PRIVATE EDUCATION

As I have been using the phrase, "liberal arts college" denotes public as well as private institutions. However, one frequently hears glowing references to the educational virtues of the *private* liberal arts colleges. The phrase has a kind of double-barreled effect; liberal arts colleges are supposed to be more liberalizing than other kinds, and private colleges are supposed to be superior to public ones. For public relations reasons, the latter thought cannot always be expressed bluntly; it is something which the other fellow (especially if he is a donor or foundation executive) should infer without your having to spell it out for him. I would like to suggest that the educational superiority of private education per se is a myth. There are good

[6] Wade Thompson, "My Crusade against Football," *The Nation*, CLXXXVIII (April, 1959), 314.

private schools at every level of education, but there is no evidence for believing that private schools per se are better or are likely to be better than public schools.

Regardless of whether they are public or private institutions, most liberal arts colleges are unable to secure adequate financial support without sacrificing their intellectual integrity. I have been in state universities where "radicals" were expected to lie low so that they would not endanger the university budget. Faculty coffee breaks were often devoted to discussing whether a faculty member had the right to make public pronouncements that might jeopardize the budget—or, if he had the right, whether he ought to exercise it. Donors take the place of legislatures in privately supported liberal arts colleges, but the result is still professorial subservience to outside pressures.[7]

As in the case of the public schools, there is wide variation from one liberal arts college to another in the dogmas and prejudices which receive academic immunity. But the closer one analyzes the situation, the more apparent it becomes that public schools and liberal arts colleges suffer from the same maladies. The fallacious notion that "He who pays the piper must call the tune," which has done so much to weaken public education, is generally accepted in higher education; the professors may not believe that it is right but they obviously don't know what to do about it. As long as they have been unable to develop independent sources of power and financial support which would do away with their mendicant status, the inability of elementary and secondary teachers to do so should be no surprise.[8]

The fact is that all types of educational institutions have found

[7] For an excellent analysis and criticism of the view that private colleges are more free than public colleges from non-academic interference, see Harold W. Stoke, *The American College Presidency* (New York: Harper & Bros., 1959), chap. IV.

[8] "I believe that the educators of America are largely responsible for the present confusion in and about education. They have felt obligated in my day to seek for money, first, last, and all the time. They have always supposed, I think erroneously, that money could be obtained only for activities that harmonized with the interests and opinions of those who had it" (Robert M. Hutchins, *The University of Utopia* [Chicago: University of Chicago Press, 1953], pp. 83–84).

it necessary to make unprofessional accommodations to their sources of funds. This fact underlies a few comments I wish to make concerning private schools below the college level. They have cultivated the idea that there is something especially liberalizing about private education below the college level. This claim should be examined carefully.

At the elementary and secondary levels, there is undoubtedly a great deal of overlap in the quality of public and private schools. My judgment is, however, that the quality of private non-parochial elementary and secondary education is widely exaggerated. I do not say this on the basis of carefully controlled evaluations of private schools (which are badly needed, by the way) but on the basis of the fact that private schools are not ordinarily subject to the same degree of state supervision as is public education.

The majority of private schools are Catholic parochial schools. Where such schools flourish, it would often be political suicide to insist that they meet the same standards as public schools. An important illustration of this is the fact that although all the states require *public school* teachers to meet certain minimum standards for a teaching certificate, only ten states require *all* elementary teachers to meet these standards and only seven require *all* secondary-school teachers to meet them.[9]

Note that the private non-parochial schools are in a much different situation than are the parochial schools. Both kinds may enjoy freedom from public supervision, but the parochial schools are part of a larger system that provides its own safeguards. I do not believe that these safeguards are as effective as those prevailing in the public schools, but this is an impressionistic judgment which it is unnecessary to argue at this point. The important thing is that there is some centralized supervision of parochial schools which is not present in the case of private

---

[9] W. Earl Armstrong and T. M. Stinnett, A *Manual on Certification Requirements for School Personnel in the United States* (Washington, D.C.: National Education Association, 1957), p. 40. Seventeen states require private elementary-school teachers and twenty-one require private secondary-school teachers to have a state certificate if the private school desires to be accredited.

independent schools at the elementary and secondary levels.

It is true that the controls over public education exercised by the states (and extralegal professional associations) are not very rigorous. There is a vast amount of poor education going on in public schools that do conform to state requirements. Nevertheless, although these requirements vary from state to state, they ordinarily make it more difficult to operate schools that lack adequate staff, facilities, equipment, supplies, sound instructional programs, and other things essential to a good education. The state controls do not generate a high level of education, but they put a floor (with many holes in it, to be sure) under public education.

Let me cite a recent experience to demonstrate what can happen in the absence of state supervision of private schools. In a university where I worked, a man 58 years of age applied for admission to our teacher-education program. This man was a retired postal employee who had attended college on a part-time basis prior to his retirement. He had recently been awarded a bachelor's degree in mathematics with honors, and he wanted to teach this subject in high school. In view of this man's outstanding intellectual achievements and his obvious strength of character and personality, he was encouraged to go into teaching despite the fear that he might have a difficult time getting a teaching position because of his age. This turned out to be the case; the man could not get a position in the public schools. As a result, he finally accepted a job in a private boarding school in a nearby state.

A few months later, he came to me, asking whether it would be ethical for him to resign in the middle of the year. He cited the following conditions in the school as the reasons why he wished to sever his connection with it as soon as possible:

1. Teachers taught academic subjects for which they had no preparation whatsoever.

2. Although the school claimed to have an outstanding guidance program staffed by trained personnel, it actually had no such program and no trained personnel in this area. This was especially shocking because the school enrolled an unusually

high percentage of problem children—those who were emotionally disturbed and those who were just dumped there by their parents.

3. There was practically complete staff turnover every year, not only because of the low salaries and unpleasant conditions, but because the school administration was apparently not anxious to have anyone learn too much about its operations.

4. Teachers often were forced to teach more than one subject at a time in the same room, skipping back and forth between two groups of pupils.

5. Students were charged outrageous prices for personal and educational services, some of which were nonexistent.

6. Parents were assured that the graduates of the school would get into college. The headmaster always encouraged the staff to give high grades to fool parents and admissions officers; he even changed grades submitted by instructors to achieve this goal. The students who got into a reputable college quickly flunked out; others were enrolled in colleges which apparently existed to meet the needs of private schools such as this one.

7. Students were abused mentally and physically; "tortured" would not be too strong a word to describe some of the things that were done.

What happened after this teacher told me about his situation is instructive. I called the state education department where the school was located to inquire about the extent to which there was state supervision of private schools.[10] In answer to my query, I was told that the state education department was helpless; the only state regulations pertaining to private schools were the following:

1. They must keep Standard School Registers if children from seven to fifteen years of age inclusive are in attendance, and also make an annual report to the State Department of Education.

2. They must be providing the required courses of instruction in citizenship and must file a copy of such courses annually with the secretary of the state Board of Education.

[10] When I set forth the conditions without naming the school, the official to whom I was talking assumed that I meant another school in the state!

3. Secondary schools which accept pupils whose tuition is paid out of public funds must be approved for that purpose specifically.

4. The medium of instruction and administration in all public and private elementary schools shall be the English language and not more than one hour in any school day may be given to instruction in any one language other than English.

5. Their buildings must conform to state laws governing safety and sanitation.

It does not take much thought to realize that these requirements provide virtually no protection for children in private schools. The requirement that not more than one hour a day be devoted to a foreign language is absurd, but it applies to public school pupils also. The value of these regulations is suggested by the following: Although a course in "the duties and responsibilities of U.S. citizenship" is required under regulation 2, there is absolutely no requirement relating to the preparation of the teacher giving such a course. No matter how inadequate such a teacher might be, there was no legal basis for state intervention to protect the pupils.

I cite this example for a reason. Wherever there are no educational standards enforced by an agency that has the power to apply powerful sanctions, some institutions will go to virtually any lengths to stay in business. This applies to every level of education, but it is more difficult to swindle the public and the students in higher education. At the elementary and secondary levels, the students are not able to protect themselves; if there are no others to do it for them, we can expect the worst. To this extent, I would modify my earlier statements to the effect that public and private educational institutions reveal the same weaknesses. In a sense, they do, but we must also recognize what is likely to happen as a result of the sweeping absence of safeguards in private education.[11]

---

[11] I have selected an extreme example which may be very unfair to the vast majority of private schools. However, shortly after writing this chapter, my attention was called to two recent publications dealing with elite private schools, the top fifteen in the country. These schools (and many others, I am sure) are far superior in every way to the private school I have just

LIBERAL EDUCATION AND THE STUDY OF
EDUCATION

Education is the major activity of one-fourth of our population. For this reason alone, the curriculum of the liberal arts college might be expected to clarify important educational problems. Who ought to be given what kind of an education? Who is receiving an education? How is and how ought education to be financed? What are the proper limits of professional decision in the educational system? What are, and what ought to be, the scope of community and parental decision in our schools? Surely a rigorous study of such educational problems ought to be as conducive to a liberal education as the study of our political or economic systems, not to mention the trivia which are part of the curriculum of most liberal arts colleges.

Reasonable as this idea might seem to the non-academic mind, it is not obvious to most professors. In our liberal arts colleges, the professors continue to croak "vocationalism" at the idea of education courses even for teachers, and to act as if a course is liberalizing only to the extent that it has nothing directly to do with man's work or his immediate problems. The schools of education have compounded the confusion by their insistence that every education course is "professional." Since all education courses are "professional," none is presumably a proper part of liberal education.

The entire controversy over education courses is a remarkable illustration of the capacity of college professors to confuse words with things and institutions with ideals. Instead of regarding

---

described. However, the publications indicate rather forcefully that even the best private boarding schools are overrated as educational institutions and that they should not be regarded as models for the public schools to emulate. See Vance Packard, *The Status Seekers* (New York: David McKay Co., 1959), chap. xvi; and E. Digby Baltzell, *Philadelphia Gentlemen* (Glencoe, Ill.: Free Press, 1958). I am also indebted to Mr. David Merrall, vice-president of one of the better private secondary schools in New York City, for the suggestion that the private schools in the National Council of Independent Schools are reasonably free from the characteristics of the worst private schools. I hope the suggestion is well taken, although at the present time I am not well enough informed either to indorse or to criticize it.

liberal education as an ideal and then evaluating courses according to their capacity to contribute to this ideal, professors have come to regard liberal education as something that can occur only in courses which are under the jurisdiction of the liberal arts college. There is no basis in theory or fact for this identification; it is purely gratuitous. Nevertheless, on most campuses it has the force of Holy Writ.

It is common today to read of the need for greater emphasis upon the liberal arts in teacher education. We are told over and over again that we require "a massive transfusion of the liberal arts." The people who talk this way generally hold to the position that our teachers are poorly educated, but they persistently ignore the fact that a large part of the training of most teachers consists of subjects in the liberal arts categories. Another fact often ignored is that our liberal arts colleges produce more high-school teachers than our teachers' colleges. If our high schools are as bad as the professional liberal arts college advocate would have us believe, one might begin to question whether a massive transfusion of the liberal arts is really the answer. Perhaps a massive exposé would be more appropriate.

The antagonism toward the study of education even for teachers, let alone as an essential part of a liberal education, has implications for the layman's attitude toward education as well as for teacher education. Offhand, it might be supposed that it is chiefly the less educated citizenry which is responsible for violations of academic freedom. In practice, the possession of a B.A. degree seems to give people a strong feeling that they ought to tell teachers what and how to teach. If anyone doubts this, he need only peruse the educational backgrounds of school boards which engage in the crudest interference with the professional autonomy of teachers.

And, after all, why should they not interfere? They have been told over and over again by the country's leading champions of the liberal arts that teaching is not a profession, that it requires very little specialized preparation. Indeed, according to a former president of the University of Chicago, "All there is to teaching can be learned through a good education and being a teacher." In context, Hutchins clearly meant that all the education a person needs to be a teacher is the same general education that everyone ought to have, that no professional training of any kind is required for teaching.[12] If this is the case, it is difficult to understand why the public should not rightfully interfere with the content and methods of teaching, since they would know as much about these things as the teachers.

Paradoxically, Hutchins has acquired a reputation as a staunch defender of academic freedom. In fact, his statements on this subject are among the best that have been made:

> Academic freedom is simply a way of saying that we get the best results in education and research if we leave their management to *people who know something about them.* Attempts on the part of the public to regulate the methods and content of education and to determine the objects of research are encroachments on academic freedom. . . . The democratic view that the state may determine the amount of money to be spent on education and may regulate education and educators by law has nothing to do with the wholly undemocratic notion that citizens may tell educators how to conduct education and still less with the fantastic position that they may tell them how to live, vote, think and speak.[13]

Of course, this rationale for academic freedom is completely inconsistent with the notion that teaching requires no special training whatsoever. It hardly makes sense to urge that we leave education and research to people "who know something" about these things and, at the same time, to argue that a good general education suffices to be a teacher. Thus while the schools of education contend that teachers are professionals and then advocate lay-professional relationships that are the essence of antiprofessionalism, an influential segment of our liberal arts

---

[12] Robert Maynard Hutchins, *The Higher Learning in America* (New Haven: Yale University Press, 1936), p. 56. In a recent discussion Dr. Hutchins asserted that my interpretation of what he had written was not correct. I am happy to know that he no longer holds to the view I have ascribed to him, but I invite anyone to check the source to see whether I have quoted him correctly and with due regard for the context. And after all, it is his published views, not those he holds privately, that have had the most influence on American education.

[13] *Ibid.,* p. 21. Italics added.

faculties insists that teachers are not professionals, and yet that they ought to have professional autonomy!

The refusal of liberal arts colleges to regard the study of education as a liberal study is partly responsible for some of the strange views of public education that seem to be endemic in these circles. I have read statements, made in utter seriousness, that the shortage of mathematics and science teachers in our high schools is due to the fact that potential teachers of these subjects balk at having to take a flock of methods courses for a teaching certificate. One even hears this in liberal arts colleges which do not require a single education course of their own mathematics and science instructors but which are experiencing serious difficulty themselves in recruiting instructors in these areas.

The irony of the situation is that the hostility toward the study of education in liberal arts colleges is simply a case of academic man cutting off his own nose to spite his professorial face.[14] In the past fifty years, the professors in liberal arts colleges have suffered a sharp social and economic decline. The prospects are that their situation will deteriorate even further. Yet of all occupational groups, the professors have the best opportunities to study their occupational problems and to build a deep and lasting case for public understanding and support. Instead of utilizing this opportunity, they have rejected it out of hand.

If educational problems are not sufficiently important to be included in the liberal arts curriculum, if they are not worthy of serious research by at least some of the professors in liberal arts colleges, it should come as no surprise that the graduates of these colleges are not particularly interested in the problems of the colleges. Granted, another course is not the solution to

[14] The governing body of the American Association of University Professors is its Council. Members of the Council are elected from ten geographical regions of the country. Two persons are nominated and one is elected from each region. A professor long active in the AAUP and one in whose integrity I have the utmost confidence told me that in order to get a Negro elected to the Council, it was decided to run him against a professor of education. I later wrote to the national office of the Association and discovered that the first Negro elected to the Council had in fact been elected over a professor of education—and had also failed to attend any Council meetings!

every problem. Still, who but themselves do professors in liberal arts colleges have to blame for public indifference to fundamental educational problems?

THE FUTURE OF LIBERAL EDUCATION

The liberal arts college is supposed to develop a common intellectual framework and a lifelong commitment to intelligent modes of behavior. For a long time, the curriculum set forth to achieve these goals was dominated by the study of ancient languages, literature, and history. By common consent, these studies precede specialized education for professional or managerial careers. In recent years, professional training has increased in duration, creating strong pressures to keep the period of preprofessional training to a minimum. Although preprofessional training is supposed to be devoted to liberal education, it actually shows a growing emphasis upon subjects related to professional work. Despite all the warnings that we must not neglect the humanities, they are declining in importance, even in the liberal arts college itself.

These movements are still in their early stages, but they have thoroughly frightened the professors in the humanities. Many of them are clutching at straws to bolster their position. Science, they say, can give us knowledge only of means. It can be used to destroy men as well as to enrich them. Men must know the purposes and the values of life or their scientific studies will be used destructively. The humanities are the subjects which tell us the purposes and values of life, hence they should be the heart of the liberal arts curriculum.

This philosophical bunk is regarded as a profound truth by many professors of every subject threatened by the increasing emphasis upon science and mathematics in the liberal arts curriculum. At the same time, however, intelligent people in all walks of life are finding it increasingly difficult to take seriously the claim that professors in the humanities know more than anyone else about the purposes and values of existence. Of course, the idea that a certain group has special insight into these things is not new. Plato's concept of the philosopher-king was based on it. However, philosophers have learned a great deal since (as well as from) Plato, including the futility of the claim that philosophers or any other academic group are experts on the purposes and values of life. Philosophy itself, by the way, is one of the more productive disciplines erroneously classified in the humanities; it is amusing to hear these pretentious "philosophical" defenses of the humanities that would be rejected out of hand by professional philosophers.

The need to develop well-rounded individuals, whole men instead of narrow specialists, is another lead-weighted life preserver for most of the humanities. To produce well-rounded individuals, you must have a well-rounded curriculum—that is, one scattered over as many fields as possible. Thus we get the game of academic musical chairs whereby every department is given a required course or two. The more departments that get into the act, the more whole and well rounded the student.

When elementary teachers talked about "teaching the whole child," this was an occasion for uproarious laughter in the higher echelons of liberal education. Although the idea was never clearly defined, it was based upon sound educational considerations, such as the need to utilize the emotional, aesthetic, and physical as well as the intellectual components of learning. It was never based upon any need to keep the academic peace or save a few subjects from extinction. Nevertheless, it was and is ridiculed by the same professors who think "the whole man" is the answer to the world's most pressing problems. Upon closer inspection, "the whole man" turns out to be the college student who has been exposed to a smorgasbord academic program. Quite often, the smorgasbord program includes a number of smorgasbord survey courses which emphasize "the broad view."

What the future holds for liberal arts colleges is difficult to say. Even if they should retain their present form, their curriculum is likely to be increasingly dominated by the professional schools. How long they can go on without drastic change is problematical. It is questionable whether the liberal arts college can continue to maintain the fiction that subjects like speech, English, and history are genuine disciplines, and that those who teach these subjects are members of the same profession as those who teach physics, chemistry, mathematics, philosophy, or economics. The liberal arts college, even more than the high school, is composed of disparate elements that bear no inherent intellectual or organizational relationship to one another.

Historically, the public schools have followed rather than led the colleges. Nevertheless, we may see a change in the historical pattern. Many educational reforms may come first in the public schools and then trickle upward to the liberal arts college. This is especially likely in the area of employer-employee relationships; the American Association of University Professors lags hopelessly behind those organizations of public school teachers that are beginning to pay serious attention to collective bargaining and teacher control over entry.

Instead of trying to assess the future of the liberal arts college, perhaps we should concentrate upon something infinitely more important, the future of liberal education. Liberal education is too important to be abandoned because our present ways of implementing it are not effective. Perhaps it is time to abandon, or at least scrutinize, the idea that liberal education belongs primarily to late adolescence. We might then try to create an educational structure that will articulate our educational resources with the major problems confronting our society. A liberally educated person is one whose education is continuous, but I question whether continuous education can be achieved by a few years of college which are supposed to be an educational generator for the rest of the student's life. The liberal arts college simply does not provide its graduates with enough momentum to overcome their lack of any organic relationship to our educational resources.

It is a mistake to think that liberal education can disregard concrete circumstances of time, place, people, and events. Whether or not education is liberal in effect depends as much upon these factors as it does upon the content which one seeks to teach. To be specific, if the American people are confronted by grave issues of foreign policy, how can we synchronize their understanding of the issues with their hour of decision upon them?

This basic educational problem will not be solved by the course-jugglers in the liberal arts colleges. More evening courses will not solve it either. Basically, the problem is how to make our occupational organizations, our service clubs, our political parties, and our religious and cultural organizations more effective educational agencies. Thus far, we have not found the structural keys to liberal education. We are, in fact, just beginning to look for them seriously. Pathetic ventures such as the Great Books program must be seen in context as a primitive effort to develop continuous liberal education. If failures such as this do not discredit the ideal of universal and continuous liberal education, we will eventually discover the ways and means to implement the ideal effectively. But the first and most important step is to grasp the fact that our present institutional means, to wit, the liberal arts college, is not getting the job done.

Chapter VIII

EMPLOYER-EMPLOYEE RELATIONSHIPS
IN A PUBLIC PROFESSION

The twentieth century has been a period of fundamental changes in employer-employee relationships. For the most part, these changes have been confined to private employment and are just now beginning to be reflected in public employment. However, their widespread introduction into public employment, including public education, is a practical certainty.

Before analyzing these changes, I wish to discuss briefly two attitudes that have obstructed clear thinking on employer-employee relationships in education in the past. First, there is the attitude that any policy associated with unions is inappropriate for a professional association. The second is that any policy which is helpful to a privately employed occupational group is inappropriate for a publicly employed one. These two attitudes must be completely dispelled if we are to understand the future of the teacher as an employee.

There are differences between unions and professional associations. There are also similarities between them. Unfortunately, people are often confused on the points of similarity and dissimilarity. The important thing is that in evaluating the appropriateness of a policy for public education, we not be misled by superficial similarities or dissimilarities between unions and professional associations.

To illustrate, suppose we are considering whether a certain practice which has worked successfully for unions should be adopted by teachers. It is a *non sequitur* to think that a "union practice" cannot be successful because "teaching is a profession." Our interest should be in the conditions that led to the success of this practice and whether these conditions prevail in education. We must always be interested in *relevant* conditions. To adopt a policy in public education merely because it has proved successful in other occupations would be equally foolish unless the conditions justifying the policy in the other occupations also prevail in education.

The logic of this point applies to policies followed in the professions as well. A policy which has proved successful in other professions would be good for education only if the conditions which led to its success elsewhere also prevail in education. By the same token, policies which were not successful in other professions may be successful in education if the conditions causing failure elsewhere are not present in education.

Let me restate the point in a different way. Education is a unique occupation. So is medicine, flagpole sitting, and every other occupation. But even unique occupations may have important similarities with others. We should never, therefore, assume that the experience of any other occupation is inappropriate for education merely because "education is unique." Neither should education blindly follow the experience of other occupational groups merely because there are general similarities among them.

To illustrate this point, let me quote from a recent publication of a teachers' association in New York City:

During October, we were asked to attend a hearing . . . regarding the institution of a union dues check-off system for teachers. This was opposed by the BTA on the grounds that teachers consider themselves professional people who are opposed to any deductions from their salary checks, and who wish to pay their dues to any organization personally and at times and in the manner determined by themselves alone. Our opposition to the plan was duly noted at the hearing.[1]

[1] *The Brooklyn Teacher,* February, 1958, p. 2.

This illustrates how a false professionalism can mislead teachers. In the first place, public employees must always give their consent for any direct deduction of dues from their salary checks. For this reason, the reference to choosing personally the time and place to pay dues misses the point—why not choose the time and place indicated by the check-off? Since acceptance of the check-off is always voluntary in public employment, it is foolish to contend that teachers would lose their freedom by paying their dues through a check-off. It would mean only that they would have chosen to exercise their freedom in this way.

The fact that the check-off is more common among unions than among professional associations has nothing whatsoever to do with professionalism. The reason that most professionals do not pay their dues by a check-off is not because of their opposition to this practice in principle. Most professionals are fee-takers; hence there is no feasible way to check-off their dues. For this very reason, most professional organizations devote a great deal of their resources to collecting dues, resources which could otherwise be devoted to promoting the interests of their members. Hence it is to the interest of the members, regardless of whether the organization is a "union" or a "professional association," to facilitate the collection of dues.

The snobbery toward unions revealed in the quotation is made even more ridiculous by the fact that some professional groups which are on salary do accept the check-off. Many non-union teachers' associations collect their dues in this way. As a matter of fact, the check-off will soon be almost as common in public employment as it is now in private employment. This change will help considerably to strengthen organizations of public employees, including teachers' organizations which are more concerned with organizational efficiency than with avoiding "union" practices.

Because of the attitudes just discussed, teachers are an extremely backward group in the area of employer-employee relations. I mean by this much more than the fact that teachers are not doing very well in terms of salaries and working conditions. I mean that their entire approach to employer-employee problems is outmoded. There will be no basic improvement in teachers' salaries and working conditions until the teachers themselves develop a new framework of employer-employee relations in education. This new framework must be accompanied by new concepts of the teacher as an employee, new attitudes toward the strategy and tactics of securing adequate conditions of employment, and new concepts of what are adequate conditions of employment.

One of the first objectives of teachers should be to end legislative determination of their conditions of employment. The teachers must realize that state-wide minimum salary laws, or state-wide tenure laws, perhaps the two dearest legislative objectives of every state teachers' association, are anachronisms. Teachers should not spend another cent toward securing these objectives by legislation.

To understand why this is so, let us examine the current strategy employed by teachers to improve their conditions of employment. This strategy is a simple one. The major effort is made at the state level. The state teachers' associations strive for legislation setting minimum levels of teacher welfare. Local school systems are free to exceed these minimums but not to go below them. For example, states may legislate minimum salaries for teachers; school districts are free to pay more than the state minimums but may not pay less.

This strategy can be extended to other aspects of employment. State legislation may require school districts to give tenure to teachers after a certain period of time, to require a fair hearing for teachers who are being discharged, to contribute to a retirement system, and so on. In each case, local teachers' associations are supposed to try to improve upon the state-wide minimums mandated by the legislatures. By and large, this is the strategy that has been employed by teachers during the past fifty years. Efforts to secure federal aid do not alter it in any essential way.

What is wrong with this strategy? First, consider the problem at the state level, using state minimum salary laws to illustrate the weakness of the entire procedure. When teachers do succeed in establishing state minimum salary laws, the minimums are rarely substantial when enacted. Substantial or not, the minimums quickly become irrelevant in an inflationary and expanding economy. Ours is an economy in which an occupational group must steadily increase its income merely to maintain its relative position vis-à-vis other occupational groups. As a practical matter, state legislatures are not able to make the continual adjustments in conditions of employment which are necessary to protect the position of public employees. This is one reason why conditions of public employment typically lag behind those in private employment.

State legislatures usually meet every year but they are not in session for long periods of time. In addition to setting minimum salaries for teachers, they are under constant pressure to set minimum salaries for many different kinds of state employees, many kinds of municipal and county employees, and many kinds of private employees in intrastate commerce. Time-consuming as this is, it is only part of the tremendous legislative jam that confronts every session of state legislatures. Legislation concerning roads, hospitals, higher education, welfare agencies, parks, conservation, and other areas must be considered during these sessions.

I have said that even the state minimum salary laws which are helpful when passed soon become irrelevant. The fact is that most of them are of little value when passed. Few communities can get good teachers at the minimums set by the states. In Iowa, which has had a minimum salary law since 1913, the legal minimum salary for a beginning teacher with a master's degree was $810 per year as of September, 1958. In North Dakota, which has had such legislation since 1905, the legal minimum for such a teacher was $1,350 per year. These states provide the most extreme examples, but there are many others.[2]

Why can the minimums not be raised every year or every few years in order that teachers may keep pace with other groups? A legislature cannot sit every year as a salary-setting agency for

[2] See NEA Research Division, "State Minimum-Salary Laws," *Research Bulletin*, XXXVII (February, 1959), 8–12.

hundreds of different kinds of employees. It is too busy. Any legislation that affects so many people in so many different ways as minimum salaries for teachers must undergo interminable hearings. From one year to the next, different legislators and different parties with different commitments are in power. Every change requires another round of hearings, subject to all the changing elements that pervade a state legislative body.

What has been said concerning minimum salary legislation obviously applies to other state legislation relating to teacher welfare. The legislation is always too little and too late. Even so, the state teachers' associations fall back exhausted once they have achieved it. By the time they have pulled themselves together for another assault upon the legislature, conditions have usually become so bad that school systems have to improve them, regardless of legislation, just to get a teacher in every classroom.

The futility of legislative determination of conditions of employment is recognized by the overwhelming majority of authorities in the field of public administration. Not all of them have specifically discussed the role of legislation in public education. Those who have are convinced that it is as outmoded a way of resolving employer-employee relationships in this field as it is in other areas of public employment.[3] Every criticism that applies generally to legislative determination of the conditions of employment applies with equal or greater force to public education. If the teachers cannot learn this much from their continuing failure to improve their economic position, they deserve a seat in the corner with a dunce cap on their heads.

Actually, emphasis upon state legislation has been an unwise strategy quite apart from the frustrations inherent in legislative determination of conditions of employment. As previously pointed out, state appropriations in many important areas are supplemented by federal appropriations.[4] This has not been true in the past in education. Thus the state dollar goes farther in other fields than it does in education. For this reason teachers

[3] See Morton Robert Godine, *The Labor Problem in the Public Service* (Cambridge, Mass.: Harvard University Press, 1951), and Sterling D. Spero, *Government as Employer* (New York: Remsen Press, 1948).
[4] See the discussion on pp. 49–50.

should give federal aid for teachers' salaries the very highest strategic priority. Such aid should be in large enough amounts to provide a strong incentive for state legislatures to appropriate funds for public education. This will not happen unless the federal government assumes a much bigger share of the costs of public education than is currently contemplated by Congress.[5]

COLLECTIVE BARGAINING
IN PUBLIC EDUCATION

What will replace the present framework for resolving the conditions of employment in education? The answer is collective bargaining. Predictions are risky and perhaps foolish, but I would guess that collective bargaining will be the established mode of resolving employer-employee problems in education in most of the states within a generation.

What is collective bargaining? In federal legislation, it is defined as:

. . . the performance of the mutual obligation of the employer and the representatives of the employees to meet at reasonable times and confer in good faith with respect to wages, hours, and other terms and conditions of employment, or the negotiation of any agreement, or any question arising thereunder, and the execution of a written contract incorporating any agreement reached if requested by either party, but such obligation does not compel either party to agree to a proposal or require the making of any concession.[6]

At the present time, school boards in most of the states are legally free to ignore the duly chosen representatives of the teachers if the boards so desire. Note that collective bargaining imposes an affirmative obligation on employers to recognize the representatives of the employees and to negotiate with them as such. In the absence of such a requirement, the employers are

[5] The National Defense Education Act, passed by Congress on August 23, 1958, does provide some incentives for the states to spend more on education, since it provides for matching federal funds for certain educational expenditures. However, teachers' salaries constitute about two-thirds of the total cost of public education, and this act did not provide any federal funds for such salaries, except for teachers who undertake certain kinds of advanced study.

[6] Labor Management Relations Act, 1947, sec. 8 (d).

160

really free to deal with each employee as an individual. Teachers must secure legislation that would *compel*, not merely *permit*, school boards to negotiate with their representatives.

For collective bargaining to take place, both sides must make proposals and counterproposals in good faith. However, they are not required to accept any specific proposal or make any specific concession. It might appear that one or the other side might continually make unreasonable proposals and thereby frustrate the collective bargaining process, but this is not really a difficult problem to resolve in practice. Whether parties are bargaining in good faith is a question of fact, and it is usually clear whether it exists or not.

The rationale for collective bargaining is that although neither side is required to accept a proposal or make a specific concession, it is likely that the parties will agree upon conditions of employment if they are required to bargain in good faith about them. In other words, it is based on the theory that if the parties are forced to adhere to certain procedural requirements, they will ordinarily agree on the issues that are the subject of negotiation. In education, this would mean that a school board would not be unlawfully delegating any of its discretionary powers concerning conditions of employment merely because it was compelled to bargain with teachers about them.

Collective bargaining will come first between local teachers' associations and local school boards. In its early stages, the boards will be permitted but not required to bargain with teachers. Then laws will be passed requiring local boards to recognize the representatives of the teachers and to bargain with them in good faith concerning conditions of employment. For reasons to be explained shortly, these laws will then be changed to provide for collective bargaining at the state level. At this stage, the legislatures will delegate to the state superintendent of public instruction the authority to negotiate conditions of employment with the representatives of state teachers' associations. These negotiations will be conducted annually or biennially as they are in industry. The agreements reached will be subject to legislative approval, but this will be a much simpler process than the attempt to have the legislatures enact into law all the provisions of such an agreement. The persons who negotiate for the state legislatures will have a good idea of their limits, just as the persons who negotiate for large companies have a good idea of what they can and cannot concede in negotiations.

It is likely that this procedure will eventually be put into practice at the national level. Representatives of the national teachers' organizations will meet with appropriate representatives of the federal government to negotiate conditions of employment. The agreements reached will be subject to congressional approval. These agreements will not attempt to state precisely the exact terms of employment for every public school teacher in the country. Some of the conditions of employment may be spelled out at the federal level, others may be left to collective bargaining at regional, state or local levels.

It should never be assumed that merely because bargaining takes place at the national level, the resulting agreement must provide for exactly the same conditions of employment in every part of the country. This point is also relevant to bargaining at the state level, which may well result in intrastate differences in conditions of employment. In industry-wide collective bargaining, differentials for people in different regions doing the same kind of work are not uncommon. There is no reason why this practice cannot be accepted in public employment when it is desirable to do so. Even now, administrators of federal projects coming under the same federal agency do not pay the same wages for the same work in every state. They are accorded the discretion to negotiate for certain kinds of employees at prevailing wages. Of course, federal educational administrators would not have a prevailing wage rate in private employment to use as a yardstick in negotiating with teachers. But the illustration does show that there could be flexibility in a federal system.

I am not contending that teachers of the same subjects and grade levels in different parts of the country ought to be paid differently, nor am I contending that they ought to be paid the same. I am merely pointing out that there is no inherent reason why teachers' salaries would have to be the same the country over if they were determined by collective bargaining at the national level.

Collective bargaining can be introduced into public education in so many different ways and with so many different qualifications that it may be foolhardy to predict its lines of development. Nevertheless, I should like to explain why bargaining will be carried on at successively higher levels of government, until there is collective bargaining by teachers at the national level.

At the present time, teachers are an extremely weak occupational group. They have no control over entry to teaching at the state level and are unable to bargain collectively at the local level. They are also handicapped by the fact that there is only one employer for teachers in most communities. Whenever there is only one employer for a particular service, the absence of any competition gives the employer an enormous advantage in setting the conditions of employment. In most occupations, a person can change employers without having to move to another community. Obviously, the fact that teachers cannot do so weakens their position. Then too, the presence of large numbers of women who are ready to leave their housewifely tasks and become teachers at any time tends to keep teachers quiescent.

Nevertheless, there are other factors favorable to teachers which they have never used properly. Within a given community, the school board is the only employer, but on a state level, there are hundreds of employers and only one state teachers' association. Thus, at the state level, the power situation is reversed, or could be. Where there is a multitude of employers and only one employee organization, the latter usually has an excellent opportunity to force any one employer to be reasonably accommodating. For this reason, teachers will have an unparalleled opportunity to gain the balance of power vis-à-vis local school boards when collective bargaining is introduced at the local level.

Let us suppose that a state legislature has authorized collective bargaining in local school systems. The state teachers' association might then set a minimum salary which would be binding upon all of its local associations; none could agree to work for less. If a community refused to pay its teachers this minimum, it would have a real fight on its hands. The state association could establish a defense fund to support teachers in the community affected. All institutions of higher education and teacher-employment agencies would be alerted not to refer any applicants to the system until the dispute was settled. Since acceptance of employment in the system during the duration of the dispute would be unethical, new teachers would not be likely to wish to step into the breach. Under these circumstances, the community would soon find the money if it did not already have it.

Collective bargaining will be much more effective in improving the conditions of employment in education if it is accompanied by teacher control over entry. Such control is necessary to prevent public authorities from winning every dispute by licensing a horde of housewives and throwing them into the breach caused by a community's unwillingness to pay its teachers a decent salary. Actually, control over entry is the more important of these two strategic objectives if a choice must be made between them. The point is, however, that with able leadership, the balance of power would shift from local school boards to the state teachers' associations. Local communities would take care before challenging the power of an organized and determined state group.

To understand what will happen next, we may again turn with profit to industrial experience. When a union became so strong that it was able to impose its will upon individual employers, the employers combined so that they could not be coerced individually. And this, I think, will happen in education. Local communities which are no match for a powerful state teachers' association will inevitably come to favor a state-wide approach to conditions of employment. Inevitably, the approach will be state-wide not only in terms of the applicability of the agreement but in the source of funds to implement it. And the same process, in attenuated form, will add to the pressures for collective bargaining at the federal level, when a powerful national organization of teachers puts pressure upon individual states.

At the state level, if not at the local, collective bargaining in public education will become multiple bargaining. I mean by this that there will eventually be other groups represented at the bargaining sessions besides the teachers and the administrators who negotiate for the state government. There will be need for technical representatives to advise on the costs of various proposals. It may be feasible to have representatives of the legislature as observers during the bargaining sessions so as to provide informed leadership in that body when its approval is required. Precautions must be taken to prevent the teachers and administrators at the state level from entering into an agreement which is unfair to the taxpayers or to other groups which must be paid from public revenues. There are cases wherein employers and employees in a particular industry have made agreements which satisfy both sides at the expense of other groups in the economy. One reason for insisting upon legislative approval of basic agreements reached in collective bargaining in the public service is to prevent such an occurrence. Other precautions, requiring the systematic representation of several groups, will also be necessary.

These considerations also suggest a reason why collective bargaining in public education is bound to come, regardless of current attitudes toward it. In modern society, competition between individuals has been largely replaced by competition between groups. People who work in an occupation which has little group strength are bound to lose out in such a situation. For this reason, they will eventually turn to collective bargaining whatever their prejudices against it. Collective bargaining enables large occupational groups to advance their interests much more effectively than they could as individuals. This is as true in public as it is in private employment.

The weakness of individual negotiation where there are large numbers of persons doing the same work for the same employer has long been apparent. In recent years, however, there have been basic changes in the nature of the groups which bargain with each other. We can take the history of collective bargaining in the field of coal mining as an example. First, there was bargaining between individual miners and the owners of a particular mine; then between all the miners in a mine and the owners of that mine; then between all the miners in all the mines under one owner and that owner; and finally between all the miners in all the mines and a council of all the owners in the industry. We can see this pattern in one field after another. There is, therefore, a tendency for the most important economic decisions to be made at the national level, not only at the bargaining tables but in Congress, in the executive branch of the federal government, and in many other ways.

The upshot of this trend is to make the strength of the national organization the crucial factor in the determination of economic position. This is true even when the national organization is not a party to the actual negotiations between employers and employees. An occupational group which is not tightly organized, which does not exert any real power at the national level, will lose out in the struggle for economic position. To be specific, if teachers do not bargain as a group, it is extremely unlikely that they will improve their relative economic position regardless of how many sputniks the Russians send flying into space. Furthermore, if teachers continue to make their main effort at state and local levels while most other large groups make theirs at the national level, the economic position of teachers will continue to deteriorate. For even where the national organization is not a party to the direct negotiations between employers and employees, its influence, or lack of it, will be reflected in the ability of its state and local groups to gain their objectives. In self-defense, therefore, the teachers will have to organize and bargain at successively more inclusive levels, until they find themselves bargaining at the national level. But it will make a world of difference whether the teachers take this step as a last desperate resort or whether they have the foresight to take positive action now in this direction.[7]

One of the most important problems which must be solved to make collective bargaining successful in public employment is the organizational basis of teacher representation. In industry the wisest policy has been to have the majority organization represent all the employees. Bargaining with two or more organizations is usually not a successful policy. Each of the competing organizations refuses to agree to anything to make sure that it does not settle for less than the other. Since the organizations are competing for members, their leaders tend to outpromise one another, thus building up impossible demands on the employers. Sometimes the employers play off one organization against another, thereby keeping them all weak. In other situations the employers often have no way of telling which of two or more competing organizations really represents employee sentiment.

On the other hand, a single organization which includes highly disparate levels and kinds of employees is almost certain to result in arbitrary treatment of some employees. For example, in New York City it would seem hardly feasible to have the same organization represent beginning teachers in the elementary schools and the high-school principals. The first-year teachers need only a bachelor's degree; they are paid $4,500 per year (in 1959). The high-school principals are experienced professional employees. All have at least a master's degree and many have doctoral degrees. They receive $15,600 per year after five years of satisfactory service.

What we have here is the old problem of craft versus industrial unionism, only this time in an educational instead of an in-

[7] The best brief treatment of many of the points raised in this section are set forth in John K. Galbraith's *American Capitalism: The Theory of Countervailing Power* (Boston: Houghton Mifflin Co., 1956). This book could be read with profit by all teachers.

dustrial context. Anyone who thinks this problem is of no concern to educators should consider the following news story:

A bill which would make the High School Teachers' Association the sole bargaining agent for teachers in the senior high schools will be introduced in Albany shortly by Sen. Harry Gittleson and Assemblyman Lentol. The measure was drafted today by the law firm of Bennenson and Israelson, counsel for the HSTA.

Under the proposed bill the State Labor Relations Board would have power to determine any controversy in connection with the representation of teachers in the senior high schools. The Board of Education would be called on to recognize, as the representative of the high school group for collective bargaining purposes, any organization which has the majority of these teachers as its members.

The bill further calls on the school board to negotiate such matters as employment, working conditions and salaries with the selected organization, and provides for the employment by the board of an impartial arbitrator to settle any disputes that may arise.

The measure provides that while the proposed plan is in effect, "no teacher subject to its provisions shall have the right to strike, whether or not such right is preserved by law or otherwise recognized for employees of the state or other employes of the city." [8]

Four days after the publication of this item, the following story appeared in a different New York City newspaper:

Mayor Wagner is considering the issuance, in the next few weeks, of an executive order giving civil service unions many of the rights enjoyed by unions in private industry. The proposed order also would set up more systematic machinery for the adjustment of labor disputes in city departments. . . .

The proposed order would guarantee the right of municipal workers to join unions of their own choosing and to bargain collectively through those unions. However, it would rule out any form of compulsory union membership for those who did not want to join.

Unions designated by a majority of the workers in an appropriate bargaining unit would get exclusive bargaining rights. However, minority groups would retain the power to present to city officials the views and requests of their members. . . .

[8] *New York World-Telegram and Sun*, January 9, 1958, p. 29. Legislation requiring school boards to confer with representatives of the majority organization of teachers has already been passed in Minnesota and Wisconsin. However, these laws do not specifically require "collective bargaining" between teachers' organizations and school boards although they do require school boards to meet with the representatives of the teachers.

Under the projected city plan, a majority union would be informed of the minority views and would conduct all negotiations affecting those views. The minority groups would be barred from participating directly in the official machinery set up by the city for the adjustment of grievances.

The determination of the appropriate unit would rest with the Labor Commissioner. He would decide whether the unit should include a whole department, several departments or various classes of workers of subdivisions within a department. . . .

The yardstick would be the grouping best calculated to assure workers the fullest freedom of union selection consistent with the efficient operation of the public service. . . .

Labor disputes that could not be settled through direct talks between departmental heads and the unions representing their workers could be carried to [the Labor Commissioner's] office. The executive order would grant him flexibility in resolving the dispute. . . .

The program would apply initially to an estimated total of 110,000 workers in departments directly responsible to the Mayor.[9]

The solution to the problem of representation will probably be along the lines suggested by these news stories. Within the educational system as a whole, there will be established broad categories of employees: professional, administrative, custodial, semiprofessional, clerical, skilled labor, unskilled labor, and perhaps a few others. Each job in the schools will be included in one of these categories. Within each, there will be elections to determine the employee organization or organizations to bargain for that category. Collective bargaining cannot be carried on effectively if all employee groups, regardless of size, are accorded equal representation. It is possible that there will be exclusive recognition of the majority organization, as in private industry. However, at first, there is more likely to be a plan whereby organizations within each category are accorded representation according to their size. Such a plan would eliminate splinter representation while giving important minority interests an opportunity to gain recognition and expression.

Within the professional category, important differences between groups of teachers will be reflected in the bargaining

[9] *New York Times,* January 13, 1958, pp. 1, 41. Executive Order 49 embodying these recommendations was issued by Mayor Wagner on March 31, 1958.

situation. For example, certain kinds of high-school teachers may choose one organization and elementary teachers may choose another. There may be a third organization which attempts to represent both groups. Eventually, there may be two or three major groupings by grade level or subject area.

Undoubtedly, it will take considerable experience to determine the appropriate units of organization. Since future developments may change the personnel structure of education at any time, it will always be necessary to avoid dogmatic adherence to a given form of representation. For example, the accepted point of view is to regard both elementary and secondary teachers as members of the same profession and the same employee group. However, as the first news item illustrates, many high-school teachers do not wish to be included in the same group as elementary teachers. They believe that high-school teaching should be paid more than elementary teaching. Since there are invariably more elementary than secondary teachers in comprehensive teachers' organizations, such organizations rarely favor a differential for high-school teachers.

Conflict between elementary and high-school teachers over a single salary schedule was primarily responsible for a resurgence of interest in the High School Teachers' Association in New York City in 1947. Until that time, the high-school teachers had enjoyed a higher salary schedule. When this differential was eliminated, the high-school teachers could not get the existing comprehensive organizations to work for its restoration. As a result, many of them split off in order to work within an organization composed entirely of high-school teachers.[10]

There is a way to protect any substantial minority of teachers within a comprehensive organization. The organization could, on its own initiative, provide for the representation of any group which would otherwise feel that its interests were being sacri-

[10] As things stand now, the teachers in New York City are fragmented into more than seventy organizations because they have not learned how to provide adequate protection for minority interests within the structure of a comprehensive teachers' organization. One would be hardpressed to find a more overorganized group, or one weaker for its size, than the 40,000 New York City teachers.

ficed in the mass. If the minority were assured of some representation at the bargaining table, it would not have to secede to protect its interests.

For instance, a comprehensive teachers' organization could provide that a certain number of its representatives be chosen by high-school teachers. A procedure similar to this was adopted by the United Automobile Workers when many skilled workers in the UAW became increasingly dissatisfied with their lot. These workers felt that too much emphasis was being placed on improving conditions for unskilled and semiskilled workers and that more emphasis was needed on maintaining the differentials between themselves and other types of workers. To meet their criticisms, the UAW adopted a constitutional amendment giving skilled workers the right to disapprove a proposed contract if it was not satisfactory to them.[11]

Thus, if certain interests are not adequately represented within an organization, they will seek such representation outside it. The ever present threat of independent outside representation will force comprehensive organizations to give some recognition to minority groups. This kind of problem clearly exists in education. All the syrupy speeches at teachers' meetings maintaining that everyone who works in the school is a member of one big happy family cannot sweep this fact under the rug.

TEACHERS AND SCHOOL ADMINISTRATORS
IN A COLLECTIVE
BARGAINING SITUATION

One of the important effects of collective bargaining in public education is likely to be a clarification of the relationships between teachers and school superintendents. Currently, it is customary for superintendents to belong to the local education associations which represent the teachers as employees. This has always placed superintendents in an awkward position. As the chief executive officer of the school board, a superintendent

---

[11] See "Contracts and Negotiations," Constitution of the International Union, United Automobile Workers, adopted at the April, 1957, Convention in Atlantic City, N.J., sec. 3, art. 19, pp. 51–52.

is clearly a managerial employee. Nevertheless, in most school systems he is also regarded as the spokesman for the teachers in a community. The result is that the superintendents are placed in a position where they are expected to represent both sides in matters pertaining to conditions of employment.

Some educators have contended this is as it should be. The superintendent supposedly rises above his partisanship for one or the other side to advocate what is fair for both. In practice, however, the superintendent's tenure in a particular community depends upon his pleasing the school board rather than the teachers. It does not take much imagination to realize that the teachers are gravely handicapped by this situation. The inclusion of managerial representatives in an employee organization is prohibited by law in private industry.[12] This is necessary to prevent employer domination and to insure that the representatives of the employees will in practice advance their interests instead of those of the employer.

The domination of teachers' organizations by school administrators was largely responsible for the formation in 1916 of the American Federation of Teachers, a union affiliated with the AFL-CIO. The AFT excludes superintendents and places a number of other restrictions on the inclusion of administrative personnel in its membership. However, the AFT is numerically overshadowed by the National Education Association, which has over 600,000 members. The NEA has always favored the inclusion of administrative personnel in the same organizations as classroom teachers despite the fact that some of its affiliated local education associations are restricted to classroom teachers. The NEA has taken the position that to exclude administrators from a teachers' organization would mean adopting a trade union practice which may be appropriate in industry but has no place in a profession.

The advent of collective bargaining in public education is likely to present the NEA with some very difficult questions of

---

[12] Technically, it is prohibited only if the employee organization seeks the jurisdiction of the National Labor Relations Board. However, most large employee organizations find it to their advantage to do so.

policy and practice. Obviously, if collective bargaining is to be prevalent in education, it becomes important whether the representatives of management—in this case, the school superintendents—are excluded from the employee organization. Certainly, it is just as important to protect the integrity of employee organizations in public as it is in private employment. It is precisely the lack of this protection that makes a mockery of trade unions in the Soviet Union. In that country, employee organizations are dominated by the government, that is, by the employer. For this reason, they are of very limited value in protecting the rights and working conditions of their members.

Authorities in the field of public personnel administration agree that when it comes to the need to protect employee organizations from employer domination, there is no valid distinction between public and private employment. The experience of organizations of postal employees in the United States bears this out. In the early 1900's, many postal employees joined AFL postal unions in order to get rid of administrator-dominated organizations. Since then, the problem has come up in scores of other organizations of public employees, and the solution has always included forbidding membership to or weakening the influence of administrators within the employee groups.

The fact that some of its own local associations exclude educational administrators is usually ignored by the NEA. Such exclusion is thought to be justified only because, in the communities affected, the school administrators did not treat the teachers kindly. The NEA has also ignored the fact that the American Association of University Professors excludes from active membership persons whose duties are half time or more administrative in character. This exclusion is even more rigid than the exclusion of school administrators from the American Federation of Teachers. Thus we have the paradox that administrators of public institutions of higher education are excluded from the organizations of professors, but the administrators of public school systems are not excluded from organizations of public school teachers. If such exclusion is necessary to protect the integrity of the AAUP as an employee organization, it would seem equally necessary in the case of organizations of public school teachers.

In defense of NEA policy, it is contended that local associations in other professions are open to all members of the profession. This is true, but it overlooks basic differences between education and these other professions. Physicians do not stand in an employer-employee relationship with one another; therefore, there is no need to exclude doctor-administrators from the local medical associations. Likewise, the practitioners in other professions are so seldom in an employer-employee relationship with each other that a policy of excluding employer-professionals would hardly make sense in a community-wide organization of professionals.

Even though most physicians are fee-takers, some are hospital administrators. It might be argued that if my point of view were sound, it would at least require the exclusion of hospital administrators from the local medical association. The fact that this is not done supposedly shows by analogy that the union point of view on administrator membership is unsound in a professional association. However, there are good reasons for not excluding medical administrators from local associations, reasons which do not apply to educational administrators.

A local medical association is not an employee organization; a local teachers' organization practically always is. A local medical association does not represent all the physicians in negotiations with a single employer, who is represented by a physician-administrator. Such a situation would call for the exclusion of the physician-administrator who negotiates conditions of employment on behalf of the employer. In other words, where an employer-employee relationship does exist between members of the medical profession, an employee organization can be organized, and it can exclude the employer-professional; but there would be no point to excluding the physician-administrator from a local medical association which does not bargain with anybody and which has no reason to do so.

In fact, where the situation confronting physicians is similar to that confronting teachers, the physicians do engage in collective bargaining. In some communities, the costs of medical services are borne largely by the health funds of unions. Because so many of their prospective patients are covered by the union's health fund, physicians who are not approved by the medical administrator of the union have no chance to practice successfully in these communities. Furthermore, the fee schedule set by the union has a strong influence on the economic position of the physicians. In these communities, therefore, the physicians must come to terms with the union in somewhat the same way that teachers must come to terms with a school board. In both cases, there is little realistic hope of professional employment other than from the one major employer.

In these communities, where the physicians are dependent upon one employer just as are the teachers, there is a growing tendency toward collective bargaining between physicians and the unions. The physicians as a group negotiate conditions of employment, even though this is technically still a matter for individual doctors and patients to decide. What is even more interesting is the fact that more and more physicians are specifically calling for collective bargaining as the best procedure to determine fees, schedules, and other conditions of employment in such situations.

Another factor in the medical situation which lessens the need to exclude physician-administrators from the medical associations is the tight control over entry which is exercised by the medical profession. This puts the individual physician in a much stronger bargaining position than the individual teacher. Administrator domination is not a serious problem in the medical profession because the individual physician is not dependent upon a particular employer in the community. The teachers, having only one employer, and lacking any effective control over the supply of teachers, lack the power to bring the employer to reasonable terms. In short, physician-employees are in an incomparably stronger position than teacher-employees; hence administrator domination of medical associations is less likely than administrator domination of educational associations.

The problem of administrator membership in teachers' organ-

izations involves much more than the status of school superintendents in local associations. Principals will want some organizational medium to protect their own interests. What will be
the status of principals—should they be regarded as managerial
employees, as another kind of teacher, as a craft union within
the employee organization, or as an independent employee group?
Perhaps it is a mistake to think of principals as a homogeneous
class of educational employees. Note that in industry, the label
"foreman" actually covers a wide range of supervisory personnel.
Some have very little supervisory or managerial responsibility,
others have a great deal. One must look to the occupational
situation, not the label, to determine their status in an intelligent way.

Similarly, there are basic differences between the principal-
ship of a New York City high school and that of a small rural
school. In the former, the principal is a powerful administrator
who supervises a school with 3,000 students and perhaps 250
teachers. The principal of a small rural school may teach most
of the day, supervise as few as 3 teachers, and be a mere rubber
stamp for the county superintendent of schools. A high-school
departmental chairman in New York City has more administrative responsibility than many principals in small rural schools.
For this reason, it is difficult to propose any inflexible dividing
line between managerial personnel and other employees. As
long as collective bargaining is conducted from school district
to school district, there will be variations in the constituency and
the framework of the teachers' organizations.

The impact of collective bargaining upon administrator membership in teachers' associations is difficult to predict. The possibilities are numerous and depend upon factors which cannot
be assessed very well at this time. For example, the extent to
which teachers are successful in achieving control over entry to
teaching will have important repercussions in their membership
policies. The more rigorous this control and the more it forces
communities to compete for teachers, the less danger will exist
of administrator domination of teachers' associations and the less
need there will be to exclude administrators from these associations.

Although there are many possible solutions to the problem of administrator domination, the National Education Association has yet to make any constructive contribution toward a sensible solution. The NEA admits that there has been some administrator domination in the past but treats all suggestions that the problem still exists as a trade union criticism beneath the dignity of professional teachers to answer. This attitude must give way to one which is more in accord with occupational realities. Some restrictions will have to be placed upon administrator membership in the organizations which bargain on behalf of teachers. There is, of course, no reason to restrict administrator membership in professional organizations which do not have any bargaining functions.

COLLECTIVE BARGAINING IN PUBLIC
EDUCATION: PROBLEMS AND
PROSPECTS

The preceding analysis has not touched upon many of the objections that will be raised against collective bargaining in public education: that it would require an unlawful surrender of the discretionary powers of school boards; that it would lead to strikes by teachers; that it would unduly hamper school administrators; that it is out of place in public education because education is not carried on for profit; that it would threaten the stability of government; that the public would never stand for it; and so on. None of these objections has any real merit.[13]

The advent of collective bargaining in public education will raise many genuine problems in addition to the few which have been discussed. It will be important to develop a structure that permits individual grievances to be handled promptly and fairly in the schools where they arise, but without placing unwarranted restrictions on school administrators. There need be no fear that teachers would abuse effective grievance procedures, for to do so would be to jeopardize the continued existence of these procedures. There must be a clarification of what is properly subject

[13] These objections, as well as many other points discussed in this chapter, are analyzed in detail in Myron Lieberman, *Education as a Profession* (Englewood Cliffs, N.J.: Prentice-Hall, 1956), chap. xi.

to bargaining. However, problems like these are already being solved every day in the largest and most complex enterprises, both public and private. There is no reason to believe that they cannot be solved in education.

Many people believe that the recent Russian successes in science and technology will automatically redound to the benefit of teachers in the United States. The public, it is thought, is now willing to provide adequate conditions of employment for teachers.

This point of view is a delusion. Nobody is going to bestow anything upon the teachers, national crisis or no national crisis. The teachers will have to fight for their place in the sun, and they will have to be much better fighters than they have been in the past. It is doubtful, to say the least, that a suddenly aroused public is going to cut down on its liquor, cigarettes, and television sets in order to pay its teachers more.

Recent events have provided teachers with a great opportunity to reverse their occupational decline. At present, the teachers are muffing this opportunity, chiefly because they regard it merely as an opportunity to get better salaries or fewer classes or more sick leave. They must realize that to struggle in the same old way for the same old objectives, different only in the higher amounts of money requested, is to insure failure. The opportunity and the task ahead is to transform the entire framework of employer-employee relations in education.

Collective bargaining will not only be a change in the way teachers negotiate their conditions of employment. It will be an orderly way of channeling the ideas and energies of teachers into their work. It will mean that the professional opinion of teachers as a group will receive consideration, not at the whim of school boards or administrators, but as a respected part of the educational enterprise. Collective bargaining may be advocated initially as an economic measure, but its ultimate justification will lie not so much in what it will do for the teachers as in what it will do for American education.

Chapter IX

TEACHERS' ORGANIZATIONS: A LOOK

AT THE RECORD

The foremost fact about teachers' organizations in the United States is their irrelevance in the national scene. Their futility in protecting the public interest and the legitimate vocational aspirations of teachers is a national tragedy, much more dangerous to our democratic institutions than the excessive power wielded by such familiar bogeys as "Madison Avenue," "labor bosses," "captains of industry," "military high brass," and the like. Because their organizations are weak, teachers are without power; because they are without power, power is exercised upon them to weaken and to corrupt public education.

Let me illustrate the justification for these statements first by a brief analysis of the National Education Association (NEA), the largest organization of school teachers in the United States. The NEA has over 600,000 members, most of whom are public school teachers. Although it was founded in 1857 as "The National Teachers Association," much of its growth in membership is a recent phenomenon. By 1907, fifty years after the founding of the NEA, there were only 2,332 members. Gains were small until 1918, when a trend toward teachers' unions spurred school superintendents into an all-out campaign to enrol teachers in the NEA. Membership jumped from slightly over 10,000 in 1918 to more than 118,000 in 1922. Except during the depression, membership increased steadily, but the largest gains have come in recent years. From 1952 to 1957, the average annual gain in membership was close to 40,000 per year.

At the Centennial Convention in 1957, NEA dues were raised from five to ten dollars per year. This action resulted in a moderate decline in membership. However, NEA dues are still much less than the prevailing dues in most national professional organizations. Its huge membership enables the NEA to support a budget ($6,927,000 in 1957–58) larger than that of any other professional association.

The size of the NEA is partially reflected in its complicated organizational structure. The NEA has thirty departments, devoted to such diverse fields as school administration, retired teachers, school secretaries, higher education, audio-visual instruction, and art education. The departments vary considerably in membership, prestige, and power. Much of the power in the NEA rests with the American Association of School Administrators (AASA), an NEA department whose membership consists largely of school superintendents. Despite the fact that its membership is only slightly over 10,000, the AASA is far more powerful than the Department of Classroom Teachers, which enrols 70 per cent of the Association's membership. There is ordinarily no requirement that one be a member of the NEA to be a member of a department, or vice versa. Thus, although the NEA works closely with the departments, the latter are often quite autonomous; they have their own membership and dues structure, permanent staff, and programs. This fact is frequently overlooked. A recent example was the widespread criticism of the NEA when the executive secretary of the Department of Secondary School Principals urged the members of his department to cancel their school subscriptions to *Life* magazine because of certain articles in it alleged to be unfair to American education. The NEA was widely and unfairly accused of advocating unethical practice in this case.

In addition to the thirty departments, there are twenty-four permanent commissions and committees operating under the nominal control of the Representative Assembly, a delegate body of about 6,000 members. There is also a Board of Directors (77 members), an Executive Committee (11 members), and a Board of Trustees (5 members), whose main function is the selection of the chief permanent officer of the Association, the Executive Secretary. There are thirteen Headquarters Divisions which operate under the Executive Secretary, who is assisted by five assistant executive secretaries and a business manager. The presidency is chiefly a ceremonial office and, by long tradition, goes to a man one year and a woman the next. The twelve vice presidencies are also largely ceremonial; their chief purpose is to reward the faithful with prestige and a few trips during the year. However, beginning in 1958, the first vice-president automatically became president the following year. The total NEA staff of about six hundred is housed in a new $9,000,000 structure completed in 1958, in Washington, D.C.

A less impressive picture of the NEA emerges from a consideration of its recruitment techniques. Although many teachers join freely, there has long been a great deal of compulsory membership in the NEA. A few years ago an official of the American Federation of Teachers, the only serious organizational threat to the NEA, suggested to me that NEA membership would be cut in half if superintendents would stop forcing teachers to join the NEA in order to get or keep their jobs. This is very probably an exaggerated estimate, but the practice of coercing teachers to join the NEA is still widespread in many states.

It is practically impossible to assess the precise extent of compulsory membership. The chief reason for this is that teachers are generally not in a secure position from which to publicize or protest the practice. In many communities, teachers have no tenure and do not dare to protest against compulsory membership. In some states, teachers are still forced to join the NEA despite explicit state laws forbidding the practice of requiring membership in a teachers' organization as a condition of employment. Even in Oklahoma, which has such a law, I have met teachers who informed me that their superintendents did not even bother to suggest membership; the deductions for NEA dues were made without any prior discussion with the teachers. Since teachers have no tenure in Oklahoma, most of them are afraid to protest such coercion. A teacher who is not rehired may find it very difficult to prove that his dismissal was due to his opposition to joining the NEA.

It is really a most remarkable thing that many school boards make, or permit their superintendents to make, membership in the NEA and its affiliated state and local associations a condition of employment for teachers. The requirement that the teacher join these organizations is often included as a part of the employment contract signed by the teacher. In other areas of public employment, there would be a tremendous outcry if public employees were forced to join a particular organization as a condition of employment. The reader need only imagine the reaction in his own community if the city administration should require all publicly employed carpenters, plumbers, and electricians to join the AFL-CIO as a condition of employment.

The public administrator, like the administrator in private industry, usually prefers a weak employee organization or none at all. Only in education do we find a large body of public employees openly required to join an organization as a condition of employment. The reason for this is that school administrators dominate the NEA and its affiliated associations. Ironically, compulsory membership in teachers' associations is most common in rural areas, where there is the most pronounced anti-labor sentiment. The superintendent and the board of education would be horror-stricken, if they stopped to think about the matter, to realize that they had instituted "a closed shop"— and without even the approval of the employees!

THE NEA AS A PROFESSIONAL ORGANIZATION

The NEA prides itself on being "the largest professional organization in the world." This may be so. But what about its effectiveness? What has it accomplished since it was founded more than a century ago?

This is not an easy question to answer. Many factors influence the quality of education and the status of the teaching profession. In particular cases, it may be impossible to ascertain the relative influence, for good or evil, of all the forces that try to shape educational policies. If teachers' salaries are low, it might seem unfair to blame the NEA, which is struggling to raise them.

On the other hand, NEA programs must be evaluated in terms of their effectiveness as well as in terms of their purposes. If teachers' salaries are low, it does not make sense to absolve the Association of responsibility because it tries, albeit in vain, to win higher salaries from an apathetic public. An important test of any occupational organization is its effectiveness in overcoming public apathy. If educational facilities throughout the country were reasonably adequate, we would expect most of the credit to go to the NEA even though other agencies might also have played a role.

But if facilities are not adequate, we should not absolve the NEA of responsibility merely because it has "fought for better schools." Its adequacy as a teachers' organization must be measured by its success in overcoming opposition, not by reference to what it would like to see done in the absence of opposition.

In order to analyze the NEA's record, we should be clear about the kinds of objectives which professional organizations strive to achieve. Traditionally, the term "professional" has been applied to occupational associations which protect clients from incompetent or unscrupulous practitioners. There are several ways by which an association can accomplish this objective. Usually it tries to secure control of admission to the profession, then to set standards which protect the public. For example, admission to the medical profession is in the hands of state medical boards, composed entirely of doctors. In most states, the medical association controls appointments to these boards. This situation was made possible only by the vigorous support given to the state associations by the American Medical Association, the national association of doctors.

A professional association can also work for high standards in the educational institutions which provide professional training. It can either upgrade or eliminate the professional training program in schools which have inadequate programs. It may also set high standards for membership (as distinct from admission to the profession), thus providing the public with some means of distinguishing the competent from the incompetent practitioners regardless of what public authorities do. In addition, it can formulate and enforce a code of ethics which subordinates the welfare of the practitioners to the welfare of the public.

Let us consider first the NEA's record concerning standards for entry to the teaching profession. With all due regard to variations from region to region, state to state, institution to institution, occupation to occupation, and person to person, the over-all picture is clear. As a general rule, teaching requires from one to five years less preparation than other professions. Many institutions have no program of selective admission, or only a nominal one, for entry to teacher education. The quantitative and qualitative standards for graduation from programs of teacher education are typically much lower than they are for medicine, law, engineering, and other acknowledged professions. The lower standards for admission to and graduation from programs of teacher training are paralleled by the decline, amounting to an almost complete disappearance, of public machinery to test the adequacy of professional training. The use of written examinations for a teaching license, a common practice fifty years ago, is practically extinct today. Such examinations are still common in other professions, and the trend is to extend their use wherever possible. In short, for the country as a whole, there is not a single step toward the teaching profession for which the standards are set as high as they are for a similar step in other professions.

The NEA deplores low standards for teaching. In fact, the standards are low because teachers have no control over them, and they have no control over these standards because the NEA does not believe in it. Since 1921 at least, the NEA has advocated non-professional control of the state boards which set the standards for teacher certification. The NEA has maintained this policy despite the fact that professional control over entry has always preceded the establishment of high standards in the acknowledged professions. This explains why every professional association except the NEA is attempting to expand its control over entry.

The really ominous fact is that in a growing number of states, teachers are *excluded by law* from the boards which control entry to teaching. To appreciate the professional decline to which the NEA is currently leading the teachers of this country, one must realize that other professions are still moving to strengthen their control over such boards. Indeed, since control over entry is a criterion of professionalism itself, the NEA's policy on this issue is essentially an antiprofessional one.

The sad truth is that NEA policies are responsible for—or unable to remedy—a situation in which the public cares less about the competence of teachers than it does about the competence of any other professional group. The basic purpose of certification, or licensure as it is called in other professions, is to protect the public from incompetent and unscrupulous practitioners. As previously pointed out, in the overwhelming majority of states, only public school teachers need be certified; those who teach in non-public schools are generally not required to satisfy any state-imposed requirements. This is in striking contrast to the prevailing situation in other professions, where there is not one set of standards for publicly employed professionals and a different set, or none at all, for privately employed ones. The protection of the public requires that *all* professionals establish their competence. This is true for physicians, attorneys, dentists, and every other profession. The NEA's desire for higher standards for teachers is sincere, but the major barrier to higher standards is its own support for, or indifference to, non-professional control of admission to teaching.

The status of professional ethics in education is another remarkable example of the NEA's preoccupation with the appearances of professionalism while it ignores its substance. The NEA has had a "Code of Professional Ethics" since 1929. Up to the present time, its Committee on Professional Ethics has formally tried exactly one person for unprofessional conduct. This took place in 1946, when Dr. William H. Johnson, the superintendent of schools in Chicago, was expelled from membership in the NEA. Johnson himself did not even bother to appear or to answer the charges of corrupt and dictatorial administration which were the basis for the Committee's action.

Since less than one-third of the teachers in the country were NEA members at the time, the punishment accorded Johnson seems rather innocuous. Nonetheless, the educational journals of the day hailed Johnson's expulsion as a historic occasion, marking the beginning of an era in which teachers would assume corporate responsibility for their professional conduct. In fact, however, the NEA's Committee on Professional Ethics merely reverted to its traditional role of issuing pious platitudes about the child, home, community, country, and profession. As with so many other NEA agencies, its main function seems to be in providing some of the faithful with a few trips each year at NEA expense.

The absence of any enforcement of the NEA's Code of Professional Ethics is more understandable when one reads the Code itself. It is a confused ragbag of platitudes and contradictions which would be quite dangerous if its enforcement were taken seriously. For instance, Section 1, Principle II, of the Code asserts that "a teacher will adhere to any reasonable pattern of behavior accepted by the community for professional persons." This presumably means that it is unethical for a teacher in Mississippi to condemn racial segregation. Section 3, Principle III, states that "the teacher will discuss controversial issues from an objective point of view, thereby keeping his class free from partisan opinions." The Committee has not yet explained how a teacher can "discuss controversial issues" while simultaneously "keeping his class free from partisan opinions."[1]

The absence of NEA leadership in developing and enforcing a code of professional ethics for teachers is reflected in the apathy of the NEA's affiliated state and local associations on this matter.

---

[1] For a more detailed analysis of the NEA Code of Professional Ethics with some suggestions for improving it, see Myron Lieberman, *Education as a Profession* (Englewood Cliffs, N.J., Prentice-Hall, 1956), chap. xiii.

The activities of these associations in the area of professional ethics usually consist of adopting the NEA Code, framing it, and then promptly ignoring its existence. The majority of teachers have probably never read the NEA Code; in fact, many teachers are not even aware that any such code exists.

TEACHER WELFARE AND THE NEA

There is no hard and fast line which divides "professional" activities from those designed to advance the welfare of teachers. Adequate salaries are desirable from a broad social point of view as well as from the teachers' point of view. But for purposes of analysis, it is illuminating to consider what NEA leadership has accomplished for the American teacher.

Such an analysis is difficult to make in a few paragraphs because the trends have not affected all educational groups in the same way. Thus from 1904 to 1953, the real income of principals and teachers in large city high schools actually declined, whereas the real income of elementary teachers increased during this period. In general, however, teachers have either suffered an absolute decrease in real income since 1904 or their real income has increased at a much slower rate than has real income in other occupations. Certain groups of elementary teachers constitute the only important exception to this statement.

Since 1929 at least, the average annual salaries of public school personnel have remained very close to the national average for all employed persons. In 1929, the average teaching salary was $1,400 and the average for all employed persons was $1,405. By 1957, the average teaching salary was $4,450 and the average for all employed persons was $4,190. Between 1929 and 1957, the average annual teaching salary was higher than the average for all employed persons in nineteen years, and in eight years it was lower. However, during this period there was never a substantial difference between these two averages.[2]

[2] Most of the data in this and the preceding paragraph is taken from NEA Research Division, *Economic Status of Teachers in 1954–55* (Washington, D.C.: National Education Association, 1954); and Beardsley Ruml and Sidney G. Tickton, *Teaching Salaries Then and Now* (New York: Fund for the Advancement of Education, 1955).

The 1950 Census gave data on 1949 incomes for eighteen professional occupations requiring at least a bachelor's degree. In twelve of these, the average income was at least 50 per cent above the average for all employed persons. Teaching ranked fifteenth among these professional occupations; in 1949, the average income of teachers was only 14.1 per cent above the median income of all employed persons, including part-time workers. As late as 1957–58, 25 per cent of all classroom teachers received an annual salary of less than $3,500. Also during 1957–58, 46,000 teachers were paid less than $2,500, a figure which is $1,690 less than the average for *all* employed persons, including persons employed only part-time, during 1957.[3]

Although there is no authoritative definition of a "professional level of income," it is usually taken to be two to three times the average annual income of all employed persons. On this basis, it is clear that the NEA has made no progress toward securing a professional level of income for teachers during the past fifty years. But even this statement does not bring out the actual extent of the NEA's failure to advance the interests of teachers. The failure of teachers to improve their salaried position relative to other occupational groups really represents a major decline in their economic status. The number of days worked per year has declined in every major occupation except education, where it has increased from 147 in 1904 to 182 in 1953. Furthermore, the number of hours worked per day has increased in education but decreased in practically all other occupations.

It should also be noted that the fringe benefits in industry are increasingly superior to those in education. Most collective agreements in industry provide for severance pay for employees who must be released for no fault of their own. Such provisions are urgently needed in education, where, for instance, the consolidation of school districts or desegregation often reduces the number of teachers needed. Nevertheless, there is no severance pay for teachers, no matter how long their service. The typical employ-

[3] I have taken the data in this paragraph from NEA Legislative Commission, *Teacher Shortages and Teacher Salaries* (Washington, D.C.: National Education Association, 1958).

ment agreement in industry includes grievance machinery according employees a full measure of protection against arbitrary and capricious changes in the conditions of employment; the typical teaching contract is completely silent on these matters. The only dimension in which teachers still enjoy some superiority over other occupational groups is in the matter of vacations, but this gap is being steadily narrowed from both directions, with longer vacations in industry and shorter vacations in education.

The NEA does work for teacher welfare, but its programs are low in aim and weak in execution. Politicians are well aware of the fact that NEA support or opposition is irrelevant at the polls. One need only compare the NEA's record with that of the American Medical Association to appreciate this. In 1950 the Truman administration attempted to pass a compulsory health insurance bill which was opposed by the American Medical Association. To defeat the legislation, the AMA raised $3,000,000 by assessing every one of its members $25.00. Compulsory health insurance, financed by federal funds, has been dormant ever since the Association's campaign against it.

Regardless of one's attitude toward the legislation killed by the American Medical Association, there can be only respect for the forceful way in which the Association achieved this legislative result. If the NEA could assess every member $5.00 and pour the resulting $3,000,000 into a vigorous, well-planned campaign for federal support of teachers' salaries, every member would get back this assessment many times over within a short time. But the NEA is incapable of moving with vigor and imagination, even when confronted by the most serious problems and challenging opportunities.

Some NEA apologists always take the attitude that the Association does its good deeds behind the scenes. It is allegedly not interested in headlines, and therefore one should not condemn the NEA for the fact that its activities are not in the public eye. For a long time I felt like an uninitiated ignoramus, criticizing the NEA only because I was not privy to innumerable good deeds which, for some unexplained reason, had to remain confidential. Unfortunately, the steady and continuing decline of the teaching profession are public facts which require public analysis.

Of course, the NEA does perform some valuable services for teachers. If a local association desires a credit union, the NEA will help to organize it. The NEA's information and research services are prompt and thorough. Many NEA publications are extremely useful. The teacher who plans a trip will get all the help he desires from the NEA's Travel Service.

Nevertheless, while freely conceding the existence of these and other worthwhile activities, it is necessary to face up to two basic facts about them. The first is that these constructive results have been achieved largely in areas which are peripheral to the basic problems of the profession. Second, even in these useful but peripheral services, the NEA often reveals a shocking inability to act on principle.

For example, the NEA Travel Service sponsors tours to Arab countries from which Jewish teachers are excluded. Despite many protests against this practice, the NEA's Executive Committee continues to permit its Travel Service to continue to sponsor these tours. The excuse given is that it is not the NEA but the countries involved which are responsible for the discrimination. On this line of reasoning, the NEA might just as well abandon the policy (adopted after one of the few successful revolts in NEA history) of meeting only in cities providing satisfactory accommodations for all delegates, regardless of race. The NEA could meet in Mississippi and contend that any inconvenience suffered by Negro delegates was due to discrimination by Mississippians, not by NEA agencies.

Every occupational organization undoubtedly has some redeeming features. However, we need to know more than the simple fact that there are good and bad aspects to the NEA. If we are to act intelligently with respect to the NEA, we need an understanding of its specific accomplishments and failures. In this context, it would be most naïve to equate mechanically NEA successes and failures. On the basic professional issues, the NEA has been a dismal failure. A general who loses an army to gain a few yards of barren land is not a success. Neither is an occupational organization which dissipates the funds and energies of hundreds of thousands of teachers for limited, even picayune, results.

STATE AND LOCAL ASSOCIATIONS

Education in the United States is largely a function of state and local government. This fact emphasizes the need for strong teachers' organizations at the state and local levels.

Let us first consider teachers' organizations at the state level. The state teachers' associations (or state education associations, as they are frequently called) vary widely in membership, resources, programs, and leadership. It must be obvious, however, that these associations share responsibility with the NEA for the condition of education in the United States today.

The lack of professional control over admission to teaching, the low standards for teaching certificates, the existence of substandard programs of teacher education, the declining professional and economic status of teachers, the absence of professional autonomy, the superficial attention to professional ethics —all these and other indications of professional failure constitute a reflection upon the state education associations as well as upon the NEA. Most of these associations have never put up a real fight for the most basic principles or the most elementary vocational objectives appropriate for teachers. They are habituated to begging for crumbs instead of fighting for loaves; more often than not, they get the back of the hand from the state legislatures.

As for the local education associations affiliated with the NEA, not even the NEA's own studies venture the claim that they typically wield any real power in their communities. Occasionally an outstanding individual stimulates a local association into significant action, or conditions degenerate to the point where the local association must act or perish. Exceptional individuals and circumstances are, however, an inadequate answer to an organizational need which is always present in every community. As it is, most local associations are not taken seriously, even by their own members. The fact that their dues are seldom more than a dollar or two a year affords some indication of the character of their programs.

A 1948 study of local associations made by the NEA's Research Division indicated that their programs were usually devoted to problems of teacher welfare, such as getting higher salaries.[4] This finding should have embarrassed quite a few NEA adherents, who are always criticizing teachers' unions for being preoccupied with teacher welfare. Of course, the fact that local associations devote most of their attention to salary problems does not mean that teachers are more mercenary than other vocational groups. It means only that they are less efficient in achieving their economic goals. It is typical of local education associations to dissipate their energies in futile efforts to improve their conditions of employment. Other than this, they give teas for new teachers in the fall and retiring teachers in the spring, and perhaps listen to a few travelogues in between.

TEACHERS' UNIONS

To understand the history and prospects of teachers' unions in the United States, it is necessary to make a few additional comments about the NEA. The NEA was founded by school superintendents and has always been dominated by them. Partly for this reason, it has never developed a vigorous program to improve the economic status of teachers. Even after 1900, an influential segment of NEA leadership believed that emphasis upon teacher welfare was unprofessional and beneath the dignity of the Association.

Under these circumstances, it was inevitable that the teachers should seek an organizational medium devoted to advancing instead of stifling teacher welfare. Many came to feel that unions were the answer, and in 1916, teachers from New York, Chicago, Gary, Scranton, Oklahoma City, and Washington, D.C., combined to form the American Federation of Teachers (AFT). Soon after its formation, the AFT was issued a charter by the American Federation of Labor. It is currently affiliated with the AFL-CIO.

[4] NEA Research Division, "Local Education Associations at Work," *Research Bulletin*, XXVI (October, 1948).

The founders of the AFT were not always hostile to the NEA. Many of them believed that the two organizations should be complementary. It was thought that the NEA would be devoted to the science and art of teaching and the AFT would be devoted to improving the economic status of teachers. However, within three years after it was founded, the AFT had more teacher members than the NEA. From 1916 to 1919, its membership increased to over 10,000. Frightened by this unexpected development, the NEA launched a powerful counterattack, beginning in 1920. Superintendents forced teachers to join the NEA and its affiliated state and local associations. Teachers were also forced to sign employment contracts in which they agreed not to join unions. School administrators found it easy to carry out these policies in the anti-labor climate which followed World War I.

By 1927, membership in the AFT had dropped to 3,500. Then, under the impetus of the depression, membership began to rise slowly. Just prior to World War II, the AFT was forced to expend most of its energies in expelling a Communist faction operating chiefly out of a few eastern locals. After the expulsion of the Communists (some of whom then joined the NEA, according to AFT leaders), the AFT again entered upon a period of steady growth. In 1958, its membership was slightly over 55,000.

The founders of the AFT shared the popular view that public school teachers should not be permitted to strike.[5] To make up for the loss of power resulting from the relinquishment of this right, it was thought that teachers needed powerful allies to overcome the strong industrial, commercial, and real estate lobbies that usually opposed higher taxes for educational purposes. The labor movement seemed a natural ally. The vast majority of wage earners could not adequately finance the education of their children by private expenditures. Union leaders such as Samuel Gompers had long been aware of the fact that equality of educational opportunity could be realized only through higher taxes upon the more favored economic groups. For these reasons, teacher affiliation with the labor movement appeared to be a

[5] The 1958 Convention passed a resolution calling upon teachers to work for the right to strike.

practical means of securing a wide base of support for the objectives of the teachers.

This rationale helps to explain why AFT publications generally put more emphasis upon the activities of other unions than they do upon the activities of professional associations; for instance, they constantly refer to the success of other unions which have utilized collective bargaining. At the same time, however, the AFT has completely ignored the need for teacher control over entry to the teaching profession. This is a surprising failure in view of the fact that many unions as well as professional associations have realized the importance of job control in raising standards of service. The shortsighted "professionals" in the NEA are quite mistaken in thinking that teachers should not soil their professional hands with tough collective bargaining, but the AFT is at least as shortsighted in its failure to understand that certain policies of the fee-taking professions, such as occupational control over entry, must be incorporated into the programs of teachers' organizations.

The failure of the AFT to advocate teacher control over admission to teaching has nothing to do with the charges often made against the Federation that it is "unprofessional." As a matter of fact, the reasons why most teachers refuse to join the AFT have little or nothing to do with the criticisms which can justly be made of it. For instance, teachers' unions have been opposed on the grounds that, as public employees serving all the people, teachers should not affiliate with any particular segment of the population. It is alleged that affiliation with the labor movement would compromise teachers in their daily work.

This, of course, is not an argument against teachers' unions as such but only against their affiliation with the labor movement. But in any case there is no reason why a teacher's affiliation with the AFL-CIO should compromise his work any more than his affiliation with any religious, political, or social organization which takes a stand on broad social issues. Authorities in the field of public personnel administration agree that this objection to affiliation with the labor movement by public employees has little merit. In fact, decades of experience with public employee unions affiliated with the labor movement have shown that affiliation is to be desired rather than feared as a matter of social policy. Parenthetically, it might be noted that although it is not officially affiliated with other groups, the NEA has on several occasions shown the most extreme partiality to certain non-educational organizations, such as the American Legion.

AFT supporters defend their affiliation with the AFL-CIO on two contradictory grounds. First, they argue that affiliation enables the AFT to secure the support of practically all organized labor for AFT objectives. This contention naturally raises the question whether other unions in the AFL-CIO can force the AFT to take an action opposed by the teachers. The AFT's answer is that it, like other federations in the AFL-CIO, is autonomous. It cannot be forced by other federations in the AFL-CIO to support policies opposed by the teachers. This defense of affiliation is valid, but it materially weakens the case for affiliation. As a practical matter, other unions in the AFL-CIO support AFT policies only to the extent that these other unions independently favor such policies. It is true that most unions in the AFL-CIO usually support AFT recommendations concerning education. However, it is doubtful whether affiliation is an important factor in securing such support.

Second, and more to the point, affiliation is really based upon the discredited assumption that the interests of teachers coincide with the interests of other unions in the AFL-CIO. Actually, with or without affiliation, other unions support or oppose AFT policies as they see fit. Furthermore, many organizations not affiliated with the AFL-CIO support such AFT objectives as federal aid to education.

Even if its affiliation with the AFL-CIO has been helpful to the AFT in some ways, it has also been a serious organizing handicap. Although affiliation does not compromise the teachers individually or collectively, many teachers think that it does and are lost to the AFT for this reason. But regardless of their logic or lack of it, there is no inherent reason why 1,300,000 teachers should need affiliation with the AFL-CIO any more than 200,000 physicians or a like number of lawyers should need it. Affiliation was attractive when teachers' unions were founded because the teachers were weak. However, their future lies in developing independent sources of power, not in continuing to rely upon the largesse of other occupational groups. It seems to me that AFT supporters have concentrated so hard upon answering invalid objections to affiliation that they have never given much thought to other objections which do have merit.

It must be emphasized that the preceding comments referred to teacher affiliation with the labor movement, not to the desirability of teachers' unions as such. However, many arguments against teachers' unions which are decisive with the teachers themselves make no sense whatsoever. Thus it is often contended that teachers should not form unions because teachers should not have the right to strike. However, the right to strike and the right to unionize are two different things entirely; it is quite possible to have one without the other. The same holds for the desirability of striking and the desirability of unionizing. The view that the strikes are a necessary adjunct of unionization is completely mistaken.

Ironically, the AFT has a very specific constitutional prohibition against strikes, whereas the NEA's constitution has nothing to say in the matter. Personally, I believe that teachers should have the legal right to strike, since they are morally obligated to withdraw their services under certain conditions.[6] Perhaps most people do not share this view. The point is, however, that many unions of public employees have constitutional provisions prohibiting strikes.

Probably the most important deterrent to teacher membership in the AFT is the reluctance of teachers to become identified with blue-collar workers. Teachers are one of the most white-collar-conscious groups in our society. They like to think of themselves as "professionals," a category higher than "union workers." AFT leaders do not like to admit that the idea of joining a "union" is repugnant to most teachers, but AFT pub-

[6] For a more thorough analysis of this issue, see Myron Lieberman, "Teachers Strikes: An Analysis of the Issues," *Harvard Educational Review,* XXVI (Winter, 1956), 39–70.

lications never cease to pound at the theme that a union can be "professional."

In any event, the statistics concerning membership tell the story. In 1959, more than forty years after it was founded, the AFT enrolled less than 5 per cent of the teachers in the United States. It has been making small gains in recent years, but they are insignificant in the over-all picture. In 1957, the NEA increased its membership by 44,000, whereas the 1957 total membership of the AFT was only about 55,000. As a result of an increase in dues from $5.00 to $10.00, NEA membership declined during 1958–59. Nevertheless, it still has over ten times as many members as the AFT.

Some union leaders have finally realized that the label "union" is damaging in organizing white-collar workers. The latter are asked to join "associations" or "guilds" instead of "unions." AFT leadership, however, is dominated by professional liberals who simply cannot accept the fact that the war cries of traditional unionism will never organize the teachers. AFT spokesmen continually refer to NEA locals as "company unions." The analogy may be sound in principle, but the reference to NEA locals in these terms is poor strategy. Teachers simply do not wish to be labeled as members of a union, and organizing strategy that emphasizes the terminology of unionization is bound to fail with them.

While teachers shy away in droves from the AFT for the most superficial reasons, the criticisms which can legitimately be made of the organization go unnoticed by members and non-members alike. Among these criticisms are the AFT's neglect of teacher control over entry, its adherence to outmoded strategies of gaining welfare objectives, its uncritical attitude toward single salary schedules, its blind adulation of the labor movement, its refusal to study and profit from the experience of the fee-taking professions, and its failure to provide for the specialized teaching interests of its members. The AFT is a courageous organization. Usually it is much quicker to act on principle, even at some risk to its own organizational strength, than is the NEA. Its sympathetic attitude toward the labor movement has enabled it to see the need for many policies which are badly needed in public education. Nevertheless, the organization would have to undergo basic changes in program, strategy, and leadership to do the organizational job that is needed today in American education.

Teachers do have much to learn from the labor movement. They also have much to learn from the fee-taking professions and from other organizations of public employees. Furthermore, teachers have interests in common, as well as some that conflict, with each of these groups. To be successful, teachers' organizations must be much more sophisticated about the lessons to be learned from these groups, and the points of common and conflicting interests, than they have been in the past.

A teachers' organization which is not affiliated with labor, which is free both from administrator domination and also from an unimaginative and unproductive hostility toward administrators, which aggressively advocates teacher control over entry to the teaching profession as well as collective bargaining, which is ready to take a new look at such shibboleths as local control of education, which is adamant on such matters of principle as the elimination of racial segregation from public education, which takes the lead instead of dragging its heels in the introduction of such things as educational television or a new personnel structure in education—such an organization might well replace the NEA as the predominant teachers' organization in the United States. In any case, the development of a teachers' organization along the lines suggested is one of the most important educational needs of this generation.

Chapter X

THE PROFESSORIAL EXAMPLE

Apart from the professional apologists for the AFT and the NEA, there is little dissent from the conclusion that existing teachers' organizations are a feeble lot. What are the reasons for this situation?

The organizational situation of the teachers of teachers, and the influence of their example, is undoubtedly a large part of the answer. This calls for a brief analysis of the American Association of University Professors (AAUP), the national organization of college professors.

Although commonly regarded as both a "professional" and an employee association, the AAUP fulfils only a few limited functions of either type of organization. At best, it fulfils these in a most cursory way. The AAUP sets forth certain principles relating to faculty participation in policy-making, tenure, and academic freedom, but these are guides only. The Association exerts no control over admission to college teaching. It enforces no educational standards for institutions of higher education. The AAUP itself exercises no corporate responsibility for the competence or the professional conduct of professors. No professor has ever been expelled or suspended from the AAUP for unethical conduct, nor are any likely to be in the foreseeable future. Politically, it is doubtful that the Association has even nuisance value. If Congress or a state legislature has ever paid any attention to the AAUP, the incident has escaped my attention.

The weakness of professorial organizations is most pronounced at the state level. When state legislatures consider appropriations for higher education, including those for professorial salaries, the professors are seldom represented before the appropriate legislative bodies. State organizations of professors exist in only one-third of the states, hence the professors ordinarily lack even the machinery to present their views on a state-wide basis to state officials.[1]

The case for or against state legislation affecting professors is usually argued by college and university administrators. These administrators are not active members of the AAUP, and according to AAUP regulations, they cannot be. Active membership is prohibited to persons whose duties are half-time or more administrative in nature, on the grounds that the interests of such persons are likely to conflict with those of the professors. To be represented on crucial issues by persons conceded to have interests which conflict with their own is a striking commentary on the practical sense of the academic community.

At the local level, the influence of AAUP chapters varies a great deal from institution to institution. In most cases, however, local chapters have little influence. They do not ordinarily enrol a majority of the faculty, and they lack official status in dealing with college and university administrators. Their dues are nominal and their programs correspondingly trivial.

AAUP conventions, publications, and programs devote more

[1] The following comment about meetings of state and regional associations of the AAUP is illuminating: "Rarely, or never, have questions of salaries, for example, or closely related financial matters, been discussed. This may have been well, for it may be predicted that a state conference is destined to failure if it permits itself to become a pressure group, or attempts to discuss salaries and financial matters in cases where some of the institutions concerned must compete for appropriations from the state legislature. The chief value of state conferences would seem to be the opportunity for informal discussions and the interchange of ideas. A decision to act should seldom be the outcome of a state conference; such decisions should be left to the individual chapters" (James Holladay, "The Role of Regional Meetings in the Work of the Association," *American Association of University Professors Bulletin*, XL [Autumn, 1954], 448). The author of this remarkable invitation to occupational suicide served as first vice-president of the AAUP during 1957–58.

attention to individual cases relating to tenure and academic freedom than they do to any other type of problem. This preoccupation may speak well for the AAUP's devotion to principle, but it is hardly a testimonial to its effectiveness as a professional organization. During its existence, the AAUP has failed to advance any broad welfare interest of the professors. I do not mean to imply that the advancement of these interests is or should be the only objective, or even the major objective, of the Association. Its primary objective should be the protection of the public interest in matters relating to higher education. Nevertheless, the advancement of the welfare of professors must also be one of its basic and legitimate responsibilities. This responsibility need not conflict with its responsibilities to the public. It is in the public interest that there be a strong organization devoted to the welfare interests of the academic profession. But what does the record show?

Consider briefly the economic fortunes of the professors since the founding of the AAUP. Shortly after it was established in 1915, the United States entered a period of inflation brought on by World War I. It was not until 1932 that college professors were able to achieve salary levels which accorded them the same purchasing power that they enjoyed prior to World War I.[2] From 1940 to 1957, the purchasing power of faculty salaries declined again. During this period, the professors lost about $2 billion of real income because their salaries failed to keep pace with rising prices. Furthermore, the rest of the population was experiencing an increase in real income during this period. The professors would have had to earn from $5 to $6 billion more than they did from 1940 to 1957 to have gained their proportional share of the nation's rise in real income during this period. To put it in individual terms, there was an average loss of $30,000–$36,000 per faculty member as a result of the inability of professors to maintain their relative economic position from 1940 to 1957.

The income level of college professors is extremely low in view

[2] Seymour E. Harris, "Faculty Salaries," *American Association of University Professors Bulletin*, XLIII (December, 1957), 590. Most of the data cited in my discussion of the economic status of professors is taken from this article.

of their long average preparation (typically, seven years of education beyond high school). The mean pay of all college professors in 1955–56 was $5,200. This was only 33 per cent more than the national average for all employed persons, regardless of ability or educational attainments.

When the income of professors is compared to the income of groups whose training is substantially equal to that of the professors, the differences are quite substantial. The $5,200 mean pay for all college teachers in 1955–56 was about one-third of the average net income of physicians in private practice in the same year. Fewer than one professor in every two hundred was paid more than $14,000 in 1955–56 whereas 57 per cent of all physicians earned $15,000 or more in that year. While the differences are not so great in the case of lawyers and dentists, these groups also enjoy a substantial economic superiority over professors.

The economic decline of the professors is not questioned by the AAUP. On the contrary, the decline has been accepted as a reason to give higher organizational priorities to improving the economic status of professors. However, the AAUP's program for achieving this objective hardly inspires confidence that the Association will be more successful in the future than it has been in the past in this regard.

Essentially, the program consists of a scale by which to grade the salary schedule at each institution of higher education. Institutions which pay full professors a minimum of $14,000 get an "AA"; institutions which pay them a minimum of $12,000 get a "A," and so on, until at the lower end of the scale, institutions which pay full professors as little as $5,250 get an "F." Other academic ranks are also graded in the same way.[3]

As a minor detail in a program to achieve higher salaries, the practice of giving institutions letter grades according to their salary schedules would not be objectionable. Unfortunately, the grading plan appears to be the major plank in the AAUP's "program" to improve the economic status of professors. Its futility

[3] For an explanation of the way in which the grading plan is supposed to work, see "Grading of Academic Salary Scales," *American Association of University Professors Bulletin,* XLIV (March, 1958), 214–36.

is obvious just from a realization of the short shrift it would get
in other occupations. Imagine Walter Reuther telling the United
Automobile Workers, "Fellows, General Motors gets a "B" this
year and Ford gets a "C." I am sure that Ford will be striving
to raise its grade to "B" in the years ahead so you men working
for Ford should not feel that your national organization has let
you down."

It is quite possible that the use of the grading scale may retard
higher salaries rather than improve them. The strategists in the
AAUP assume that institutions which receive low grades will
be encouraged to raise their salaries. Although this may happen
to some extent, the grading scale is likely to have an adverse
effect upon salaries at the top of the scale. If an institution is
at the top of the scale, its trustees and administrators may use
that fact as an excuse not to raise salaries. Not that this is my
fundamental criticism of the grading proposal; the whole business
is so naïve and so completely ignores the crucial role of organizational pressure and power that its crashing failure can be taken
for granted.[4]

The inability of the AAUP to exert effective pressure is not the
sole cause of the economic decline of the professors. However,
many of the other causes could be eliminated or mitigated by
a reasonably alert professional organization. For example, the
AAUP gives little serious attention to ways and means of increasing the productivity of professors. It typically bases its appeals for higher salaries upon the increases in the cost of living
during recent years. On the other hand, economists generally
believe that salary increases should be tied as much as possible
to increases in the productivity of occupational groups, not to
increases in their cost of living. An alert professional organization would be active both in increasing the productivity of its
members and in making certain that they received a fair share

[4] Between 1940 and 1950, non-academic salaries in institutions of higher
education increased 110 per cent, whereas academic salaries increased only
54 per cent. At least one well-known economist has interpreted this fact as
evidence that the organizations of professors are weaker than the organizations of janitors and other non-academic employees. See Harris, *op. cit.*,
p. 587.

of the benefits of their increased productivity. The AAUP has been practically useless along both of these lines.

The AAUP has no status as a bargaining agent for the professors. Administrative authorities are not legally compelled to negotiate with the AAUP about anything. The fact that administrators and boards of regents frequently consult with AAUP representatives is not too important. It makes a considerable difference whether an employer is compelled (by law or by the organizational strength of the employees) to negotiate with employee representatives or whether the employer talks to employee representatives as a matter of charity. The difference, of course, is reflected in the quality of the agreements reached. Employee organizations which compel recognition from the employer achieve greater gains than those which have no recognized legal status as bargaining units and which are too weak to compel employers to recognize them in this capacity.

THE AAUP, TENURE, AND ACADEMIC FREEDOM

The real tragedy of the AAUP is not that professors have fallen behind the Joneses. It is the AAUP's shocking incapacity to protect the integrity of higher education. The industrial worker needs free speech, but it is not as a rule necessary for him to do his job. Again speaking in broad terms and allowing for much qualification, the industrial worker is concerned functionally with physical processes, not conflicting ideas. On the other hand, the professors who formed the AAUP specifically recognized that their jobs often required a frank treatment of new and upsetting ideas. Yet the fact is that the typical industrial worker has more freedom on the job to speak his mind freely than the overwhelming majority of college professors who require such freedom to do their job properly.

If the state of academic freedom seems better today than it did during the heyday of the late Senator McCarthy, the reason is not in what the AAUP has done. It is that a combination of factors over which the AAUP had no control, such as the decline and death of the senator, helped to mitigate the cruder forms of interference with academic freedom. The fact that a demagogue like the late senator from Wisconsin can throw the academic community into great turmoil indicates how weak academic freedom really is in the United States.

The fallacy of supposing that academic freedom is growing stronger merely because one particular threat to it has subsided is apparent from the situation in the South. In many Southern institutions of higher education, academic freedom on matters relating to racial segregation has all but disappeared. The professors in these institutions realize that all the local, state, and national branches of the AAUP are too weak to protect individual professors who criticize racial segregation, either in their role as citizens or in the legitimate exercise of academic freedom.

Because many professors tolerate the most extreme violations of academic freedom in order to keep their jobs, it is a grave error to evaluate the AAUP's record with respect to tenure and academic freedom merely by reference to the cases which become matters of controversy. Indeed, even in cases where unjust dismissal actually occurs, the professors involved are often unwilling to appeal to the AAUP for help. They may believe, and with good reason, that the AAUP is incapable of restoring them to their positions. Since an appeal to the AAUP may destroy a professor's chances of securing a position elsewhere, appeals are not often made. Thus few tenure cases officially arise, because the AAUP is so weak an organization.[5]

[5] ". . . I was dismissed from a university after several years service as an assistant professor. I was informed that my department was overstaffed, but an additional instructor was employed in that department for the next academic year. What the real reason was I do not know to this day. I submit that such things are outrageous, but they are not very rare. A similar case was investigated by Committee A of the American Association of University Professors, but far more numerous are the cases that are never reported by the victims. They conclude, as I did, that they will have a better chance to get back into academic life if they avoid publicity" (E. H. Sturtevant, "Selection and Retention of Faculty Members," *American Association of University Professors Bulletin*, XXV [October, 1939], 421). I quote this statement not for the evidence it bears but for the commonsense reasoning it represents. For a systematic study of the extent to which academic freedom has been impaired without any protest or action by the professors, see Paul F. Lazarsfeld and Wagner Thielens, Jr., *The Academic Mind* (Glencoe, Ill.: Free Press, 1958).

Why has the AAUP never developed a broad and realistic program to promote the welfare of college professors? What has prevented it from becoming a powerful occupational organization, serving effectively to protect the integrity of higher education and at the same time to advance the welfare of the professors?

Paradoxically, one reason for its failure to protect academic freedom is that the organization is devoted chiefly to this purpose. Thus its appeal is largely confined to those who already have a strong interest in the matter. Many professors see little sense in joining an organization which is preoccupied with academic freedom and which is not particularly effective even in this limited area.

The AAUP's failure to grasp the fundamental importance of recognition is also part of the explanation for its unimpressive record. As things stand, each chapter of the AAUP must devote a great deal of its time and energy to achieving an integral place in the structure of employer-employee relations at its institution. The AAUP seems content with a strategy which calls for an institution-by-institution approach to achieve this objective. But success, if achieved at all, is due to the efforts of outstanding individuals or to the friendly attitudes of particular administrators, and when these people disappear, the influence of the chapter does also. Professors refuse to join because the chapters have no assured status, and the fact that they do not join makes it more difficult for the chapters to achieve such status.

The institution-by-institution approach to recognition can be compared to the industrial scene before the New Deal, when every union had to devote most of its energies to force employers to negotiate conditions of employment. If recognition were assured, the chapters would be free to concentrate upon professional and economic problems instead of organizational ones. This goal can be achieved in different ways. One way would be to give the highest priority to legislation that would require college administrators to negotiate with the duly chosen representatives of the professors on matters of employment.

This strategy will seem absurd to many professors. After all, it presupposes that professors have to become a pressure group and get into the political arena like everyone else. It presupposes also that it is futile to wait for society to bestow wealth and power on academic man; he will have to fight for these things or go without them. This is not a pleasant thought, especially since professorial political incompetence has long been characteristic of American politics. Of course, this fact cannot be conceded, publicly at least, by the professors. The evils of becoming a "pressure group" provide a face-saving rationalization for their political incapacity.

The alleged evils of being a pressure group frequently find expression in the long-standing controversy within the AAUP over whether it is or ought to be a "trade union." As is the case within the NEA, the professors find it necessary to formulate elaborate and wholly gratuitous distinctions between their activities and those of "trade unions." The distinctions reveal little understanding of unions, but what is more important, professorial strategy is weakened by the requirement that it be different from that adopted by blue-collar workers. How much it is weakened can be seen from the following incident. A friend of mine who was a delegate to the 1959 AAUP Convention told me that her expenses were shared equally by her chapter and her university. While she was in the office of the university president prior to the convention, he urged her to go to the convention and "put some guts" into the Association. Imagine a president of a coal company paying the expenses of a miner to the annual convention of the United Mine Workers and urging the miner to "put some guts" into the UMW! As the saying goes, "We should live so long!"

The professorial compulsion to avoid the appearance of trade unionism is reflected in the following paragraphs in a report recently issued by the AAUP's Committee Z on the "Economic Status of the Profession":

ALLEGED TRADE-UNION PRACTICES

The Committee is aware of the unfavorable reactions which its program has aroused in several quarters. Members of administrations and governing boards of colleges and universities have expressed themselves, sometimes in angry words, concerning the "trade-union practices" to which the AAUP is supposed to have resorted.

The comparison of our activities with trade-union practices might by many members of the profession be interpreted as a recognition of the effectiveness of our activities; some might even accept it as a flattering comparison; others may resent it, reject it, or be embarrassed. Be this as it may, we should note at least one essential difference between trade-union methods and the methods employed in our program. Trade-union pressure achieves its greatest effectiveness by utilizing some monopolistic or bargaining advantages; our methods, however, involve nothing but publicizing three indexes of salary payments for each institution. Public knowledge of prices or wages paid is one of the prerequisites which economists regard as essential for the functioning of a free competitive market. The quest for public information on the salary conditions at different institutions can certainly not be considered an improper demand.[6]

Another important reason for the weakness of the AAUP at all levels is that local chapters cannot count upon immediate and effective support from the national organization in a time of crisis. This is apparent from a consideration of the feeble sanctions employed by the AAUP. These sanctions are more appropriate for a ladies' aid society than for a professional organization.[7] For example, when the gauntlet is thrown down to the AAUP by an institution of higher education and an issue must be resolved by an all-out test of strength, the most drastic action taken by the AAUP is a vote to censure the administration of the institution concerned. Such action, often taken years after the event which precipitated the controversy, has been the limit of AAUP action

[6] "Report of Committee Z to the 45th Annual Meeting" (Washington, D.C.: American Association of University Professors, 1959), p. 15. Duplicated material.

[7] I wrote this sentence before attending the 1959 annual national convention in Pittsburgh. In their reliance upon wrist-slapping statements of censure instead of deeds and their fear of using, or appearing to use, pressure tactics, the delegates at that meeting were nothing if not enfeebled. The atmosphere was really not much different from that of an NEA convention.

in cases involving the most fundamental opposition to the Association's policies.

In censure cases, the professorial victim often suffers a severe setback, regardless of his innocence in the matter. Of course, not all grievances are carried to the point where they involve a vote of censure by the national organization. Some are settled on a basis favorable to the professors but without publicity by the national office. Nevertheless, these cases do not justify a belief that the AAUP has been an effective professional organization. The conditions confronting the academic community as a whole are too unsatisfactory to accept such a conclusion.

Some of the most basic reasons for the weakness of the AAUP are rarely discussed in academic circles. Professors have yet to face up to the fact that it is unrealistic to regard all college teachers as members of the same profession. Failure to confront this issue and to take the organizational steps required by a realistic answer to it are a basic cause of the weakness of the AAUP.

If you ask a medical professor his occupation, he is more likely to think of himself as a physician than as a professor. True, he is both, but the relative emphasis is crucial. The professor physician is more likely to be interested in the American Medical Association than in the AAUP. Likewise, the chemistry professor regards himself as a chemist and the American Chemical Society as his professional organization. The mathematics professor regards himself as a mathematician and gives his organizational priorities to the American Mathematical Association.

In short, most professors are primarily interested in organizations which concentrate upon developments in their fields of specialization. There is, however, a vast difference between the various specialized organizations to which professors belong. The medical professor need not worry about the weakness of the AAUP because the American Medical Association has a very effective program to protect the independence and economic status of physicians. Furthermore, physicians need not be professors. They can make out very well apart from any university connection. Thus the universities are forced to bargain with individual physicians who wish to teach, and to respect the autonomy of the medical professor. However, the AAUP is irrelevant as far as this outcome is concerned. On the other hand, most professorial organizations are study organizations and only that. And since professors tend to join them instead of the AAUP, they really have neither a professional nor an employee organization.

We may use history professors to illustrate this point. They regard the American Historical Association as their "professional" organization. Now whatever the American Historical Association may be, by no stretch of the imagination can it be regarded as a professional organization. According to an Association publication, "The American Historical Association welcomes to its membership anyone who subscribes to its purposes"—and pays $7.50 in dues. The Association sets no standards for admission to teaching history or being a "historian." It exercises no control over the training of historians. It neither formulates nor enforces a code of professional ethics. It is at most an organization of people interested in history; it is no more "professional" than a society of stamp collectors. The very fact that history professors pompously refer to the American Historical Association as their "professional" organization tells us a great deal about the organizational naïveté of these academicians.

The same analysis applies to the various regional and state historical associations. Only persons hard up for status symbols would dream of calling them professional organizations. Note, however, what happens when history professors concentrate their organizational activities upon these associations. The various historical associations do not represent the professors as employees. Only a small minority of professors at each institution teach history. University administrators are not going to negotiate separately on conditions of employment with each history department, and, indeed, the history professors themselves do not advocate that they should. The upshot is that the "professional" associations of history professors have no impact whatsoever on conditions of employment for history professors. Equally important, these associations are completely devoid of the professional controls and sanctions which might give individual history professors a measure of bargaining power and occupational protection vis-à-vis their employing institutions.

We can summarize the situation in this way: A truly professional organization is concerned with both the work of the profession and the conditions of employment of its membership. Some professors, such as those in medicine, are members of non-academic professional organizations which effectively serve these two kinds of interests. Most, however, confine their organizational activities to such organizations as the American Chemical Society, the American Physical Society, the American Historical Association, the American Sociological Association, and so on. The programs and activities of these organizations are devoted exclusively or in large part to a field of knowledge; they have practically no impact upon conditions of employment in higher education.

The AAUP is supposedly the comprehensive organization of professors which *is* concerned with conditions of employment. However, since the AAUP has no subject divisions or sections, it lacks one of the basic appeals of a professional organization. Some professors divide their time and energy between the AAUP and their subject organizations, but this is an inefficient procedure. Because many do not join the AAUP at all, or because those who do join divide their organizational energies between several incomplete organizations, the AAUP is fatally weakened as a professional and as an employee organization. The employing institutions dictate to a disorganized group of individuals instead of negotiating with strong organizations of professionals.

These comments about the AAUP are not intended to excuse the weaknesses of organizations of public school teachers. Nor are they intended merely to show that certain problems confronting teachers below the college level are also prevalent in higher education. It is the causal relationship in the situation that is important. Teachers tend to look to professors for leadership; when the latter are so incapable of solving the kinds of problems which concern teachers also, professorial leadership becomes a case of the blind leading the blind.

A PRESCRIPTION

The organizational mess in education can be cleaned up; to think otherwise is to despair of the future of American education. In order to clean it up, we must first dispel two basic misconceptions concerning the dynamics of educational reform.

I have already alluded to one of these misconceptions. This is the notion that because certain issues are for the public to resolve, the teachers are absolved from responsibility for the decisions made by the public. This misconception is based upon a formalistic instead of a strategic conception of the relationships between a profession and the public it serves. Having discussed this point at some length in previous chapters, I shall not elaborate upon it here.

The other misconception is not as obvious, but it is more pervasive. This is the notion that school systems and institutions of higher education are in the best position to initiate and carry through needed educational reforms. The people who are subject to this misconception are aware of the need for educational leadership. The trouble is that they overemphasize leadership by educational administrators and neglect the crucial role of organizational leadership.

Education textbooks, especially those in school administration, resound with appeals for educational statesmen. It is clear from the context, however, that superintendents or principals are expected to fill this role. A heavy emphasis upon instructional leadership also stands out in educational literature; I would estimate that of all the books and articles on the subject of educational leadership, less than a hundredth part is focused directly upon leadership in teachers' organizations.

The same mistaken emphasis prevails in higher education. This is apparent from such things as the pattern of foundation grants. Enormous sums are granted to strengthen educational institutions; very little is spent to strengthen educational organizations.

The foundations have made some grants to educational organizations for the avowed purpose of raising their level of effectiveness. For example, in November, 1958, the Fund for the Republic made a $10,000 grant to the Academic Freedom Fund of the AAUP. The money is to be used for investigations of alleged violations of academic freedom, the support of professors whose means of livelihood have been cut off in such cases, legal expenses, and appropriate publicity. These are worthy causes but thoroughly typical of the tendency to concentrate upon a few visible cases while the entire academic community sinks deeper into the abyss.[8]

What must be done? Some things have been pointed out, or are implicit in the preceding discussion; others will be suggested in subsequent chapters. At this point I would like to make a proposal that goes beyond any specific area where reform is needed. The proposal is applicable to all major educational organizations, but I shall use the AAUP for illustrative purposes.

The AAUP should draft, or cause to be drafted, a proposal for a thorough, critical, no-holds-barred evaluation of itself. Regardless of who drafts the proposal, it should provide that the evaluation not be under the control of the organization; it should be conducted under other auspices with the consent and co-operation of the AAUP. The evaluation should cover every important aspect of the Association—its goals and goal-setting procedures, dues, membership requirements, publications, personnel, business procedures, relationships with local chapters, legislative programs, state and regional groups, national conventions, strategy and tactics; in short, the Association has to be put through a wringer. This is not likely to happen if the organization itself controls the evaluation.

The evaluation should be prospective as well as retrospective; that is, it should be programmatic. For example, from the evaluation there might emerge sound proposals that the present $8.00

[8] Frankly, it is difficult for me to understand why the Fund for the Republic should have made this grant. The professors ought by this time to be able to fight their own battles and take care of their own wounded. If they cannot, the foundations ought to help them discover and eliminate the reasons for their incapacity. But it is not the business of a foundation to provide support for routine cases which should be an organizational responsibility.

dues be raised to $50.00 or even $100. These proposals would be accompanied by specific suggestions as to the way the money should be spent and the results to be expected.

The evaluation, including action proposals, should become the Association's agenda for the next few years. If the evaluation is carried out as suggested here, a number of vested interests in the Association are going to get hurt. I do not mean the paid staff necessarily, but many points of view long advocated and followed in the organization will have to be abandoned. This fact underlies the need for outside evaluation; whatever recommendations emerge will have a better chance of being accepted if they come from expert but disinterested sources.

The important task is to get a program accepted by the membership as a basis for action. Presumably there will have to be modifications of the proposals emerging from the evaluation, but the directions to be taken should be fairly clear. The re-education of the membership can be achieved through the *American Association of University Professors Bulletin,* special publications, and local, regional, and national meetings. To speed up this process, there should be a series of Institutes on Educational Leadership held at leading universities throughout the country. These institutes should be designed to re-educate chapter and regional leaders on the findings and recommendations of the evaluation. They should not presume to make chiefs out of Indians but to give the present leadership at local, state, and regional levels a new conception of what their organizations can and should do.

A program of the kind just outlined should be designed to change our image of professorial organizations in a relatively short time. Such a program would not cost more than a few million dollars at most; even if it were to cost this much, the amount would be small compared to those the foundations are currently pouring into rearranging and integrating courses, institutional self-surveys, and the other dry wells of foundation drilling. I am convinced the money can be raised if and when the AAUP makes a genuine effort to get it for this purpose.

These comments concerning the need for and the strategy of

organizational reform in higher education apply with equal force to organizations of public school teachers.[9] Some schools of education must challenge the present emphasis on strengthening school systems and concentrate upon strengthening teachers' organizations. Needless to say, however, "strengthening" teachers' organizations is not the same thing as helping them to enrol more members to pay more dues to be thrown away on the same old objectives.

In order to strengthen their organizations, educators must demand and support a level of leadership higher than that prevailing. They must get rid of the leadership that has led them to the current impasse and must put in positions of power and responsibility leaders who will produce results. This is not unreasonable; results *can* be achieved with able leadership.

Contemporary educational leadership reminds me of a basketball coach described to me by a friend. When his team was losing badly at the half, the coach's half-time counsel was, "Make those baskets!" This advice was about as helpful as advice to teachers that they deserve higher salaries. Higher salaries for teachers are not a program—they are one of the objectives of a program. Mere reiteration that teachers should receive higher salaries or have better training or be accorded more respect does not constitute leadership worthy of teacher support. Leadership consists of finding ways and means to achieve these objectives.

Unfortunately, the record shows not only a steady decline of the teaching profession but also that the full-time leaders of state and national teachers' organizations are practically never fired, no matter how little their organizations accomplish. In teachers' organizations, it seems that nothing succeeds so well as failure.

Let me illustrate what must be done in terms of the state teachers' associations. The executive secretaries of these associations are the authorized spokesmen for the teachers. These spokesmen should command the utmost respect, by virtue of both their position and their personal qualifications. Their position should

[9] The NEA recently employed a private consulting firm to make a survey of itself. The results were some improvements in the business operations of the Association, but the survey did not really come to grips with the more basic problems of organizational goals, strategy, and achievements.

be regarded as of equal or greater importance than the presidency of a major university or the top educational job in the state government. Furthermore, the qualifications and rewards for this position should be consistent with this point of view.

In fact, teacher leadership at the state level is often tragically weak. Teachers who would hire the very best lawyer to be their advocate in a legal case show the most shortsighted reluctance to hire the most effective occupational advocate that money can buy. A conservative estimate of the difference between effective and ineffective state leadership would be several hundred dollars per year per teacher. This being the case, a salary of $50,000 a year would be cheap for a really able leader of a large state teachers' association. In a state like New York, such a salary would amount to less than fifty cents per year per teacher if all teachers belonged to the association. This kind of salary is needed to attract and support top caliber leadership, but only one of the state associations pays as much as $25,000 to its chief executive. The teachers, who do so much talking about the importance of our investment in human resources, are the least inclined to make such an investment out of their own pockets.

Instead of waiting for scattered individuals in scattered organizations over the country to take a few timid steps to remedy this situation, there must be launched a massive nationwide effort to create a new concept of this position. I recognize the enormous difficulties involved, including the obvious threat to many of the present leaders. There are states in which the teachers would be well advised to retire their present officers on full salary in order to get on with the job. But once the teachers grasp the importance of organizational leadership, they will find the ways and means of getting it.

In conclusion, let me affirm my conviction that the weakness of teachers is a catastrophe for the country as well as for the teachers. The educational world is full of professional liberals who are always ready to denounce the power of the American Medical Association, the American Bar Association, the National Association of Manufacturers, the AFL-CIO, and other occupational organizations. Meanwhile, the educators are helpless to protect the integrity of their own work or their own legitimate vocational interests. Whatever abuses of power may justly be attributed to such organizations as the American Medical Association, one must question whether the country would be better off, medically or otherwise, if the AMA were as weak as the AAUP, the NEA, or the AFT. Conversely, if the country is not so well off educationally as it ought to be, our educational organizations must bear the major responsibility for this situation. It is time to put aside the cliché that the public is only getting what it deserves—that is, what it is willing to pay for—in the field of education. Our concern should not be with the public but with the educational organizations which fail to provide leadership that will be respected and followed by the public.

Chapter XI

THE STRATEGY AND TACTICS OF
EDUCATIONAL CHANGE

It is unrealistic to expect the public to initiate basic educational reforms or to provide the driving force needed to effectuate them. Intelligent non-professional action is essential at certain stages, but the major and enduring responsibility for improving our schools lies with the people who work in them.

This view calls for a reassessment of current strategy designed to improve education. My analysis will deal first with this strategy, which in my opinion misconceives the role of the public in bringing about educational improvements. It will then move on to some suggested changes in the role to be played by the public. The last part of the chapter will be devoted to specific problems of strategy confronting the teachers. These problems are important to everyone, since they involve the nature and limits of occupational action in areas of fundamental public concern.

To illustrate current strategy for achieving educational improvements, and my criticisms of this strategy, I propose to analyze the development and implementation of the "Conant report." [1] The background of the report is as follows: Dr. Conant was approached by the Carnegie Corporation to see whether

---

[1] James B. Conant, *The American High School Today: A First Report to Interested Citizens* (New York: McGraw-Hill Book Co., 1959).

he had any interest in returning to the field of education after completing his duties as ambassador to the Federal Republic of Germany. Pursuant to the discussions between Dr. Conant and representatives of the Carnegie Corporation, the latter made a grant to the Educational Testing Service to enable Dr. Conant to study certain problems relating to comprehensive high schools in the United States. In Dr. Conant's own words, "comprehensive high schools" are those "whose programs correspond to the needs of *all* the youth of the community."

Dr. Conant did not attempt to conduct a broad survey of American high schools generally, or even of comprehensive schools. His overriding interest was to ascertain

whether, under one and the same roof and under the same management, it is possible for a school to fulfill satisfactorily three functions: Can a school at one and the same time provide a good general education for *all* the pupils as future citizens of a democracy, provide elective programs for the majority to develop useful skills, and educate adequately those with a talent for handling advanced academic subjects—particularly foreign languages and advanced mathematics? The answer to this question would seem to be of considerable interest for the future of American education. If the answer were clearly in the negative, then a radical change in the structure of American public secondary education would be in order. . . . On the other hand, if the answer is in the affirmative, then no radical change in the basic pattern of American education would seem to be required.[2]

Note that if Dr. Conant were able to locate at least one comprehensive school satisfactorily fulfilling the functions he deemed appropriate for them, he would be able to provide a definitive answer to his basic question. The existence of one such school demonstrates that it is possible for a comprehensive school to fulfil these functions. (Actually, Dr. Conant regarded eight of the 103 schools visited by him or his staff as adequately fulfilling these three functions.)

Dr. Conant's report was published in February, 1959. A major part of the report is a series of twenty-one recommendations for improving public education. The range of these recommendations is indicated by some of their headings: "The Counseling

[2] *Ibid.*, p. 15.

System," "Required Programs for All," "Ability Grouping," "English Composition," "The Academic Inventory," "Homerooms," etc. In some cases, the recommendations made under these headings are very specific. For example, Recommendation 6 reads:

> The time devoted to English composition during the four years should occupy about half the total time devoted to the study of English. Each student should be required to write an average of one theme a week. Themes should be corrected by the teacher. In order that teachers of English have adequate time for handling these themes, no English teacher should be responsible for more than one hundred pupils. . . .[3]

We thus have the following situation: A man who is a distinguished scientist, an outstanding university president, a successful diplomat, and a devoted supporter of public education in and for our democratic society is liberally supplied with funds to enable him to study a basic problem of American education. He carries out the study and writes a report which receives unprecedented publicity; approximately 200,000 copies of it were sold or otherwise distributed within six months after it was first published. For the most part, the educational recommendations in the report would improve public education. Although I disagree with some of them and admit incapacity to evaluate others, nothing that I have to say depends upon any criticism of the educational recommendations in the report. The report itself is intelligent, reasonable, and without a trace of the hobby-horsing or ax-grinding that characterizes most books on education written for the general public. It comes at a time when it is difficult to get men of Dr. Conant's stature seriously involved in the problems of public education. What, if anything, is wrong with the situation?

Perhaps nothing—as I have described it thus far. But let us look at the way in which the report is being implemented. According to Dr. Conant: "When I first planned the study, I had in mind formulating my conclusions in such a way that they could be presented in various states to the citizens committees concerned with supporting good public education." And later he states, "Since, however, the school boards, almost without excep-

---

[3] *Ibid.*, pp. 50–51.

tion, do have a great degree of freedom in managing the local school, I have addressed this report *in the first instance to school board members.*" [4]

In attempting to implement the recommendations emerging from his study, Dr. Conant met with school boards and citizens' committees over the entire country. He also worked with various professional organizations, but the focus of his persuasive efforts was on the school boards.

What would have been the reaction to the procedure followed by Dr. Conant if someone had utilized it in higher education? Surely, Dr. Conant would have been the first to protest if, while he was president of Harvard, the trustees had notified him that they wanted certain changes in the curriculum and in "the requirements for admission to advanced courses" put into effect at the beginning of the school year. Presumably, these things are a professional prerogative at Harvard. I see no reason why they should not be so in public education as well—and this brings me to one of my reasons for thinking that the net impact of the report may be harmful despite the merits of its educational recommendations. The procedures used to implement the report reinforce the prevailing notion that school boards ought to decide professional matters, such as what subjects should be offered and at what grade levels.

The matter of professional autonomy is not confronted squarely in the report. Those comments which do relate to it are rather ambiguous. We read that:

Other recommendations [those not involving a budgetary increase] concern the details of school organization and curriculum; in the first instance, these recommendations belong in the province of school administrators. . . . Some of the recommendations listed below can be put into effect at the beginning of the school year without upsetting in any way the morale of the teaching staff. Other recommendations, however, can be effective only if a majority of the teachers are convinced of their wisdom. . . . I have in mind particularly the controversial subject of ability grouping, any recommendations in regard to marking or grading, and the requirements for admission to advanced courses.[5]

[4] *Ibid.*, pp. v and 9. My italics.
[5] *Ibid.*, pp. 43–44.

These comments are not too clear, since there is no explicit statement of what curriculum matters are for the school board to decide and what are "details" for the professional staff to decide. Furthermore, the need for school boards to convince the teachers of the wisdom of certain changes raises some interesting questions. Teachers should be persuading school boards of the need for changes in class size, ability grouping, and requirements for admission to advanced courses; is there not something amiss when the persuading on these matters is the other way around?

To change the curriculum, persuade those who have the power to change it—the school boards. In this sense, Dr. Conant's procedure is sound; there is no point in persuading the teachers first, since they could only recommend action to their school boards. But if you believe, as I do, that our most serious curriculum problems flow from the fact that teachers do not have the operating power to make the professional curriculum decisions, then you do not try to bring about changes by means of a strategy that reinforces the prevailing antiprofessional power structure of public education.

To clarify this point, consider two of the proposals in the report. Its major recommendation calls for the elimination of small high schools. Dr. Conant states: "I should like to record at this point my conviction that in many states the number one problem is the elimination of the small high school by district reorganization." Later, he says: "I can sum up my conclusions in a few sentences. The number of small high schools must be drastically reduced. Aside from this important change, I believe no radical alteration in the basic pattern of American education is necessary in order to improve our schools. And "Unless a graduating class contains at least one hundred students, classes in advanced subjects and separate sections within all classes become impossible except with extravagantly high costs . . . [;] the same conclusion has been reached by a committee of the American Association of School Administrators." [6]

The fact that small schools are wasteful and that their consolidation ought to be given very high priority has been a re-

[6] *Ibid.*, pp. 38–40, 77–78.

curring theme of textbooks in secondary education and school administration for decades.[7] However, before analyzing the implications of this fact, let us look at one other proposal and Dr. Conant's comments concerning it. Recommendation 18 reads in part as follows:

The school board should be ready to offer a third and fourth year of a foreign language. The guidance officers should urge the completion of a four-year sequence of *one* foreign language if the student demonstrates ability in handling foreign languages. . . . The main purpose of studying a foreign language is to obtain something approaching mastery of that language. And by mastery is surely meant the ability to read the literature published in the language and, in the case of a modern language, to converse with considerable fluency and accuracy with an inhabitant of the country in question.[8]

Dr. Conant then makes the following comment:

I have met no teachers of foreign language who felt that anything approaching mastery could be obtained by the study of a foreign language for only two years in high school, nor have the students felt that two years of study had given them any real working knowledge of the language . . . [;] the foreign language teachers with whom I talked were almost unanimous in agreeing that two years were quite insufficient and that a very small residue, if any, was left in the student's mind after such an exposure.[9]

Dr. Conant does not claim originality for these recommendations. Indeed, it is precisely because they are not original with

[7] See R. Emerson Langfitt, Frank W. Cyr, and N. William Newson, *The Small High School At Work* (New York: American Book Co., 1936), esp. pp. 42–61; William M. Alexander and J. Galen Saylor, *Secondary Education* (New York: Rinehart & Co., 1950), pp. 196–99, 474–75; and Rudyard K. Bent and Henry Kronenberg, *Principles of Secondary Education* (3d ed.; New York: McGraw-Hill Book Co., 1955), pp. 97–102; and Paul R. Mort and Walter C. Reusser, *Public School Finance* (2d ed.; New York: McGraw-Hill Book Co., 1951), pp. 582–86. Literally dozens of other textbooks as well as scores of articles in educational journals also emphasize the need to eliminate the small school. A recent yearbook of the American Association of School Administrators was devoted largely to the problem of eliminating schools or school systems which are too small to operate efficiently. See American Association of School Administrators, *School District Organization* (Washington, D.C.: American Association of School Administrators, 1958).

[8] *Conant, op. cit.,* p. 69.

[9] *Ibid.,* p. 69.

him that the attention given them demands our own attention. John Gardner, president of the Carnegie Corporation, says about the report: "If the reader . . . is in the mood to roll up his sleeves and say 'precisely what can we do tomorrow morning to improve our schools?' this is the book." [10]

In view of the fact that the major recommendations of the report have been made for years by professional educators, it seems to me that some important questions are going unanswered —perhaps because unasked—in this situation. Take Mr. Gardner's reader who is "in the mood to roll up his sleeves" and go to work "tomorrow morning to improve our schools." Why were his sleeves not rolled up ten or twenty years ago, when the reforms now recommended by Dr. Conant were first made by the professionals in his community? Is it desirable, is it necessary, that school boards should have to be convinced by an outside figure of great prestige to carry out reforms advocated by the overwhelming weight of professional opinion in their own community?

Mr. Gardner goes on to say: "Hundreds of thousands of Americans all over the country are concerned about their schools, wondering what to do about them, seeking answers, hoping for guidance. Mr. Conant has provided that guidance." [11] I yield to no one in my estimate of what one man can do, in education or any other field. Nevertheless, I am skeptical of the man-on-horseback approach implicit in the preceding quotation. I suggest that a fruitful course for a foundation to follow would be to analyze the reasons why those proposals in the Conant report long advocated by professional opinion should have lain dormant through the years. For what it is worth, my own view is that the strategy of implementing educational reforms exemplified by the Conant report has so weakened the power and prestige of educators that what they say no longer counts.

The dangers of this strategy will be more evident if we pay due regard to the specificity of the recommendations in the re-

[10] *Ibid.*, pp. x–xi.
[11] *Ibid.*, p. xii.

port. The report points out that it takes three or four years of study to master a foreign language. This can change. Teachers may find it feasible to provide short periods of intensive study which materially shorten the over-all time needed to master a foreign language. The ease of travel to foreign countries, international television, or new developments in teaching may also have this result. In short, it may be that two years will be deemed sufficient for the mastery of a foreign language. But if so, where will Dr. Conant be? He specifically points out the probability that some of his recommendations may need revision in five or ten years. But this misses the point. If school boards do not *now* accept the recommendations of their professional staff concerning the amount of time needed to master a foreign language, what reason is there to believe that they will be more willing to accept such recommendations in the future?

The Conant report is an eloquent plea for the continuation and strengthening of comprehensive schools on the grounds that such schools are an essential bulwark of social cohesion in the United States. It is nontheless clear that Dr. Conant himself is (or was) far behind professional opinion on the extent to which these schools lack social cohesion and contribute to the stratification of American society. He writes:

> Somewhat to my surprise, I found that almost without exception those students elected to the student council or as officers of the class were in the group of the more academically able students who were preparing to go on to college. Such was the case in each of these schools, although the reader must remember that this collegebound group was always in the minority.[12]

Now this is itself a surprising statement. Educational research going back at least twenty years has demonstrated that college preparatory students tend to monopolize class offices and other prestigeful positions far out of proportion to their numbers. These students are also favored in grading, in discipline, and in the various academic, musical, and literary contests which characterize large comprehensive schools. These points are made in

[12] *Ibid.*, p. 18.

many textbooks in the sociology of education and in secondary education. Principals of comprehensive high schools always expect to encounter this phenomenon.[13]

The favored position of children from the upper classes in comprehensive schools obviously weaken Dr. Conant's thesis that such schools are a sort of melting pot for children from different social classes. The children from different socioeconomic classes may be together physically in the comprehensive school, but they are not necessarily getting to know and like one another better as a result.

These considerations do not necessarily invalidate the ideal of a comprehensive school. In my opinion, they only point to specific problems which must be solved in order to effectuate the ideal. But the fact that the country's leading supporter of comprehensive schools was so obviously unaware of important data bearing upon the ineffectiveness of these schools suggests the dangers and the futility of relying upon one man, no matter how outstanding, to provide "the" answers to complicated educational problems on a hit-and-run basis. The question, therefore, still remains— how can we articulate professional opinion in the structure of public education so that it is reflected in practice within a reasonable period of time, and what strategy should be followed to achieve this goal?

[13] Examples of research studies which bear directly upon this point are David Wright, "Participation in Extra-Class Activities According to Economic Status" (master's thesis, Stanford University, Calif., 1937); Elizabeth J. McElroy, "Participation in Extra-Curricular Activities as a Welfare Phenomenon" (master's thesis, Stanford University, Calif., 1937); Harold C. Hand, *Principal Findings of the 1947–48 Basic Studies of the Illinois Secondary School Curriculum Program* (Springfield, Ill.: Office of the Superintendent of Public Instruction, 1949); and A. B. Hollingshead, *Elmtown's Youth* (New York: John Wiley & Sons, 1948). The last reference, which devotes considerable attention to the phenomenon which surprised Dr. Conant, is one of the most widely read books in the country in the fields of sociology, adolescent development, and education. For an example of a textbook in secondary education which deals very specifically with the domination of school offices by children from the upper classes, see Harold C. Hand, *Principles of Public Secondary Education* (New York: Harcourt Brace & Co., 1958), pp. 99–104.

THE STRATEGY OF SCHOOL-BY-SCHOOL
IMPROVEMENT

Let me turn next to another strategic fallacy in the Conant report. This fallacy may be more pervasive among the public at large than among educators, but I believe that it overwhelmingly characterizes the strategic thinking of both groups. I refer to the faith in a school-by-school approach to educational reform. In Dr. Conant's words:

> The improvements must come school by school and be made with due regard for the nature of the community. Therefore, I conclude by addressing this final word to citizens who are concerned with public education: avoid generalizations, recognize the necessity of diversity, get the facts about your local situation, elect a good school board, and support the efforts of the board to improve the schools.[14]

The plausibility of this advice, especially for parents, is obvious. The individual parent is most interested in the education of *his* child at *this* time in *this* school. Furthermore, he cannot go to Washington or to his state capitol to remedy shortcomings in his school system. His interest may be great, but his individual circumstances render such action prohibitive. Since he can affect the school system attended by his children more easily than he can a state legislature or Congress, he tends to focus his educational efforts on the local school boards. These agencies alone provide immediate results.

The school-by-school (or community-by-community) strategy rests upon the assumption that local school boards have the power to bring about basic educational reforms. Unquestionably, they have the legal power to bring about some of them. But they do not have, nor are they likely to have, the operating power to bring about many of the important reforms which are needed.

We have already discussed (in chapter iii) the various reasons why it is no longer possible to rely upon local (and state) sources of revenue to finance the rising costs of public education. Even where substantial sources of revenue are physically located within a school district, they are frequently not available for educational

[14] *Ibid.*, p. 96.

purposes because of features of the tax structure not subject to local control. Furthermore, there are many communities which just do not have sufficient revenue.

The limitations of the community-by-community approach are also obvious from the standpoint of teacher education. There is a nationwide shortage of teachers in several crucial areas. This problem cannot be solved on a system-by-system basis—the various systems are simply dividing up the scarcities. No single system, except possibly the very few largest, can affect the over-all supply and demand situation. Raising salaries in one system to get certain kinds of teachers, e.g., physics teachers, merely creates a shortage of such teachers in other systems. Furthermore, raising salaries means raising taxes, and this brings us back to the financial plight of most school districts.

School boards are political creatures of the state legislatures, which can eliminate, expand, or modify the powers of these boards at any time. Some legislatures and constitutions have placed a ceiling on the tax rate that can be levied for the public schools. No matter if all the citizens in a particular district are willing to double their taxes for schools, they cannot legally do so. They must first get action at the state level to be able to act at the local level.

The limitations of the community-by-community approach constitute one of the major problems in reorganizing small school districts in order to get schools large enough to be efficient. As Dr. Conant himself points out, where such reorganization depends on a majority vote in all the districts to be reorganized, it is often rejected by the voters of one district. This is likely to happen if one district does not possess resources commensurate with the number of children it would contribute to the consolidated district. The citizens of the wealthier districts do not wish to pay higher taxes for the education of the children from the poorer districts. Clearly, this problem can be solved only by adopting a broader strategy than the community-by-community approach to educational reform.[15]

[15] In general, some type of mandatory legislation is needed at the state level to expedite the consolidation of small and inefficient school districts.

I do not wish to underestimate what a good school board can do. Neither do I wish to exaggerate it. When the standard advice given to those who work for better education is to concentrate on electing and supporting good school boards, I feel most strongly that the potential of these agencies to improve public education is being vastly overrated.

It is no answer to point to what an exceptional school board has achieved. Our attitude toward school boards must be based upon what we can reasonably expect them to be and do, given a wide range of circumstances affecting their membership and their freedom—both legal and practical—to take action. Strategy should take into account what exceptional people do, but can it be sensibly based upon the assumption that everyone will be exceptional? Suggestions that citizens "get the facts" and "elect a good school board" have been made for a long, long time in American education, and the results are not impressive.[16]

For these and other reasons, I disagree with the belief that the most important election for the education-minded citizen is the local school board election. In the short run, and for rather limited goals, sometimes; in the long run, the educational views of governors, state legislators, Congressmen, and presidents are more important than the views of local boards. A governor who realizes the need for a new framework of educational controls in his state is more important than a hundred school boards, good, bad, or indifferent. A president who is aware of the national stake in public education and is prepared to take whatever federal action is necessary to protect that stake is more important to the future of public education than thousands of school boards.

Why not work for all of these things—education-minded school boards, legislators, governors, and presidents? By all means, let us do so. But let us also be clear that the priorities lie where the power lies. When you advise people to work for better schools

---

See American Association of School Administrators, *School District Organization* (Washington, D.C.: American Association of School Administrators, 1958).

[16] See Neal Gross, *Who Runs Our Schools?* (New York: John Wiley & Sons, 1958).

by telling them to concentrate upon their local situation, you direct their energies to the most visible but not necessarily most important agency of educational reform. School systems operate in a context which limits what can be achieved on a purely local basis. Failure to understand this context is the reason for the sincere but misguided faith that people have in the possibilities of local solutions to educational problems.

My criticism of a community-by-community strategy should not be interpreted to mean that I favor a policy of citizen inaction. The usual modes of citizen support for public education are inefficient, sometimes even harmful, but citizen participation and support is essential for its improvement. If, for example, the citizen is a member of the American Legion, he can resist Legion pressure on the school board to conduct misguided essay or athletic contests. He can try to get his local post to end the Legion's systematic interference with American education on a national basis. Similarly, in their churches, unions, professional and trade associations, and other affiliations, citizens can resist the efforts of these organizations to achieve a favored place in the schools. At the same time, they can enlist the aid of these organizations in developing an effective system of public education.

To the superintendents who ask, "What should we teach?" they can say, "If *you* don't know, we'll hire someone who does." They can participate intelligently in school board elections; they can help even more by making constructive educational policy an important criterion of fitness for high political office. They cannot do this unless they know what is constructive; here, teachers' organizations and liberal arts colleges have failed badly. In any event, whether the citizens do these things, or many others that might be suggested, depends primarily upon what the teachers do. For this reason, let us turn to some of the strategic problems which the teachers must solve to lead the way.

THE MERGER OF THE AFT AND THE NEA

The first thing teachers should do is put their own organizational house in order. This will require a merger of the

AFT and the NEA. All teachers can and should help to achieve this goal. To do this, they must understand why this merger is essential and the basis upon which it could be accomplished. They can then support leaders who will work toward the merger and remove from office those who wish to continue the present unproductive stalemate between the two organizations.

Some educational writers have expressed the view that the competition between the two organizations is a good thing. This point of view overlooks the realities of organizational competition. With two competing organizations, attention is devoted to belittling the opposing organization instead of concentrating on the constructive work that needs to be done. The efforts of teachers are dispersed, and outsiders play one group off against the other. Quite frequently, the competition has the most disruptive effects upon a school faculty or upon the administration of a school system. A single organization by no means eliminates all organizational problems, but it is usually better than the existence of two or more competing organizations.

With imaginative leadership in either organization, the present unproductive stalemate might be ended. There is certainly a logical and constructive basis for merger. Essentially, there are two basic issues which divide the two organizations. One is the fact that the NEA has no restrictions upon administrator membership. The other is the AFT's affiliation with the AFL-CIO. It seems to me the proper resolution of these issues is so apparent that only organizational inertia and the existence of vested interests in the present situation serve to perpetuate it.

On the side of the AFT, there must be a recognition that the policy of affiliation with labor has reached a dead end and must be abandoned. Whether the AFT has the courage to face up to this fact is an open question.[17] With some AFT members, affiliation with the labor movement has become a sacred cause instead of a means to be evaluated according to its utility in facilitating certain ends. Some members of the AFT have been passed over

[17] Personally, I have often wondered what AFL-CIO leaders think privately about the AFT's affiliation with the AFL-CIO. It is difficult for me to visualize any advantages to the AFL-CIO in having 55,000 teachers affiliated with it.

for promotion because of their loyalty to the organization. Many were active in the long and bitter struggle during the late 1930's and the early 1940's to expel a Communist faction. People who have been identified for many years with an organization and who have risked a great deal for it cannot be expected to abandon it casually. Indeed, I am not advocating that they abandon it at all, except under certain conditions. It is at this point that some educational statesmanship from the NEA is badly needed.

As much the larger of the two organizations, the NEA might take the attitude that any merger must be on its terms. However, such an attitude would be a grave strategic mistake. The concessions to be made in a merger cannot be based solely upon the size of the organizations to be merged. They must take into account the logic of the arguments involved and the direction of events. Grant practically every criticism made of the AFT, but you cannot escape the fact that the organization has endured because of its adherence to a principle that must eventually be recognized in teachers' organizations generally. As employees, teachers must have organizations reasonably free from domination by school administrators.

Freedom from administrator domination is not just a matter that concerns two competing teachers' organizations. It is, or ought to be, a matter of fundamental public policy. Teachers' organizations, like those of most other government employees, must be free from administrator domination. Unless such a policy is adopted and implemented, there is a danger that this country will drift into a totalitarian state. It does not make sense for the government to protect the integrity of employee organizations in private industry by restricting managerial membership in them and then fail to provide the same protection for organizations of public employees.

The odd part of the situation in education is that approximately one-fourth of the local associations affiliated with the NEA already do exclude administrative personnel. Some of these associations have an even more rigid policy to this effect than do some of the local unions in the AFT. The point is that minimal restrictions upon administrator membership are required of every local federation affiliated with the AFT. On the other hand, the NEA has no national policy to this effect. It will accept affiliation by local associations whether or not they have any such restrictions.

The problems of effecting a merger would be most difficult where an NEA local permits unrestricted administrator membership. Yet even in these cases, there is no insoluble problem if common sense and a respect for occupational realities are present. Actually, most school superintendents are more interested in the publications and activities of the American Association of School Administrators than they are in those of the NEA. Other kinds of administrators, such as high-school principals, are frequently more interested in the specialized associations devoted to their kind of work than to the NEA. Administrative personnel need not give up their professional affiliation with the NEA at the national level, but they should get out of local associations which represent the teachers as employees. In the long run, this will be to the advantage of administrators as much as teachers. No one should be fooled by the thought that these administrators are usually not very active in the local associations. Administrative personnel do not have to be very active to destroy the effectiveness of a local employee organization.

The fact of the matter is that the AFT has itself never grasped the implications of its policies relating to administrator domination. In some communities, it has become necessary for the teachers to designate an organization to represent them in negotiations with the school board. In such elections, teachers have been allowed to name a local education association which allows free and unrestricted membership to the managerial employees of the school system. This situation should be prohibited as a matter of public policy. The worker in private industry cannot choose between an organization which includes managerial employees and one which is free of them; neither should teachers be allowed to choose between the employer-dominated teachers' organizations and organizations free from such domination. Nevertheless, the AFT does not make any systematic appeal to school boards and state legislatures to exclude organizations permitting unrestricted administrator membership from the ballot in elections to decide which organization shall represent the teachers.

For the NEA to procrastinate any further in recognizing the importance of this issue could be disastrous. Collective bargaining is coming in public education, and it will require independent teacher organizations. If the NEA persists in its present policies, it is possible that the AFT will make substantial gains as collective bargaining becomes more widespread. And if AFT membership increases, it will mean the development of many more vested interests which would be opposed to a single teachers' organization. The difficulties of merging the two organizations will be increased many times over, and they are bound to dissipate their energies in fighting each other. This is why no greater mistake could be made by the NEA than to assume it should ignore the AFT merely because at this time it is approximately twelve times as large.

The terms I have outlined would enable the two organizations to merge honorably and with good grace. The AFT would be giving up only the illusory benefits of affiliation; the NEA would only be accepting a condition which will eventually be forced upon it in any case. Naturally, any merger should scrupulously respect the rights of all officers and paid staffs of the two organizations.

At the present time, the NEA is not making a strong effort either to support or to block collective bargaining by teachers. This indifference is bad enough, but it might change to active opposition if the Association is unable to change its membership structure so as to accommodate collective bargaining by teachers. For this reason, a strong case can be made for strengthening the AFT despite the futility of its affiliation with the AFL-CIO and despite the possibility that a substantial increase in its membership might make it more difficult to unite teachers later on. An increase in AFT membership might be necessary to jolt the NEA leadership into the realization that there is nothing unprofessional about collective bargaining and that employee organizations, whether of professionals or ditch-diggers, must be free from administrator domination.

In most national occupational organizations, the representation from the large urban centers in the North provides the liberal strength and leadership. Generally speaking, the teachers from these urban centers are more aggressive than those from other regions and from rural areas. The membership of the AFT is concentrated primarily in them—in Chicago, New York, San Francisco, Denver, St. Paul, and Detroit. For this reason, the existence of the AFT represents more than the mere absence of 55,000 teachers from the NEA. It represents the abandonment of the NEA by a group whose potential influence is much greater than is indicated by their numbers.

It is also a matter of some importance that the influence of the teachers now in the AFT is likely to be exerted on behalf of a more liberal policy on issues pertaining to the civil and professional rights of teachers. This is illustrated by the constitutional provisions of the two organizations concerning segregated locals. The NEA's constitution originally provided for only one state association in each state, but Negro teachers who were NEA members were excluded from these associations in the South. Because representation in the NEA is through affiliated state and local associations, Negro teachers were, therefore, unrepresented in the NEA. To afford them representation, the NEA finally authorized the affiliation of Negro state teachers' associations.

On the other hand, the AFT adopted the following amendment to its constitution in 1952:

No charter of the American Federation of Teachers which defines or recognizes jurisdiction on a basis of race or color, or permits the practice of such jurisdiction, shall be recognized as valid, and the practice of any local in limiting its membership on account of race or color shall render its charter void.[18]

---

[18] Constitution of the American Federation of Teachers, art. IV, sec. 8, correct as of January 1, 1958. The 1958 Convention of the AFT turned down an appeal for reinstatement by Chattanooga Local 256. The charter of this local had been revoked for its failure to make any effort to enrol Negro teachers within its jurisdiction.

We thus have this striking contrast: the NEA amended its constitution to allow for segregated state associations, and the AFT amended its constitution to abolish racially segregated locals.

Although the existence of competing teachers' organizations is to be regretted, and although I see no hope that the AFT will become the majority organization of teachers as long as it adheres to affiliation with the labor movement, there is thus valid reason to encourage its existence. From an organizational point of view, it is much easier to change the basic policies of the AFT than those of the NEA. If certain changes were made in AFT policy and strategy, and if it were to show substantial increases in membership for a few years, the result might be to hasten these same changes in the NEA and also to speed a merger between the organizations.

TEACHER CONTROL OF ADMISSION TO TEACHING

With or without a merger of the AFT and NEA, teachers' organizations must give high priority to teacher control over admission to teaching. The strategic advantages of teacher control of entry would be tremendous. The professions typically exert their group strength at the point of entry. As a result, the employer, whether a public or private one, must pay well to get the services of the professional. On the other hand, non-professional control of teacher certification has made it easy for people to become teachers. After the flood gates are down, the teachers try to improve their status through negotiations with school boards or through state minimum salary laws. This is locking the barn door after the horse is stolen. It is precisely why the AFT emphasis upon collective bargaining, unaccompanied by teacher control over entry, is only half a program, and probably not the most important half at that. Collective bargaining is never very effective unless the employees have some degree of job control. The AFT apparently has yet to learn this principle, which is taken for granted in unions as it is in professional associations.

236

The current emphasis upon minimum salary laws and the failure of teachers to accord high priority to teacher control of entry illustrates the shortsighted strategy followed by teachers' organizations. Public opinion is easily aroused against legislation which provides adequate professional salaries. People do not like to support laws calling for specific and substantial salaries for public employees. Nevertheless, most persons who oppose high salary schedules would not get especially aroused over legislation calling for teacher control of admission to their own profession. I do not say that there would be no opposition, but this is not the kind of thing that stirs the man on the street to determined opposition. And because teacher control of entry is inherently reasonable, a determined effort by teachers to achieve it should be successful. The teachers might very well join with other groups seeking a similar objective and co-ordinate their efforts to achieve a sensible framework for state licensure.

EDUCATIONAL PUBLIC RELATIONS

At the present time, educational public relations are dominated by a policy of "educating the public." In the minds of most public school personnel, "educating the public" means not to make a move before getting public approval and to respond like a Geiger counter to every shift in public opinion.

At teachers meetings one often hears exhortations to teachers to win the respect of the public. It is generally assumed that the teachers will be paid better only as they gain a larger measure of public respect. Aside from the fact that respect usually follows rather than precedes high salaries, the exhortations are typically used to justify the very things that create disrespect for teachers. Thus teachers are persuaded to accept after-school assignments without pay in order to win respect. In the gushy ideology of cracker-barrel philosophers of education, teachers must be "professional" to gain respect; being "professional" is equated with contributing your services for nothing.

"Educating the public" has also led to an ineffectual buckshot approach to educational problems. The evaluation of strategy is concerned with how many times a movie was shown, how many brochures and pamphlets were mailed out, and how many people attended how many conferences. While there is something to be said for efforts to create a climate of opinion, this should not be a substitute for unremitting pressure on strategic individuals and agencies who have the power to take action ahead of, or even in opposition to, public opinion. A thousand PTA's convinced of the need for higher salaries for teachers are not as valuable as one congressman who knows that the organized teachers can mobilize enough votes to unseat him at the next election.

Thus far, teachers have miseducated the public very effectively, by their spineless abdication of professional autonomy, by their failure to enforce high standards for entry and performance, by their political impotence, and by their moral evasion. It is time for teachers to develop different concepts of how and for what they shall educate the public.

The teachers might begin by demonstrating to politicians that opposition to the sound professional recommendations of teachers is an invitation to political disaster. The best way to conduct this kind of demonstration is to deliver the votes. Teachers might try to educate the public to the importance of academic freedom by withholding their services where there are serious violations of it. These techniques have not been tried on a large scale, but they may be more effective than the techniques currently in use. The mass distribution of movies or literature cannot be effective while the everyday performance of teachers demonstrates that they are a weak and inconsequential group.

RELATIONSHIPS BETWEEN LOCAL, STATE,
AND NATIONAL ORGANIZATIONS

There are local, state, and national organizations of teachers. Obviously, it is important that there be a functional distribution of work among these levels. If the national organization attempts to solve problems which should be handled locally, it will be less effective in advancing the objectives and interests

238

of teachers at the national level. On the other hand, it is equally disastrous to leave national problems to local organizations, since the latter do not have the resources to grapple with them.

One important reason for the ineffectiveness of educators is their continuous failure to develop an organizational strategy within which local, state, and national organizations can operate with maximum effectiveness. For example, the NEA will ordinarily intervene in a local situation only if such action is requested by the local association and approved by the appropriate affiliated state education association. Obviously, approval is not forthcoming when, as often happens, the local and state associations are dominated by administrators whose policies and practices would likewise suffer from an objective investigation by an outside agency.

However, the most important weakness of NEA policy lies in the nature of its participation in state and local situations even when it does have the support of its affiliated state and local associations. For example, in tenure cases, its participation is almost always limited to making investigations and recommendations which seldom alter the course of events. Even when the recommendations are good ones, they are rarely supported by the mobilization and deployment of NEA resources in such a way as to strengthen materially the efforts of local associations to implement them.

Let me illustrate these points by analyzing the potential role of the NEA in tenure cases. Let us suppose that a school board has unjustly dismissed a teacher. Let us also suppose that the NEA adhered to the following policies:

1. If an investigation by the NEA itself indicated that a teacher was unjustly fired, the NEA would guarantee him an income until he was restored to his position or found suitable employment elsewhere.

2. Any educator who knowingly offered or accepted employment as a replacement for a teacher unjustly fired would be tried for unprofessional conduct. If found guilty, the NEA would so publicize the results that his professional career would be in serious jeopardy.

3. The school system involved would be designated as an unprofessional place to work. All employment agencies would be requested not to refer teachers to that system. Vigorous action would be taken to see that teachers did not register with any agency which continued to send applicants to the system. All school systems would be alerted not to accept applicants from any agency which knowingly referred applicants to positions created as a result of unjust dismissals.

4. The NEA would provide substantial assistance to those forces in the community which opposed the unjust dismissal. Such assistance might well include all-out support for new candidates for the school board.

5. The NEA would bring pressure to bear upon accreditation agencies to have the school system in question deprived of its accreditation.

6. Legal assistance at NEA expense would be provided the teacher unjustly dismissed.

If the NEA were to adopt such policies, the final agreements in this type of situation would still have to be worked out at a local level, but these agreements would be profoundly influenced by the policies of the NEA. A school board which knows that its actions are leading straight to an all-out contest with a national organization of teachers is not likely to invite such a contest unless it is sure of the merits of its case. Furthermore, it is one thing for a local board to carry public opinion when the teachers have neither the funds nor the facilities for making a sustained appeal; it is quite another matter when the resources available to the teachers far outweigh those available to the board.

Why should not the teachers follow this strategy? One might suppose that it would embroil the national organization in a multitude of local disputes and lead eventually to the dissipation of its energies and resources in matters which do not advance the interests of all teachers or of society as a whole. However, this point of view confuses cause and effect. We have many of these incidents now precisely because there is no powerful national organization of teachers, the very presence of which would serve to change the character of local solutions to educational problems.

A powerful national organization ready to step into local situations when a matter of principle is involved would serve a preventive function. The more determined it was to hurl its resources into local situations where the teacher's case was clearly justified, the less need there would be for it actually to do so. Of course, there would be such a need at the beginning so that everyone would know that the national organization meant business. But after that, local boards would think carefully before violating the basic professional and civic rights of teachers.

The probability that the proposed strategy would not result in endless intervention in local situations is borne out by the experience of the National Union of Teachers in England. The National Union of Teachers has long followed a policy such that if a teacher is dismissed for reasons found to be unwarranted by the organization, it pays the salary of the teacher until he resumes work, either in the system from which he was unjustly dismissed or in another system. The National Union guarantees this salary no matter how long it takes to secure employment for the teacher unjustly dismissed. Adherence to this policy has not led to its widespread involvement in disputes over individual teachers. The readiness of the Union to intervene if necessary has influenced local school boards to dismiss teachers only for good cause. The boards do not risk a test of strength when they have a weak case on the issues involved.

The relationships between local, state, and national organizations should facilitate and encourage the settlement of disputes at local and state levels. But the way to achieve this objective is not for the NEA, or for any national association of teachers, to turn its back on "local" disputes. This policy "facilitates" their settlement by insuring settlements which are at the expense of the teachers and the long-range interests of the public. "Local" problems are always settled in one context or another. A context which includes a powerful national organization, ready, willing, and able to intervene aggressively on matters of principle, will result in solutions at the local level which are much different from those reached in a context where the national organization is weak and where it hears no evil and sees no evil.

This suggested strategy is not at all invalidated by the fact that teachers are publicly employed. The strength of the national organization of employees is as crucial in public as it is in private employment. National organizations of publicly employed persons cannot always support their local associations in precisely the same way that national associations of privately employed persons support their local affiliates, but the similarities far outweigh the differences. For example, a national organization of publicly employed persons can work for federal legislation favorable to its members, just as the AMA and the AFL-CIO strive to achieve the same result for their members. Indeed, it is doubtful whether there is any major difference in the strategy and tactics which can and should be used by public, as distinct from private, employees.

It is also crucial to see that the strategy suggested is not limited to any particular type of problem which involves teachers as employees or as a professional group. If a local teachers' association refuses to accept a salary schedule, and if investigation by the national organization supports this refusal, the strategy of bringing the full power of the national association to bear upon the local board should be effectuated. This strategy is not limited to economic objectives; it is just as applicable to problems involving academic freedom or racial integration.

The NEA takes the position that integration is something to be worked out at state and local levels. Its resolutions on integration in the public schools from 1955 through 1959 have included the statement: "It is the conviction of the Association that all problems of integration are capable of solution at the state and local levels by citizens of intelligence, saneness, and reasonableness working together in the interests of national unity for the common good of all." In the light of this resolution and the almost complete absence of any active support for integration by the NEA, it is clear that the Association regards it as a problem which can be resolved without the active intervention of teachers at the national level.

It is unrealistic to think that integration can be carried out without face-to-face negotiations at local and state levels, and in this sense integration is indeed a state and local problem. But this is not to say that the actions of a national organization cannot influence the solutions reached and the rapidity with which they are carried out. This is why the NEA policies on integration are hypocritical. They sound vaguely like support for integration but actually leave intact the power structure which perpetuates segregation.

"Intelligence, saneness, and reasonableness" should prevail at the local level, but it is naïve to think that this is likely to happen without some outside assistance when dealing with integration. A school board would be in a much better position to eliminate segregated schools and a segregated profession if it could say to its community, "Look, regardless of what we believe on this issue, we have to treat our Negro teachers fairly or we'll lose many of the white teachers we have, we'll be unable to recruit new teachers, and our schools will lose accreditation."

It is true that there are some states and communities where teachers' organizations cannot influence the immediate course of integration. But there are many others all over the country where a trace of professional fortitude on this issue by national organizations of teachers would achieve tremendous results. NEA leaders who point to local opposition to integration as the excuse for their do-nothing policy ignore the fact that much of this opposition would never have arisen if teachers' associations, and especially the NEA, had lived up to their professional responsibilities in the first place. In and out of education, it is the people who do not wish to see integration come at all who sanctimoniously affirm that integration is a state and local problem.

Of course, if the NEA is to change the context within which issues are resolved at state and local levels, it must adopt concrete measures to achieve this end. For example, the Association would have to create a multimillion-dollar defense fund to back up its interventions. Again, I wish to emphasize that the very existence of such a fund, coupled with a firm determination to use it, would obviate the need to use it in most situations.

NEA leaders continually proclaim the virtues of negotiation and persuasion, apparently in complete ignorance of the fact that these are not substitutes for a position of strength. The teachers will be persuasive only when they have enough power to command the respect of school boards. Until that situation prevails, the power which other groups command will continue to frustrate the public interest in a better school system and the legitimate welfare objectives which the teachers have set for themselves.

Chapter XII

THE ROLE OF THE FOUNDATIONS

To bring about fundamental changes in American education, people must be brought together to plan and to implement such changes. Long and costly experiments must be carried out. Many different kinds of studies must be made, and their results disseminated to the public and the teaching profession. The things which must be done will cost money, and some will cost large amounts of money. Who will finance the activities needed to change the status quo in education?

One possible source is the philanthropic foundations. It is the business of the foundations to support activities likely to produce constructive change—the more far-reaching the change, the better. Of course, not all change is constructive. Nevertheless, it is an avowed purpose of some important foundations to support projects intended to shake the educational status quo. Since these foundations are currently the largest source of funds for this purpose, it is desirable to consider the role they might play in the years ahead. This will entail some consideration of what they have done in the past and of their current situation.

Foundations vary enormously in endowment and purposes, and generalizations about them have to be qualified. For example, they vary in size from the Ford Foundation, with assets of approximately $500,000,000, to those whose assets are practically nil or whose liabilities actually exceed their assets. According to a recent study, the assets of the seven largest foundations in 1954 were as follows:

Ford Foundation	$493,213,842
Rockefeller Foundation	447,686,573
The Carnegie Corporation	178,861,599
W. K. Kellogg Foundation	109,812,214
The Duke Endowment	109,522,000
The Commonwealth Fund	105,993,035
The Pew Memorial Fund	104,987,129 [1]

The larger foundations have typically been active in the field of education, broadly considered. However, until the establishment of the Fund for the Advancement of Education in 1951, there was not one whose resources were devoted primarily to strengthening elementary and secondary education.[2] The relative disinterest of the foundations in public education is a result of many factors, most of which need not detain us here. However, one possible reason which deserves more scrutiny than it has received thus far relates to the constituencies of their boards of trustees. A recent study revealed that of 202 trustees in the larger foundations, 46 per cent held degrees from Yale, Harvard, or Princeton, and only 20 per cent held degrees from state-supported institutions. According to the author of the study, "The typical trustee emerging from this composite picture is a man who graduated from one of the eastern Ivy League liberal arts colleges and went into business or law." [3]

Since education is not regarded as a worthy field of study in some Ivy League colleges, we should not expect their graduates to be especially concerned about it. We have also to consider the fact that liberal arts college presidents are frequently selected as members of foundation boards, whereas persons holding comparable positions in public education, such as superintendents

---

[1] Wilmer Shields Rich, *American Foundations and Their Fields* (7th ed.; (New York: American Foundations Information Service, 1955), p. xxii.

[2] The Fund has received all of its financial support from the Ford Foundation, but it is at present an independent organization with its own officers and board of trustees.

[3] F. Emerson Andrews, *Philanthropic Foundations* (New York: Russell Sage Foundation, 1956), p. 76. This book is probably the best general treatment of the foundations currently available.

of large city school systems, are practically never so selected. Without in any way advocating any particular geographical or occupational breakdown of these boards, I think it would be surprising if the heavy representation of foundation trustees with a private liberal arts college background were not a casual factor in their grant-making patterns.

To say that this is such a cause is not to condemn it. I happen to believe that public education is underrepresented in the larger foundations, in the sense that its needs and potentialities are not accorded the attention they deserve. No doubt many able and sincere individuals believe that the situation with regard to representation is as it should be. It must be conceded that there are good reasons to expect some concentration of trustees from, and of grants to, particular universities. Foundations should not distribute their funds to a wide range of institutions just to avoid the appearance of partiality. In fact, they are being criticized for being nice to everyone as well as for being over-generous to a few favored institutions. I think there is some justification for both criticisms, but the issue is not an easy one to resolve.

SOME REFLECTIONS ON GRANTMANSHIP

To avoid utopian expectations of the foundations, one must be aware of the difficulties confronting them. As tax-exempt organizations, they must be wary of the many legal limitations on their activities. They must make their grants to non-profit organizations or they run the risk of losing their own tax-exempt status. For the same reason, they must not become active in promoting legislation. They are frequently targets of irresponsible political abuse. They operate under subtle but heavy pressures to spread their grants geographically, religiously, and to different types of institutions. Their conservatism or alleged conservatism may be deplorable but under these circumstances it is understandable.[4]

---

[4] Most people in the foundations to whom I have talked agree that these pressures tend to make the foundations cautious. But why should founda-

In the field of public education, there is another important difficulty. The foundations do not receive a sufficient number of good proposals to support. I am referring now to proposals concerning teacher education, curriculum revision, teaching methods, teachers' organizations, the legal and administrative aspects of education, and the economics of public education. In the field of public education, broadly conceived, constructive ideas worth substantial foundation support are rare.

This point is never conceded, publicly at least, by the foundations. When requests are turned down, the reason given to the applicant is never that his ideas are poor. It is that the foundation is concentrating upon some other line of activity, or some other reason which casts no reflection upon the proposal is given. One cannot legitimately criticize the foundations for taking a public position that they receive many more worthwhile requests than they can possibly fulfil. This posture is a practical necessity. However, it should not mislead anyone into expecting more from the foundations than they can deliver.

Bear in mind that the foundations must spend their income or it will be taken by the tax collector. Furthermore, they cannot spend less during years when fewer good proposals come in; they have to spend their income on a regular basis. Thus the fact that unpromising proposals receive foundation support does not *ipso facto* justify the inference of poor judgment on their part—unless, of course, one expects them to turn their income over to the Collector of Internal Revenue rather than allocate it to less promising projects. One can imagine the howl that would be raised all over the country if one of the larger foundations should do this.

In education, the situation can be gauged in part from the weakness of the laboratory schools operated in conjunction with leading schools of education throughout the country. The physical facilities and staff for these schools have cost many millions of

___

tion trustees be cautious if their personal fortunes are not at stake? When I put this question to one foundation president, he replied that trustees don't care about money or power; they just want to be popular, and this calls for a policy of something for everybody.

dollars during the past few decades. Most of them have been unable to produce a single significant piece of research during their entire existence. With only a few exceptions, they have become schools where prospective teachers do student teaching or where graduate assistants can support themselves while working for a doctoral degree.

It is really surprising how few proposals of any kind are submitted to the foundations. Of course, they receive many more proposals than they can possibly support, but these come from only a small portion of the individuals who might reasonably be expected to submit them. There are many faculties of education which do not include one person who has submitted a serious proposal to a foundation. The foundations may themselves be partly to blame for this situation, since they have not done much to remove the atmosphere of mystery concerning their operating procedures. It would take very little effort on their part to eliminate the feeling at some institutions that they are remote and inscrutable institutions. Publications and a wide dissemination of information on the kinds of proposals they are interested in and on how to go about applying for grants would be helpful.

A useful technique of the Fund for the Advancement of Education is to send a field representative to various institutions. Anyone who wishes can discuss his ideas or problems of procedure with this representative. Listening to eight or ten professors a day explain how they can save the world—with the help of a few hundred thousand foundation dollars, of course— must be a punishing experience, but the practice has much to be said for it. For one thing, it clears away the red tape between the people who have proposals to make and the foundation. Some proposals which do not appear promising on paper actually have tremendous potential. Foundation personnel may lose interest in a written proposal because of objections which could be cleared up easily in face-to-face conversation.

Sometimes people have excellent ideas which they are unable or unwilling to implement themselves. They may be too busy, they may not be in an appropriate location, or their institution may be hostile to the idea. In these cases, the individuals may not care to devote a great deal of time to drafting a proposal but they might be willing to discuss their ideas on a conversational basis. Some of the best ideas for educational projects have come from individuals who were personally not in a position to implement them, even with a grant. For this reason, they did not bother to draft any proposals embodying these ideas. A simple visitation procedure might tap these ideas.

From the standpoint of the foundations, there is an understandable reluctance to establish a large staff which would reduce the funds available for grants. On the other hand, if their staffs are small for the volume of proposals that should be given careful consideration, there is the likelihood that propinquity and other fortuitous factors will determine which proposals receive support. In the larger foundations, these considerations lead to a policy of supporting large grants. If a foundation has $5 million to spend every year, it is administratively much easier to choose among fifty proposals, each asking for $200,000, than among two thousand proposals, each asking for $5,000.

Some foundation officials have condemned the "scatteration" of foundation funds in a host of small grants. I think, however, that it is a mistake for a foundation to begin with any preconceptions about the size of grants which are within its means. Such important discoveries as insulin and penicillin were made by individuals working on grants of less than $10,000. It is possible that discoveries of great importance in education could be made on the basis of relatively modest grants. For this reason, foundations should have great flexibility in this matter.

A LOOK AT SOME CRITICISMS

A common criticism of foundations is that they are dominated by people who have preconceptions about the kind of projects that should receive support.[5] This criticism is pointless. If a person came to a foundation job without any idea of what should be supported, he would be a poor choice indeed.

---

[5] In the following analysis, I have purposely omitted any discussion of whether the foundations are supporting subversive or "un-American" activities. This nonsense should not be dignified by a refutation.

Every person who has a genuine interest in research and experimentation has at any given time ideas which he believes to be worthy. He neither can nor should divest himself of these ideas.

This criticism really posits a kind of non-human entity which somehow chooses the "best" proposals quite apart from the preferences of the chooser. Instead of trying to find people without preconceptions, it is more realistic to find those who are realistic about their preconceptions. The fact that a proposal is the brainchild of the foundation gatekeepers is irrelevant to whether it deserves support. Some of the best as well as some of the worst proposals supported by foundations have originated with their own staff. It is, in any case, a fallacy to believe a person must have no ideas of his own about a topic to be objective about it.

In the case of the larger foundations, this criticism is pointless for still another reason: it is practically impossible to confine grants to the hobbyhorses of foundation personnel. The fact is that foundation officials do not always agree among themselves as to what is worthy of support. Foundations are human institutions much like others that we know, and their independence is not absolute. They are under strong pressures to support institutions of different denominations, regions, character, and approach to the same problems for which foundation support is requested. It is not unusual to find the same foundation supporting mutually exclusive approaches to the same problem.

The test of whether a foundation is doing a good job cannot lie in the source of the ideas and proposals it supports; it lies only in the quality of the proposals actually supported. Of course, if foundations automatically reject proposals because of their source, or automatically support others for the same reason, they would be subject to legitimate criticism. Such policies would inevitably be reflected in the lower quality of the results.

Another frequent criticism of the foundations also seems to me to be out of order. This is the charge that the foundations unjustifiably interfere with the internal operations of the institutions which apply for or receive grants. It is alleged that they attempt to dictate personnel policies and even specific appointments as a condition of making a grant. This criticism is often launched by academic personnel who believe that the foundations are using potential grants as a club to dictate all sorts of things which are properly the province of the universities themselves.

Such incidents may indeed occur. But what is in fact surprising is not how much the foundations throw their weight around but how much latitude they give grantees and how little regulation or supervision they undertake once a grant is made. For every incident in which a foundation has attempted to dictate a matter which was not its appropriate concern, there must be dozens wherein the grantees have substantially violated the letter and spirit of their grant and the foundations have looked the other way.

Actually, there is no clear-cut framework within which foundations and grantees act. A government grant for research ordinarily involves a much more highly regulated relationship than does a foundation grant. Institutions receiving grants often take advantage of the lack of a structured operating relationship between foundations and their grantees. This is partly intentional, but the results are frequently deplorable.

Here again, the problem involves the difficulty of applying principles which are sound in themselves. Foundations cannot administer their grants, nor do they wish to stand over anybody's shoulder or require so many detailed reports that projects bog down because of red tape. Nevertheless, their own laissez-faire attitude inevitably leads to a casual attitude on the part of the agencies requesting grants. "Say anything to get the grant and then do whatever you want"—this strategy is the predictable outcome of lack of regulation by the foundations once a grant is made.

The absence of supervision by the foundations during the life of a project would be a sounder policy if the foundations were to engage in critical and vigorous evaluation of the projects they support. I am referring now to evaluation of the results; there is already considerable evaluation of proposals as they come in. If there were critical study of the results of activities receiving support, there might be a different emphasis in the kinds of projects which foundations would support. Of course, there is always some evaluation by foundations of the enterprises they support. However, the resources devoted to this purpose are almost always much less than the resources devoted to evaluating the original proposals out of which the projects developed.

While most foundation grants of any size do provide for evaluation, such evaluation is usually controlled by the agencies receiving the grants. This is often a fatal weakness. An institution hiring some outside, "independent" evaluators is not likely to go out and employ complete strangers who might turn out to be severe critics of the entire project. Nor is a severe critic likely to receive many invitations to serve as an evaluator.

In any case, it is not easy to say publicly, even if one is so convinced, that a project costing hundreds of thousands, sometimes even millions of dollars, has been a waste of time and effort. Such a judgment reflects not only on the institution but also on the foundation supporting the project. For this reason, the evaluators are likely to render their judgments in more dulcet tones. And there are other obvious factors which tend to weaken the effectiveness of "independent evaluation" that is sponsored by the institution which has operated the project itself.

One reason we get so little evaluation of projects in education is that educators have a distorted sense of success in research and experimentation. "Success" has come to mean that the researcher has proved a hypothesis to be true, whereas it should mean either that the researcher has proved a hypothesis to be true *or else* that he has proved it to be false.

In other fields, such as medicine, the possibility that some promising hypotheses are false is taken for granted. In finding them false, the researcher has added to medical science and is satisfied. In education, however, every hypothesis has to be "true." Every experiment has "to work." The disease has even spread to the point where much educational "research" is devoted to proving the obvious.[6] Imagine what our medical

[6] For example, a recent U.S. Office of Education grant to Teachers College, Columbia University, was made to ascertain why male teachers leave the profession.

situation would be like if every piece of medical research had to be successful in the sense of finding a cure or else the researcher could not get additional funds for research.

We badly need to accept routinely the fact that some promising projects will not come up with anything better than what we have. When this happens, educators ought to be in a position to admit it without endangering their chances of getting another grant. If they must (or think they must) claim "success" for every foundation project in order to get subsequent grants, the whole level of research is debased.[7]

The answer to this problem lies largely in the hands of the foundations. If their staffs feel the same compulsive need for "success" in every grant, the people in the field will also. The whole process is a kind of chain reaction, whose terminals are the man in the field at one end and the foundation trustee at the other. The latter is the most important, since he has the money. The people in the field behave in whatever way is necessary (or they think is necessary) to get it.

WHAT FOUNDATIONS CAN DO TO
STRENGTHEN PUBLIC EDUCATION

It is impossible to assess precisely the impact of foundation projects in the field of public education. No one can be certain what the situation would be like in their absence. Even when foundation projects are devoted to goals which are achieved, it is extremely difficult to assess the importance of foundation activity. Perhaps the goal might have been achieved a little later or with a heavier expenditure of non-foundation resources. However, conceding the difficulties of evaluation, I am convinced that the foundations active in public education are not emphasizing the kinds of proposals which, under present conditions, can result in widespread changes.

[7] Sometimes a willingness to face unpleasant facts has surprising results. The School of Education at the University of Wisconsin recently published a research study showing that a surprisingly low proportion of its graduates thought they had profited from their education courses. I am told that the reaction elsewhere in the university was not one of derision but of admiration for the honesty and courage displayed by the School of Education in making the results public.

To be specific, the foundations are not giving enough attention to proposals concerned with the power structure of education. Their current interests are in educational administration, teacher education, the curriculum, and teaching methods and techniques (and especially educational television). My reasons for thinking that these kinds of projects are not likely to result in fundamental changes at this time should be clear from the preceding chapters. No matter how worthwhile their results may be, it is practically impossible to get them accepted on a national basis under the present system. For this reason, the major emphasis of the foundations should not be upon the content and methodology of education or of teacher education. It should be upon the legal, administrative, and organizational structure of education. Unless basic changes are made in these areas, attempts to stimulate improvement in content and methods by pilot projects will be like trying to change the color of the ocean with an eyedropper.

Let me illustrate this point by a reference to the classic example of a foundation's impact upon a profession. In 1908, the Carnegie Foundation authorized Abraham Flexner to make a study of medical education in the United States and Canada. Flexner visited every medical school in the two countries. He then set forth his findings of fact, his criticisms, and his recommendations for future action in a historic report entitled *Medical Education in the United States and Canada.*[8]

In his study, Flexner went far beyond merely reporting on the physical, financial, and personnel resources of the medical schools then in existence. Nor did he confine himself to recommendations about what facilities should be required, or what changes should be made in the preprofessional and professional training of students. At the time of his report, many states excluded doctors from the state boards which licensed doctors, just as some states now exclude teachers from the boards which license teachers. Flexner recommended that the state boards be composed of doctors instead of laymen. He realized that it was useless to

[8] Abraham Flexner, *Medical Education in the United States and Canada* (New York: Carnegie Foundation for the Advancement of Teaching, 1910).

propose higher standards in medical education as long as there was no change in the structure of the boards which licensed doctors and accredited medical schools. He also realized that it was hopeless to expect the medical diploma mills to improve their facilities to the point where they should be permitted to exist. For this reason, he emphasized the need to create a new structure for medical education and licensure, a structure that would make it possible to establish and enforce high standards.

When the Flexner report was published, it immediately became a rallying point for overhauling medical education and licensure in the United States. Eventually, changes in these areas led to sweeping changes in medical practice. The elimination of substandard schools, the initiation of rigorous state board examinations, the removal of unwarranted non-professional interference with medical education, licensure, and practice—these were the direct results of the Flexner report. The indirect results were tremendous improvements in the actual practice of medicine. That is, the Flexner report led to a new framework of medical controls within which the science and art of medicine was able to make tremendous progress in the next few decades. The most fundamental changes in medical practice were thus brought about by a man who was neither a physician nor a scientist. Flexner was simply a keen and fearless observer whose contribution lay in getting the medical profession to eliminate the legal, administrative, and organizational weaknesses which hampered medical education, licensure, research, and practice.

The parallel between medicine in 1910 and education today is striking. There is the same chaotic variation in standards of professional training and practice from state to state and institution to institution, the same need for professional control over licensure, the same absence of high standards for admission to practice, the same widespread existence of substandard institutions providing professional training, and the same urgent need for an unimpeachable rallying point to serve as the basis for drastic changes.

My thesis here, however, is not merely the need for an ed-

ucational Flexner report.[9] It is merely to emphasize the fact
that one relatively inexpensive foundation project exposed the
power structure which constituted the chief obstacle to advances
in the actual practice of medicine. Anyone who reads the
Flexner report will see at once that it really went far beyond
medical education and actually proposed a new framework for
the medical profession itself. Likewise, the crying need in education today is not for research on curriculum or teaching
methods. It is for the elimination of the structural roadblocks
that have retarded educational progress during the past half-
century.

Studies of these roadblocks are important but they do not
necessarily lead to their elimination. Herein lies a problem. We
must remember that Flexner did not revolutionize the medical
profession all by himself. Once his report was published, it was
necessary for interested parties to implement it. Legislation had
to be drafted and supported. Local, state, and national medical
associations had to take appropriate action. In short, all sorts
of things had to be done to implement his recommendations.

This raises a crucial question for the foundations. Assuming
that they were to support comprehensive, no-holds-barred studies
of the legal, administrative, organizational, and technological
barriers to educational progress, what are the prospects for
implementing the recommendations of such studies?

Candor compels the admission that implementation would be
very difficult. On many issues, it would require vigorous action
by educational organizations, and their record is certainly not
one to inspire confidence in the outcome. Some worthwhile
projects supported by the foundations have been greeted with
outright hostility by teachers' organizations. The reactions of

[9] At least one foundation (the Fund for the Advancement of Education)
has given some thought to such a report on teacher education. The Fund
finally concluded, after getting the views of Flexner himself, that this would
not be feasible. It is true that a critical and comprehensive survey of teacher
education would be confronted by many difficulties which Flexner did not
have to face in making his study of medical education. Nevertheless, I believe such a survey to be quite practicable. The major problems would not
be in making the survey but in implementing its recommendations.

the NEA and the AFT to the teacher aide experiment at Bay City, Michigan (see page 100), are one example. To my knowledge, neither the NEA nor the AFT has ever made a proposal of their own to explore the possibilities of a different personnel structure in education. In fact, for all of its criticisms of foundation projects and its verbal support for experimentation and research, I doubt whether the AFT has ever made a proposal on any subject to any major foundation.

In the abstract, all teachers favor research and experimentation; in fact, many of them have a diffuse fear of any development that might justify drastic changes in their habitual ways of doing things. This fear frequently finds expression in overreacting to specific experiments while affirming a general interest in research. Few teachers are really prepared for the kinds of changes that would be necessary if there were important alterations in the personnel structure of education.

Some of the foundations have spent millions in exploring the potentialities of educational television. These foundations have been accused of making exaggerated claims about its results and potentialities. "Educational television will never replace the classroom teacher"—this cliché has become an article of faith for teachers' organizations. Whatever exaggerated claims for educational television may have been made by the foundations are insignificant compared to the dogmatic pronouncements of teachers' organizations concerning its limitations.

Some teachers are vaguely worried that educational television will make it possible to get by with fewer teachers. Instead of encouraging every effort to achieve this result, their organizations have concluded in the infancy of educational television that it must not reduce the number of teachers required for our schools. If their attitude had prevailed in other occupations, it would have been impossible to develop the high levels of productivity which characterize the American economy.

Educational television and efforts to change the personnel structure of education are significant for another reason. I have asserted that if we first make certain changes in the structure of American education, desirable changes in its content and

258

methods will soon follow. It is also possible that desirable changes in the structure of American education will follow from changes in the content and methods. The Industrial Revolution was not simply an alteration in the way things were manufactured. This was first in point of time, but it also meant, or led to, the most profound changes in employer-employee relationships, employee organizations, and the social and economic status of various groups. It is possible that educational television or the development of a personnel hierarchy in education could lead to basic changes in other dimensions of education. This is why I ask for a different emphasis rather than for a complete about-face in foundation policy.

The foundations are currently supporting some proposals directly concerned with the structure of public education. They are supporting others which may alter the structure of American education, although this is not their primary purpose. The point is, however, that a comprehensive restructuring of educational controls is needed and that we are not likely to get it unless it becomes a focal area of foundation support.

I do not advocate that the foundations first decide what changes are needed and then spend their resources to get them accepted. It is only necessary that they recognize the crucial importance of changes in the power structure of American education. Clear recognition of this point would lead to ways and means by which they could help to remove the most important roadblocks to a better educational system.

A FOUNDATION APPROACH
TO MERIT PAY

To illustrate a number of points in this and preceding chapters, I would like to suggest a possible way for the foundations to help public education reach a better solution to the problem of merit pay. This problem is one of the old reliables of educational controversy, partly, I think, because people interested in the problem have always favored a community-by-community approach to resolving it. The foundations are in the best position to initiate a broader approach to the problem.

"Merit pay" (or "merit rating") is really a cluster of problems growing out of one major issue confronting public education. As pointed out earlier, most school systems pay all teachers strictly according to their level of training and years of experience. This policy is commonly referred to as "the single salary schedule." As a rule, the policy makes no allowance for the subject or grade level taught. An elementary teacher, a teacher of driver education, and a physics teacher, each with an M.A. degree and five years of teaching experience, receive the same salary in communities adhering to single salary schedules.

Single salary schedules vary from community to community. They may differ in their minimums, their maximums, the size of the increments from year to year, the number of steps on the schedule, the allowable credit for prior teaching experience, and other factors. Nevertheless, wherever they are used, teachers are not paid according to any judgment of their effectiveness as teachers. They are employed, retained, or fired on the basis of such judgments, but fewer and fewer are compensated on this basis. In 1956–57, less than 5 per cent of the public school teachers in cities of 2,500 or more population were employed under salary schedules which made any provision for merit pay. Less than half of the school systems which authorized or specified higher pay for superior service were actually paying any teachers for such service.[10]

Single salary schedules inevitably result in relatively low maximum salaries. Since all teachers are eligible to receive the maximum, and since teachers are a large occupational group, any schedule with high maximums encounters strong community opposition. Communities are, or may be, willing to pay outstanding teachers outstanding salaries, but they are not going to pay *every* teacher such a salary.

Teachers' organizations and probably most school adminis-

[10] This statement is based upon an estimate made in a letter to me from Hazel Davis, Associate Director, Research Division, NEA, dated August 25, 1958. The best recent summary of the extent and nature of merit pay may be found in NEA Research Division, *Superior-Service Maximums in Teachers Salary Schedules, 1956–57* (Washington, D.C.: National Education Association, 1957).

trators are opposed to salary differentials among teachers on the basis of merit or alleged merit. Merit rating is usually a divisive factor among teachers themselves, because there appears to be no commonly accepted procedure to implement it. If school administrators decide who gets the merit raises, teachers become unduly subservient to the administrators, and there is always the possibility if not the fact of favoritism in awarding merit increases. Many school administrators do not relish the task of singling out the "better" teachers for salary purposes, especially if they have to work with those who are turned down for merit increases. If teachers decide who get the merit raises, they end up wrangling among themselves.

A school system might conceivably employ consultants or an outside agency to evaluate its teachers. This procedure presents a dilemma. In order for the outside evaluators to make competent judgments, they would have to observe the teachers several times a year. However, if each teacher were visited only once a month by an evaluator, the costs would be enormous. As an illustration, consider the costs of evaluation in New York City, which has approximately 40,000 professional employees, of whom well over 30,000 are teachers. Sound personnel policy would require that the evaluators be at least as well qualified, and presumably as well paid, as the teachers they evaluate. The costs of visiting each of 30,000 teachers ten times per year would be prohibitively high under these circumstances.

It would be possible to reduce the over-all cost of merit rating by operating on a somewhat different plan. A school system might consider for merit raises only teachers who had been employed a certain number of years, and fewer than ten visits per teacher per year might be required. However, teaching is not an assembly-line operation. Even good teachers have their share of bad days. For this reason, few teachers would care to have important decisions about their future made on the basis of only a few visits a year. It is obvious that the fewer the visits, the more likelihood that non-merit factors will determine who gets the best ratings.

Earlier, I stated that merit rating was really a cluster of problems rather than one narrow and well-defined problem. A workable plan for merit rating must solve such issues as who shall do the rating, what shall be the criteria for rating, how often shall rating be carried out, who shall be rated, how much of the salary budget shall depend on merit rating, and what differentials are to be paid for what differences in rating. Practically all plans for paying teachers according to merit have eventually been rejected because one or another of these problems was not solved to the satisfaction of school boards or teachers or both.

Although there is no unanimity of opinion on any of these matters, the biggest stumbling block has probably been the question of who shall do the rating. Regular administrative personnel in a school system, such as department chairmen or principals, could do it without heavy additional expense, because their routine work usually requires them to evaluate teachers. Also, their daily presence in the school affords them many excellent opportunities to do so. However, reliance upon ratings by regular staff personnel is not likely to become widespread; too often severe tensions and poor morale are the outcomes of this solution. Administrator domination of teachers, even in their non-classroom activities, is also pronounced under this procedure. And since the employment of outside personnel is too costly, the situation appears to be hopeless. This stalemate has been a disaster to the teaching profession.

The opponents of merit rating have often contended that it is a device to reduce school budgets. High salaries for the few are allegedly used to justify low salaries for the many. This argument overlooks the historical fact that the economic position of teachers has been declining for several decades and that this decline has taken place during a pronounced shift away from merit rating to single salary schedules. Also, plans for paying teachers according to merit vary in so many ways that there is little point to blanket condemnations of merit rating. Nevertheless, such condemnations are the rule at teachers' conventions where the subject is considered. In taking this attitude, teachers have failed to realize the harm done to our educational system by the absence of high top salaries in teaching (I am referring to salaries in the $10,000–$25,000 range, not the $8,000–$10,000 range which seems to concern most teachers).

So far as I know, not a single public school teacher in the country receives $15,000 per year, which is a conservative estimate of the average income of the medical profession. There are well over 1,000,000 public school classroom teachers in the United States, but it is unlikely that more than 200 of them make $10,000 per year from their regular teaching salary. What is even more crucial is the fact that there are no income ceilings in medicine, law, engineering, and most other occupations which compete with education for personnel. Thus education fails to get its proper share of the most able, energetic, and aggressive persons. Since there are about 1,300,000 persons engaged in public education, it is obvious that many of them must have outstanding ability. Nonetheless, the tremendous disparity between top salaries in teaching and in other fields drives away from teaching many individuals who would pull up the entire group.

One cannot measure the loss to education merely in terms of the number of good teachers lost in this way. One must visualize it in terms of its impact upon the professional standing of teachers and upon the loss of able educational leadership. For these reasons, even those who criticize current proposals for merit rating should be exerting every effort to develop a feasible way of implementing it. Certainly, we should not waste any time on those who believe that good teachers are immune to economic considerations.

What, then, is the solution to the problem of merit pay? A partial solution may be found in the establishment of national specialty boards comparable to those in the medical profession. The latter provide special recognition in the form of a diplomate to physicians who achieve outstanding levels of skill and knowledge in a particular field, such as surgery or psychiatry. The procedure for acquiring the diplomate in a given field is handled by the national organization of specialists in that field, e.g., the American College of Surgeons sets the requirements and processes the examinations for the diplomate in surgery.

In education, such a plan might work in this way: The national organization of teachers in a given field, for example, the National Council of Teachers of Mathematics, could set up an examination procedure for the diplomate in their field. These examinations should be comprehensive and rigorous. They should test the applicant's knowledge of his subject and his ability to diagnose and prescribe for various kinds of teaching problems. They should include observation of the applicant in actual teaching situations and also evaluation of any instructional materials prepared by applicants. The entire procedure should be such that only outstanding teachers are "board certified."

The use of board certification would eliminate favoritism, bootlicking, horse-trading, and all the other evils inherent in merit rating procedures whereby teachers are rated by other personnel in their own school system. Since it would not be possible for anyone in the system to give or take away board certification from a teacher, the basis for the undesirable practices just mentioned would not exist. Furthermore, the fact that a teacher could carry his board certification with him to a new position would mean that his professional advancement would not be tied to the subjective judgment of particular administrators in particular school systems. The standards for board certification would have to be high and distinctive enough so that both the non-certified teachers and the public would regard board certification as a defensible basis for salary differentials. This would happen if there were a nationally recognized body which administered the board examinations under conditions scrupulously designed to achieve this purpose.

Notice also that a system of board certification should eliminate the opposition to merit rating by teachers' organizations. School administrators would not be in a position to coerce teachers' organizations by granting or withholding merit pay to particular teachers. There would be little occasion for squabbling within a teachers' organization over who should receive merit pay.

Opposition to merit pay based upon board certification might develop in the AFT if the organizations which administered the specialty board examinations were departments of the NEA. AFT members might fear that examinations under the control of organizations affiliated, albeit rather loosely, with the NEA might be prejudicial to AFT members.[11] I believe this organizational problem could be solved in several different ways. The examinations might be administered by an independent testing agency, such as the Educational Testing Service, or they might be administered by subject-matter organizations not affiliated with the NEA, such as the American Physical Society or the American Mathematical Association. Certainly, if any teachers' organization were to oppose such a plan merely out of its organizational fears, it would be rendering a great disservice to American education.

Specialty board certification should not become part of the state certification structure. It should be an extralegal process, so that the specialty boards could make necessary changes from time to time without going through legislative channels. It would also be essential that the specialty boards rigidly adhere to a single standard for teachers all over the country. In this way, any school system or college which employs a board certified teacher would be assured of getting a highly qualified professional employee.

A system of specialty boards would meet many of the objections to current proposals to pay salary differentials to superior teachers. The specialty boards would eliminate the morale problems inherent in having teachers and administrators evaluate their colleagues for salary purposes. Using board certification as the basis for merit pay would also eliminate the expense to school systems of evaluating teacher competence for purposes of salary differentiation. With a national specialty board, the cost of the examinations would be borne by the teachers, just as the cost of board certification in the medical profession is now borne by the doctors. The reason would be the same— the board certified teacher would receive substantial benefits from his new status. All that would be required of the school system is a policy decision to pay higher salaries to board certified

[11] At the 1958 Annual Convention of the AFT, I suggested the introduction of educational specialty boards to several AFT leaders. None objected to it *in principle* as a merit rating plan.

teachers. The salary differentials for such teachers would have to be large enough to make it worthwhile for them to strive for board certification at their own expense. I believe that many school boards would pay such differentials if they had confidence in the specialty board procedures.

The establishment of educational specialty boards might also help to solve some of the most pressing problems of teacher education. In chapter VI, I pointed out that teacher-training institutions have yet to solve the problem of providing adequate supervision for student teachers. The supervising teachers in the schools are usually persons who lack advanced training. They are often selected haphazardly, without any real inquiry into their ability to help beginning teachers. To supplement the supervision they give, the teacher-training institutions send out supervisors who go to a different school every day to catch a fleeting glimpse of prospective teachers in action. This is a costly and inefficient procedure; the colleges cannot stand the financial burden of providing effective daily supervision for every student teacher. As a result, student teachers are seldom observed more than once every three or four weeks by a college supervisor.

If educational specialty boards were established, student teachers could receive their practical training under the guidance of board certified teachers. As supervisors, the board certified teachers could be treated as adjunct professors of the teacher-training institutions. Indeed, the extent to which a school system employed board certified teachers would be an indication of the caliber of that system. This would also follow medical practice, where the extent to which a hospital or clinic employs board certified specialists is widely accepted as an indication of its caliber. Many other professions have established procedures to identify their most competent practitioners.

Let us turn next to the problem of how to transform the idea of educational specialty boards into an operating reality. The proposed solution will illustrate the role which the foundations might play in remaking the structure of American public education.

First of all, the foundations might bring together the leaders of a few national organizations of specialists in certain fields. The most effective procedure would be to bring together leaders of the national organizations of professors and public school teachers in the same field. Thus in the field of mathematics there should be representation from both the American Mathematical Association and the National Council of Teachers of Mathematics. If the leaders of these organizations were agreeable, as I am sure they would be, the foundation could make relatively modest grants, say of $75,000, to these organizations to draw up proposed plans for board certification in their fields.

In due course, these organizations should draw up fairly complete plans for the operation of a specialty board in their subject. The plans would include provisions for who would conduct the examinations, the nature of the examinations, where and how often they would be given, the budget for the specialty board, the fees to be charged, the qualifications required of applicants, and so on. The foundation grants would make it possible for the organizations to secure the very best advice on these matters from teachers, leading scholars in each subject, and others with ideas to contribute.

When the plans are completed, they should be disseminated to school administrators and school boards over the country. The participating foundations might then convene a large number of leading classroom teachers, school superintendents, and school boards to assess their reactions to the proposals, either in a series of regional meetings or in national conferences or both. At these meetings, educational personnel would become fully acquainted with the proposed boards. After everyone concerned had ample opportunity to study the proposals, and after they had been changed in whatever ways seemed desirable in the light of these reactions, the issue of participation should be put squarely up to teachers' organizations, superintendents, and school boards. Naturally, local, state, and national organizations would be expected to encourage lay and professional acceptance of the proposed specialty boards.

At this point, the attitude of the foundations should be something like this: Whenever a given number of school systems agree to pay at least a specified higher salary to board certified teachers, an additional grant would be made to cover the costs of specialty board operation for several years. After that time, the specialty boards would have to be self-supporting or supported by other sources. And if it were not possible to get a number of school boards to pay a substantial differential to board certified teachers, the foundation should indicate that it would abandon the enterprise.

This is only a skeletonized version of the strategy which might be employed to effectuate specialty boards, but it does illustrate some important points. One is that the foundations supporting such a project would not be trying to ram a particular change down anybody's throat. They would be making it possible to develop an idea, to discover whether it had widespread support, and to put it into effect if it did have such support. They would be foolish to push the idea of specialty boards past a certain point without support, but they would be fully justified in giving the idea an opportunity to catch on.

It would be easier to introduce board certification as a basis for merit pay on a national basis than on an isolated, local basis. It is always easier to get a school board to approve a change when many other boards have also approved it. Teachers are not likely to undertake the intensive study needed to pass their board examinations before they know how much more school systems will pay teachers who pass these examinations. School systems are not likely to pay an adequate differential to board certified teachers unless the boards are launched with unimpeachable professional and public support. All of this requires national planning and publicity.

The establishment of educational specialty boards would not be a complete answer to the problem of rewarding superior teachers. For one thing, the boards would not be geared directly to the teacher's actual performance on the job from year to year. A teacher who had passed his board examinations might nevertheless lie down on the job. Some outstanding teachers would never get around to securing board certification. Despite these and other potential weaknesses, the specialty boards could provide a reasonably objective way of distinguishing and rewarding outstanding teachers. The big danger would be the degeneration of board standards, such as would take place if board certification were based upon the accumulation of credits, travel, service to the community, and criteria of this nature. It might be feasible to begin with boards which examined only the teacher's knowledge of his subject. This seems to me to be unduly restrictive, but it would be better than no boards at all.

In evaluating the idea of educational specialty boards, one should not assume that the idea is not feasible unless the boards provide an unerring guide to teacher competence. Nor should it be thought necessary that the boards remove all need for evaluative judgment within a school system. Merit is not always rewarded in other occupations. Some persons receive more than their due in every occupation. It would, however, be a blunder to reject merit rating in principle because no current way of implementing it promises absolute accuracy. For that matter, even the supporters of the single salary schedule admit that it results in many inequities. We are urged to endure these inequities only because nothing better has been proposed. This may be, but the long-range harm resulting from single salary schedules should stimulate everyone to search for a better plan to compensate teachers.

My proposal for educational specialty boards has two objectives: first, to illustrate a possible answer to an important problem of professional compensation, and, second, to illustrate how the foundations might act to change the structure of American education. Let me conclude by discussing the latter objective briefly.

Like the people in the field, the foundations are characterized by an unwarranted faith in a community-by-community approach to educational reform. In their case, it is reflected in an emphasis upon "demonstrations" or "pilot projects." This faith is all the more plausible since, for some purposes, demonstrations or pilot projects are the only feasible way to get improvements. Nevertheless, reliance upon demonstrations and pilot projects has a tendency to narrow the scope of needed foundation activities.

At the national level, you cannot demonstrate the wisdom of certain changes by "pilot projects"; you either make the change or you don't.

The changes which the foundations must support will threaten vested interests of all kinds—professional, religious, political, racial, and economic. A great deal will depend upon the foundation trustees. They must provide the climate within which the permanent staff of the foundations can support the bold action that is needed. For this, the trustees must have a vision of what public education can be, and they must be persons not easily bluffed by legislatures, investigating committees, disgruntled applicants, or vested interests of any kind. Their difficulties and dangers will be great, but their opportunity is immeasurable.

Chapter XIII

BEYOND THE CLICHÉ BARRIER

In this concluding chapter, I should like to summarize the educational program set forth in previous chapters. Before doing so, a few words of caution and explanation seem appropriate.

Ordinarily, any educational improvement is cumulative. Raising the standards for a teaching certificate is likely to bring about improvements in classroom performance, in teachers' salaries, in the reduction of teacher turnover, and in other aspects of education. The reverse is also true; low standards anywhere along the line turn the interdependence of educational factors into a vicious circle. For this reason, we should be skeptical of single-factor explanations of, and solutions to, important educational problems. Such explanations and solutions raise expectations which cannot be fulfilled and which narrow our insight into the levers of educational improvement.

A realistic program must be specific; at the same time, such a program must not be a collection of itemized recipes incapable of general application. For instance, the development of collective bargaining between teachers and school boards will undoubtedly require vigorous campaigns by the state teachers' organizations. In some states, these organizations are so weak that it would be futile for them even to raise the issue at this time.

Where this is the case, the teachers might be better advised to concentrate upon organizational problems. In other states, the state organizations might be capable of conducting an effective campaign but may not be doing so because of the opposition of their leaders. Here, the task is to educate or to replace these leaders. In still other states, teachers' organizations may already be working for collective bargaining in public education but there may be opposition from various non-professional sources, which must be counteracted. In still other states, collective bargaining by teachers may be partly achieved, and the task is to extend it.

It is sometimes possible to list educational reforms in order of their strategic importance, but this order cannot fit the circumstances of each individual. The development of a strong national teachers' organization is much more important than the development of strong local citizens' committees for the public schools, but particular people will find themselves in a position to implement the latter but not the former objective. A person who has a position of authority in the United States Chamber of Commerce can do more to help public education by modifying some of the educational policies of this organization than thousands of citizens could accomplish by breathing down the necks of their school boards once a month.

In brief, regardless of the strategic importance of particular issues, the steps to be taken by each person can be decided only by reference to the concrete circumstances of his situation. These considerations do not mean that no priorities can be established. They mean only that priorities may be different from situation to situation. The basic educational goals will be the same for everyone, but people confronted by different obstacles and opportunities will have different things to do to help us reach our goals.

With these thoughts in mind, I have summarized in outline form the recommendations made in previous chapters. In some cases, recommendations not previously mentioned have been included, either to provide more specificity or simply as recommended proposals which could not be analyzed adequately in this book.

TEACHERS' ORGANIZATIONS

1. The leadership positions in teachers' organizations must be made attractive enough to compete with any other type of educational position, and with top-level positions in industry, the professions, government service, and other fields. The chief executive of such organizations as the NEA and the AAUP should be paid not less than $50,000 per year.

2. Teachers should pay at least $100 per year in dues, with perhaps $40.00 going to the national organization, $40.00 to the state organization, and $20.00 to their local organization.

3. There should be at least one full-time representative of the teachers wherever there are at least 2,000 teachers in a school system or combination of systems. The national and state organizations should set minimum professional and employment standards for these representatives and be ready to assist local organizations in employing them on a permanent basis.

4. There should be a merger of the NEA and the AFT on the basis of (*a*) an abandonment of affiliation with the labor movement and (*b*) adequate organizational safeguards to prevent administrator domination of the merged organization.

5. There may be a group of teachers' organizations differentiated according to their teaching fields of specialization, but there should be only one organization to represent the same kind of teachers in employer-employee affairs.

6. Organization dues should be collected by a check-off system at the source of payment.

7. Membership in the comprehensive teachers' organizations must be mandatory, though on an extralegal basis. One possible way to achieve this is for the organizations to be aggressive supporters of high administrative salaries; in return, administrative personnel must do everything they possibly can, such as instituting the check-off system, to strengthen the teachers' organizations. Such a *quid pro quo* would not mean administrator domina-

tion of the organizations but would be a natural alliance based upon mutual strength and respect. Every effort should be made to make membership attractive through cheap insurance, credit unions, and similar inducements.

8. The membership structure of teachers' organizations must reflect in part the certification regulations for different kinds of educational personnel; those persons with no training in common and with widely disparate levels of training should not be lumped together into one vast industrial union type organization.

9. Superintendents and other top-level managerial employees should not be allowed to join organizations which represent teachers in matters of employment.

10. Teachers' organizations should establish and enforce a code of professional ethics that would be nationwide in scope.

STRATEGY AND TACTICS

1. Long-range strategy must de-emphasize the community-by-community approach to educational improvements; there should be a correspondingly greater emphasis upon improvements at the state and national levels.

2. Teachers must rely more upon organizational pressure on school boards and other elected officials and less upon "educating the public" in the way typified by present-day PTA activities.

3. The power of national and state professional organizations must be utilized systematically to affect the outcome of negotiations between teachers and school boards at the local level.

4. Professional control over entry and collective bargaining must be given a high organizational priority; the present emphasis upon minimum salary laws should be abandoned.

5. Strategy which explicitly or implicitly weakens the professional autonomy of teachers should be avoided at virtually any cost.

6. Strategy should be based upon the premise that employee benefits are ordinarily not given freely by employers; they are *taken* by employees. Teachers should not be perturbed over anguished cries from the school boards or legislatures or private citizens when they take aggressive action to achieve their just

employment demands. Employers never jump for joy in these circumstances, no matter how justified the employee arguments may be.

TEACHERS AS EMPLOYEES

1. School boards should be required to recognize and negotiate with the majority organizations of teachers concerning conditions of employment; if it appears desirable to have different organizations representing different types of teachers, only the majority organization for each type should represent the teachers.

2. Teachers and school boards should sign master contracts which cover the following subjects:

Scope and purposes of the agreement
Definitions of terms used
Recognition of the bargaining unit
Regular schedule of meetings
Membership in the bargaining unit
Checkoff
Obligations of the various parties
Legislation limiting the agreement
Duration of the agreement
Provisions for termination and renegotiation
Salary schedule
Number of paydays
Travel pay and allowances
Pay for special duties (coaching, etc.)
Hours of work (normal school day)
Class schedules
Number of preparations
Sick leave
Absenteeism by teachers
Rest and lunch-hour periods
Vacations
Promotions
Transfers
Substitute teachers
Leaves of absence
Seniority
Decrease in personnel
Safety provisions
Pupil discipline
Military service credit
Suspension and discharge procedures
Grievance procedures
Supplies to be furnished
Time off for professional meetings
Procedures for handling parental complaints [1]

3. Procedures for changing the conditions of employment should be spelled out in the master contracts; it should be im-

[1] From Myron Lieberman, *Education as a Profession* (Englewood Cliffs, N.J.: Prentice-Hall, 1956), p. 357.

possible for school boards to make substantial changes by unilateral action.

4. Grievance procedures should protect the rights and dignity of teachers without providing unreasonable restrictions on the managerial discretion needed to run a school system efficiently.

5. Application forms for employment and promotion should omit references to race, religion, nationality, or lineage.

6. Unnecessary restrictions upon the mobility of educational personnel should be eliminated; for example, requirements that a state superintendent of schools be a resident of a given state for a certain number of years prior to election or appointment should be abolished. Ways must be found to overcome the immobilizing effects of forcing teachers to give up substantial pension or retirement benefits if they should move.

TEACHERS' SALARIES

1. Since teaching is essentially a cluster of different occupations, despite their common label, we should expect some salary differentiation according to the teaching field; this does not mean merely the elementary-secondary dichotomy, which is unrealistic as a basis for differentiation.

2. Top teachers must be paid $10,000–$15,000 a year as a minimum, through the use of educational specialty boards. Such boards may provide for more than one rank of superior teacher.

3. Teachers should not be required to teach full-time or not at all; older teachers should be allowed to decrease their load and salary, and we should utilize potential teachers who can teach only part-time.

4. Teachers should be given a direct economic stake in the efficiency and productivity of the school system. They should receive a fair share of the difference between the estimated and the actual costs of operating the schools at an agreed-upon level of educational achievement.

5. A school system should not be forced to give raises on a permanent basis or not at all; the salary structure should be sufficiently flexible so that systems can pay non-recurring raises.

6. The notion that the public will not pay high salaries is a

rationalization of teacher weakness and must not be accepted as the final state of the public mind on the subject. The businessman who knows it is to his business advantage to pay high salaries for good personnel can hardly deny the validity of this argument to the business of the public.

7. All salary data should be easily accessible to the public.

TEACHER EDUCATION AND CERTIFICATION

1. There must be national standards for teacher certification; the legal form of their implementation is important but not necessarily decisive.

2. Teacher education must be confined to institutions of higher education which are centers of research.

3. There must be day-to-day articulation of theoretical and practical training in teacher-education programs.

4. There must be unified control of teacher education and of the schools in which prospective teachers receive their practical training.

5. The academic course structure must recognize that not all education courses are professional and that some of the courses in the teaching field of specialization are of this non-professional nature.

6. There must be an examination system interposed between graduation from accredited teacher-preparing institutions and actual entry to teaching. This can be initiated with examinations in the teaching field of specialization, prepared by specialists in each field. All states should be encouraged to use the same examination, prepared and evaluated on a national basis.

7. Requirements for a teaching certificate must not be enacted into law by state legislatures but should be delegated to an agency responsible to organized professional opinion; the requirements of this agency should have the force of law.

8. The number of teacher-training institutions should be drastically reduced. This should be the natural consequence of raising the standards for admission, retention, and graduation along with a system of state board examinations for entry.

9. Certification requirements should be highly prescriptive and

allow relatively little room for electives in a total program of teacher education.

10. Teachers must learn to see their stake in high standards of entry and why this requires them to assume the control over teacher education which has passed by default to the colleges and universities.

11. The persons who teach methods courses and supervise the practical training of teachers of academic subjects should be members of the appropriate academic departments in their subject fields.

12. The practice of spelling out the requirements for a teaching certificate in terms of a given number of course credits must be replaced by a system which indicates the specific content which must be mastered, regardless of courses taken.

13. The most constructive step that liberal arts colleges can take for public education is to put their own house in order. This means eliminating course proliferation, curtailing emphasis upon non-educational activities, setting up a new framework of employer-employee relations, insisting upon high standards for admission, promotion, and graduation, stopping the intensive recruitment of high-school athletes, and otherwise setting a better example for education at lower levels.

14. The study of education as a social institution must be included in the general education program for all students.

THE FOUNDATIONS

1. Thorough studies must be undertaken of what will be required to eliminate the academic retardation of underprivileged socioeconomic groups.

2. A series of substantial awards should be given for outstanding theoretical contributions in such fields as educational psychology, elementary education, school finance, and so on. These awards should provide a substantial incentive for professors to publish something better than rehashes of previous textbooks in their fields.

3. An Institute for Educational Leadership could be estab-

lished to concentrate upon the re-education of organization leaders.

4. Preliminary studies of educational specialty boards should be initiated; if these studies indicate that such boards are feasible, the foundations should underwrite the necessary measures to effectuate them.

5. There should be a national program involving the National School Boards Association, the American Council To Improve Our Neighborhoods, the American Association of School Administrators, and other appropriate agencies, to insure that schools and school systems are given a respected place in the vast urban renewal movement which is going to remake the face of this country in the next few decades.

6. Studies should be made of the way in which students at various grade and ability levels spend their time—time and motion studies, if you will. We are undoubtedly operating with a very haphazard educational structure in terms of the number of courses and credits deemed feasible for students to carry. Similar studies are needed for teachers of different subjects and grade levels.

7. There should be a grant program, the ultimate objective of which is the establishment of national standards for doctoral degrees in fields which do not now have such standards. These programs should consider the feasibility of de-emphasizing the institution-by-institution approach to the improvement of doctoral programs.

8. Studies and action programs should be designed to bring about much heavier expenditures for educational research and experimentation. We need to develop a clear idea of how much ought to be spent on educational research on a nationwide basis and what sources should support this research and at what levels.

9. An Institute for Educational Theory could be set up which would concentrate upon studies of the institutional aspects of education. This institute might provide funds and facilities for a small number of persons to study such subjects as the economics of public education, the composition and operation of state

departments of education, the dynamics of educational legislation, how, why, and what news about education gets into the mass media, the influence of textbook publishers and of privately sponsored educational materials on the curriculum, and the internal operations of educational organizations. The institute might have only a few permanent members; others could be brought in on a rotating basis, as is done at the Center for Advanced Study in the Behavioral Sciences at Palo Alto and the Institute for Advanced Study at Princeton.[2]

10. An Institute for Educational Technology might be established which would be devoted to research and experimentation with the most advanced forms of technology for educational purposes.

11. Foundations must take the initiative to improve the quality of the proposals they receive. To this end, they should sponsor a series of conferences at least every few years to review their operations and evaluate their effectiveness. This should be done jointly with institutions of higher education, school systems, and teachers' organizations. The foundations should provide for systematic, independent evaluation of their activities, just as they urge others to undergo such evaluation. For example, they should find out what able individuals do not submit proposals (there are some!) and why they do not. If handled properly,

[2] This suggestion seems especially appropriate because the research centers just mentioned do not operate as if the problems of education are important. Thus in the first four years of its existence (1954–58), the Center for Advanced Study in the Behavioral Sciences invited persons from the following fields: Political science, psychology, history, anthropology, law, literature, sociology, biology, psychiatry, and others. Except for one professor holding a joint appointment in sociology and education at Harvard, no professor of education or person whose major field of study is educational theory was a fellow at the Center. It is difficult to see the justification for excluding persons interested in educational problems from a center for advanced study in the behavioral sciences. The Institute for Advanced Study has also invited professors from a wide range of the social sciences and the humanities, but it has never invited anyone to participate in the advantages of study at the Institute for the purpose of studying educational problems. There is a certain measure of irony in this situation also, since the Institute was founded upon the advice of Abraham Flexner, a man whose brilliant and deserved reputation as a scholar was built largely upon his studies of higher education. I do not think I am misstating the case when I say that Flexner himself would never have been invited to study at the Institute under present conditions and most certainly not if he were labeled a professor of education!

this suggestion would strengthen the foundations politically as well as increase their effectiveness.

1. Local control of education by laymen should be limited to peripheral and ceremonial functions of education. However, the rights of individual parents and students to make certain basic choices (for example, whether the student takes a college preparatory or a vocational program) must be carefully protected.

2. Laymen can ordinarily make their most valuable contribution to public education in their non-educational organizations. As members of organized groups, laymen can help to protect the integrity of the school program by opposing efforts to use the schools through special holidays, contests, activities, or subjects to advance organizational interests which are not necessary for the educational welfare of students.

3. In view of the fact that the people most active in educational affairs are usually from the upper classes and tend to favor policies which are unfair to less privileged groups, citizens should support school budgets which make all subjects and activities freely available to all students who have the capacity to profit from them. School-wide activities which are theoretically open to all students but which are usually not attended by poorer children, such as junior proms requiring formal dress, should be eliminated unless economic and social class factors in participation can be removed.

4. Laymen should support proposals to give teachers more authority over students and over parental behavior relating to school problems. A request from school authorities for a parent to discuss a school problem relating to his children should not be something the parent is free to ignore, as is almost everywhere the case at the present time.

5. Citizens should support school boards which are willing to negotiate conditions of employment with representatives of the majority organizations of teachers, provided such organizations have adequate safeguards against administrator domination.

6. School boards should provide contracts of perhaps five years' duration for superintendents. Superintendents hired for shorter periods are too busy building their political fences (to insure reappointment) to provide effective educational leadership; they frequently pass every controversy on to the public, regardless of the professional nature of the issues involved.

7. Citizen participation, like the work of the teachers, needs to be evaluated periodically and critically. It might be salutary for superintendents to reveal the record of citizen participation in their community for each past year. A great deal of this participation consists of pressure to fire an athletic coach after an unsuccessful season, protesting because one's child is not in an accelerated group, criticizing the school cafeteria for not providing home cooking, attempting to get the school bus to make a more convenient stop, and sundry other matters of this nature. Citizens tend to underestimate how ineffective the schools are; at the same time, their own participation and influence upon the school program is often the cause rather than the result of this ineffectiveness.

8. Citizens' committees on public education, PTA's, school boards, and other individuals and groups interested in improving public education should work with teachers through the systematic evaluation of student achievement, diagnoses of what must be done to improve performance, and support for the measures needed for improvement.

9. Respect for teachers should be reflected in support for adequate conditions of educational employment, rather than in annual "Teacher Recognition Days" (which often embarrass the teachers and certainly do not help them materially).

10. Citizens should make an inventory of what parents are doing to help or hinder the educational progress of their children. This inventory should be conducted with due regard for the economic status and living conditions of the families involved. School boards, perhaps in conjunction with PTA's and citizens' committees, should conduct this inventory. The sort of questions to be answered include the following: (a) Are pupils sent to school with an adequate breakfast? (b) Are pupils accorded a time and a place to do homework at home? (c)

How many children work after school and on weekends? At whose insistence do they work, how many hours do they put in, and how is school performance affected by this employment? (*d*) How many pupils have an automobile or the free use of an automobile? (*e*) How late do pupils stay up the night before a school day? (*f*) Are students readily provided with funds for school supplies and equipment? (*g*) How many pupils are absent on school days before and after holidays? (*h*) How often are children absent or tardy for trivial reasons with parental knowledge? (*i*) Do parents have a reasonably adequate understanding of their children's academic aptitude and progress in school? (*j*) Are the educational policies of citizens groups formulated with due regard for the less powerful and less articulate groups in the community?

11. Citizens should recognize that the concept of "participation" is one of the vaguest of the many vague terms that make communication difficult in education. Laymen "participate" in helping to solve the medical problems of their children, but the nature and limits of this participation are well understood. Everyone has a stake in a clear-cut delineation of parental, public, and professional authority in public education. It is probably more important that the delineation be clear to everyone than that it be a perfect division of labor between professionals and non-professionals.

12. Insofar as elective officials are concerned, the rule is clear: for short-run, relatively minor, but more immediate improvements, concentrate upon local school board elections; for long-range major improvements, concentrate upon the state and national election of education-minded legislators and executives who have the power to shape the context and limits of local action.

13. Laymen who become active in the field of public education should bear in mind the fact that the worst evils of public education are more often due to teacher acquiescence in public opinion than teacher resistance to it.

Past experience in discussing these proposals leads me to anticipate certain reactions. One is that these proposals would take education away from the people who pay for it and would destroy public interest in it. This reaction is usually based on the premise that local control has been responsible for a strong grass-roots concern with public education. "The schools are close to the people"—this is now part of the folklore of American education.

This folklore persists in the face of the strongest kinds of evidence to refute it. Elections to school boards usually have a smaller turnout than elections to any other public office, local, state or federal. Statistics on the subject are not available, but my guess would be that as a rule less than 5 per cent of the eligible voters turn out in a school board election.

The reality is that public education is not in the mainstream of American life. For example, one cannot think of a person working in the field of public education who is a nationally known personality. The field of labor brings to mind names like John L. Lewis, Walter Reuther, or George Meany. In medicine, one thinks of Dr. Jonas Salk, of Dr. Paul Dudley White. Similarly, in the arts, government, law, theology, industry, and many other major fields, one can quickly name several persons whose names are known all over the country. Not all are known for desirable reasons, but they are people who make national and even international news. It is a measure of the public indifference to our schools that there are no such names in the field of public education. Even in the segregation crisis, educators are secondary figures. Politicians, journalists, NAACP leaders, and some students are more important personalities than the professional school people, who are more or less puppets in the whole situation.

Newspapers have daily interpretive columnists who write on politics, economics, fashion, family life, the arts, literature, and many other fields. To my knowledge, not a single newspaper has a daily column devoted to education. There are columnists on home and family life, but none of them is capable of serious interpretive writing about education even if he wished to do so.

It must be conceded that professional educators are not ahead of the public on this problem. For example, current education textbooks are seldom critical of local control. These textbooks tell us that the schools are "close to the people," an example of "grass-roots democracy" at its best, a thrilling example of the virtues of good old-fashioned town-hall Americanism. Turn the pages and you read a seemingly endless list of techniques to overcome public apathy toward school needs. Educators have really become enfeebled by their own propaganda; many of them think that it is flirting with totalitarianism to regard local control as a dangerous anachronism.

The centralization of public education, in whatever form it comes, will bring public education into the mainstream of American life. Centralization means that some people are going to make educational decisions that will be important in every community. When this happens, education will be news and educational leaders will be nationally known, for good or evil as the case may be. When this happens, public education may become close to the people, but in a new and more fruitful sense than it is now.

At the present time, public education presents a paradox: the work of teachers is dominated by political considerations but the teachers themselves are political nonentities. The need is to transform teachers into political animals so that their work can be based on professional instead of political considerations. Without political power, teachers will never be able to protect the integrity of their work.

Along with political power, what teachers need as much as anything is a spirit of adventure. For all their talk of change, teachers have changed their occupation less than virtually any other major occupational group. It is almost frightening to notice how much teachers take for granted in their approach to education. Over and over again, they try to solve problems within a framework that is the root cause of the problems themselves. Their perpetual frustration in trying to improve their conditions of employment through minimum salary laws is only one such example.

Educational leaders seem resigned to the fact that the salaries of public employees usually lag behind salaries in private employment during periods of inflation. Instead of regarding this lag as a practical problem, to be solved by a diagnosis and an action program, their approach has been to cite the lag as a reason for not expecting very much. However, the reasons why the salaries of teachers lag behind those in industry are not immutable laws engraved in stone. They are causes which can and should be eliminated by intelligent group action.

Many teachers have one final crushing answer to a proposed change: it is against the law, or it will require some changes in the law. To teachers, this often seems an impenetrable barrier which relieves them of the necessity to think any further. Proposals to change the legal structure of public education are dreamy utopian stuff to many teachers. Most of them are too busy running on the treadmill of community-by-community improvement to realize that there is no local solution to the basic problems of public education.

This will appear to be a message of despair to many people who work for better schools. They cannot even influence local school board elections, and now they are told that these are not as crucial as they have always supposed. The really important elections are at state and national levels, where their influence will be even more attenuated than it is on the local scene. But this thesis is a message of despair only if we assume that the present political impotence of teachers and citizens interested in public education is an unchangeable fact of life. The latter assumption would indeed be a message of despair, but I, for one, do not accept it.

The tendency to take for granted the present structure of public education weakens teachers at one important point after another. For example, to hear teachers ask in puzzled tones how they are to get control over entry or collective bargaining, one might suppose that no occupational group had achieved these objectives. Granted, the changes needed will involve some difficult problems of strategy and tactics. Nevertheless, the difficulties are not primarily strategic; they lie mainly in the failure of teachers to realize what changes are in fact needed. The strategy to be used to secure these changes is basically no different from that utilized in scores of other occupations, professional and non-professional, public and private, to achieve the same objectives.

The fact is that the essentials of the forthcoming revolution in education are already evident in other fields. For this reason, sweeping changes in education are not a remote prospect. If, for example, teachers were the only group of public employees interested in collective bargaining, there would be strong reason to doubt its eventual acceptance in public education. But this is not the case. Collective bargaining by public employees will soon be so common that its widespread introduction into public education will appear to be a reasonable development to persons who reject it now.

Apart from the merits of any proposals made in this book, their chances of gaining acceptance should not be judged according to the attitudes which people currently may have toward them. People have vowed that they would close down their public schools rather than support integrated ones, but when confronted by the realities of this policy, they have accepted integration, albeit under protest. Later, their acceptance of integration became so matter of fact that they would have been surprised to learn that they had vowed last-ditch resistance to it only a short time ago. Utopianism is, of course, to be avoided, but so is the error of assessing future attitudes in the light of present instead of future realities. This error leads to a kind of conservatism that is as unrealistic as utopianism.

From this perspective, it would be surprising if we were to continue to have a national policy for industry, finance, labor relations, transportation, communications, and other areas of contemporary life, while public education remained primarily a matter for local control. The pressures generated by the life we lead and the kind of world in which we live will not permit this inconsistency to endure indefinitely. This conclusion in no way presupposes that we are headed for a totalitarian state or one in which all the decisions are made in Washington. It presupposes only that our interdependence will be reflected in our educational as well as our political and economic policies.

The problem in education, as in so many other areas, is to maintain the substance of democracy and a high level of efficiency while modifying an important social institution so that it takes into account the conditions of modern life.

My final comment relates to the convictions set forth in the first chapter of this book. Public education constitutes one of the important occupational frontiers in American life. This frontier requires pioneers, every bit as resourceful as those who conquered geographical frontiers in an earlier day. It is a frontier on which many roles are wandering in search of leaders who understand the problems and the potentialities of public education. My firm conviction is that a handful of such leaders can bring about a revolution in education, a revolution such that the practice of free public education in the United States will stand as its major contribution to the human community of the future.

INDEX

Academic freedom, 42, 53–55, 141, 204
Adler, Irving, 61
Administration: and professional autonomy, 60–61, 67; as separate profession, 91; training for, 91. *See also* Administrators; Lay-professional relations; Local control of education; School boards; Teachers' organizations
Administrators: and authority, 222, 224; certification and preparation of, 91; and collective bargaining, 171–77, 273–74; membership of, in teachers' organizations, 182, 232–34; and merit rating, 262, 264–65; and professional autonomy, 60, 67; relationships of, with teachers, 171–77, 232–34; specialized training of, 91. *See also* Administration
Affiliation. *See* American Federation of Teachers; National Education Association
American Association of School Administrators, 180, 222, 223, 233, 279
American Association of University Professors: and academic freedom, 204–5; and collective bargaining, 152; effectiveness of, 213–14; local and state chapters of, 200–201; membership in, 173, 209–11; prejudices in, 149; as a professional organization, 199–206; program of, 202–3, 214; strategy followed by, 203–4, 206–8; and tenure, 205
American Federation of Teachers: administrator exclusion from, 173;

affiliation with labor, 193–96, 231–32; and collective bargaining, 234; Constitution of, 232, 235; future of, 198; history of, 192–93; membership in, 197, 232–35; merger of, with NEA, 230–36; and merit rating, 264–65; no-strike policy of, 193, 196; professional inadequacies of, 197–98, 236–37; and racial segregation, 235–36; and teacher aides, 258; teacher attitudes toward, 197–98; and teachers' salaries, 265
American College of Surgeons, 263
American Council To Improve Our Neighborhoods, 279
American Federation of Labor–Congress of Industrial Organizations, 182, 194–95, 216. *See also* American Federation of Teachers
American Historical Association, 210–11
American Legion, 64
American Mathematical Association, 265–66
American Medical Association, 51, 106, 189, 209
American Physical Society, 265
Anderson, Archibald W., 16
Andrews, F. Emerson, 246
Armstrong, W. Earl, 103, 142
Athletics, 136–40
Authority, 34–38. *See also* Education, at state level; Federal government and education; Local control of education

Baltzell, E. Digby, 146
Benne, Kenneth D., 16
Bent, Rudyard K., 223

PRINTED IN U.S.A.